Empowered Filmmaking

Edited by

Laura Thomas

Cover Design

Mayra Toscano

Book Layout and Formatting

Gracie_Anderson

ABOUT THE AUTHOR

Sarah Moshman is an Emmy Award-winning documentary filmmaker and TEDx speaker whose work has been featured on Netflix, Upworthy, Marie Claire, CNN, and *Good Morning America.* After directing two short documentaries about female empowerment in young women, (*Girls Rock! Chicago* (2010) and *Growing up Strong: Girls on the Run* (2012)) she set out to direct her first feature doc *The Empowerment Project: Ordinary Women Doing Extraordinary Things* (2014) which has been screened over 700 times around the US and around the world in schools, groups, organizations and corporations starting conversations about gender equality. Sarah's second feature doc, *Losing Sight of Shore* follows the incredible journey of four women who rowed across the Pacific Ocean. The film was released globally in 190 countries on Netflix in May 2017. *Nevertheless* is Sarah's third feature documentary which takes a look behind the headlines of #MeToo and Time's Up to shine a light on the sexual harassment crisis and use the power of cinema for change. Sarah is dedicated to telling stories that uplift, inform and inspire as well as showcase strong female role models on screen.

Sarah was born and raised in Evanston, IL where her love of filmmaking began. She made her first documentary for a high school English class at the age of 16 and loved the feeling of making something that she could share with an audience. She took those passions to film school and attended the University of Miami in Coral Gables, FL where she did NOT get a tan, but rather spent her weekends making narrative and documentary films with her classmates learning very important film jargon like "C47's," "10-1," and "cucoloris." She received a Bachelor of Science in Communication in 2008.

Prior to focusing on documentaries, Sarah worked as a field producer on the hit ABC show *Dancing with the Stars* for 10 seasons as well as shows on NBC, MTV, Lifetime, Bravo and the Food Network. She also directs branded content for EllenTube, Tastemade, Mattel, AT&T and more. Sarah is an inspiring public speaker, an adjunct professor in documentary film and author, passionate about empowering the next generation of storytellers and travels the globe to do so!

Sarah currently lives in Los Angeles with her husband Ryan, their daughter Bryce (featured on the cover) and as of December 2020, a son as well. And although Sarah loves watching and making documentaries, most nights you can find her curled up on the couch bingeing reruns of *Parks and Recreation*, dreaming of a world where Leslie Knope rules.

CONTENTS

OVERVIEW OF FILMS: ix

INTRODUCTION: xv

CHAPTER ONE: You And Your Voice Matter 1

CHAPTER TWO: Finding Inspiration 4

CHAPTER THREE: I Have An Idea…Now What? 10

CHAPTER FOUR: The Legal Side 29

CHAPTER FIVE: Fundraising 101 45

CHAPTER SIX: Pre - Production 97

CHAPTER SEVEN: Production 104

CHAPTER EIGHT: Camera Basics 116

CHAPTER NINE: Audio Basics 131

CHAPTER TEN: Lighting Basics 141

CHAPTER ELEVEN: Interview Techniques 148

CHAPTER TWELVE: B-Roll And The Visual Language Of Docs 161

CHAPTER THIRTEEN: Post-Production 169

CHAPTER FOURTEEN: Defining Success For You 188

CHAPTER FIFTEEN: Distribution For Independent Film 193

CHAPTER SIXTEEN: Impact 204

CHAPTER SEVENTEEN: Marketing And Promotion 216

CHAPTER EIGHTEEN: It's Your Turn! 232

ACKNOWLEDGEMENTS: 234

OVERVIEW OF FILMS

Before we begin, I want to give you the quick backstory and context of each of my feature-length films which I will be mentioning frequently throughout the book. These three films have truly been my education and the reason I have extensive knowledge to share. Each one was a labor of love, and I poured everything I had in to each one. I am credited as Director and Producer on each of these films, but as you know a filmmaker wears many hats as they bring their projects to life. If you haven't heard or seen these films yet, I hope after reading this book you will feel inspired to watch them as well!

THE EMPOWERMENT PROJECT: ORDINARY WOMEN DOING EXTRAORDINARY THINGS (2014)

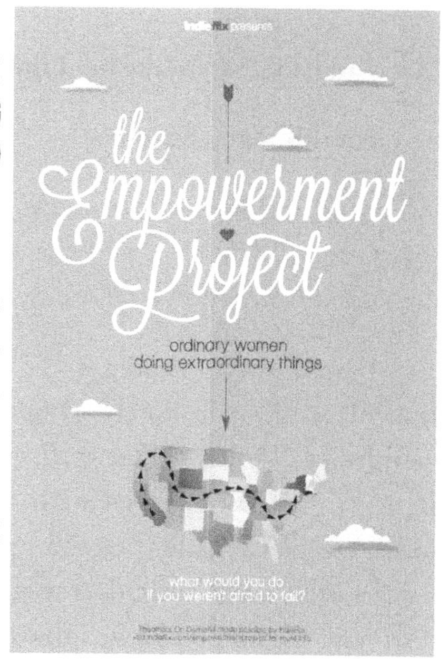

The Empowerment Project is the incredible journey of a crew of female filmmakers driving across America to encourage, empower, and inspire the next generation of strong women to go after their career ambitions. Driving over 7,000 miles from Los Angeles to New York over the course of 30 days, the documentary spotlights 17 positive and powerful women leaders across a variety of lifestyles and industries. From a pilot, to an athlete, mathematician, astronaut, and Four Star Admiral – the film shines a light on underrepresented stories of positive female role models. The film challenges the audience to ask themselves, "What would you do if you weren't afraid to fail?"

Why I Had to Make This Film: I was tired of the way the media portrays women. Every time I would go to the movies, turn on the TV, open up a magazine or listen to the radio the same messages were being sent – women are objectified, over sexualized and ignored all together. I wondered, where are the stories of the strong female role models I had in my life? Why aren't their stories being shared? And why aren't more women behind the camera as decision-makers? I decided to take matters in to my own hands and create the film I wish I had seen growing up and set off on a road trip across America with 4 other incredible female filmmakers and together we had quite an empowering experience.

Total Run Time: 99 min + 50 min (two versions)

Production: September 2013 (30 days)

Completed: April 2014

Total Time to Make the Film: 1.5 years

Total Budget: $50,000

Fundraising Route: Successful 60-day Kickstarter campaign in 2013 - we raised $28,590 from 404 backers, from there we got a $25,000 private donation through our fiscal sponsor.

Distribution Strategy: We worked with educational distributor Indieflix to bring the film to schools, groups, organizations and corporations worldwide. We have done well over 700 educational screenings through Indieflix. We also worked with brands like Nordstrom, American Girl, Microsoft and Charles Schwab to sponsor screenings in innovative ways. 3 years in to our distribution strategy we signed with Gravitas Ventures to distribute the film on Hulu, iTunes, Amazon, Vudu, Google Play, and many more platforms. It has been over 6 years since finishing this film and the impact and revenue continue.

How to Watch Now: iTunes, Amazon, Google Play, Vudu, and more. Anyone can host a screening in their community by purchasing our educational kit.

For More Information: empowermentproject.com

LOSING SIGHT OF SHORE (2017)

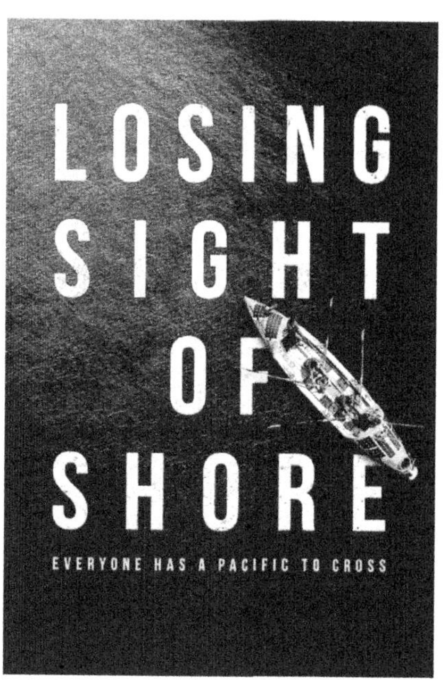

Losing Sight of Shore follows the extraordinary journey of four brave women known as the Coxless Crew that set out to row the Pacific Ocean from America to Australia unsupported. As they row over 8,000 miles during their 9 months at sea, they face extreme mental and physical challenges they must overcome in order to go down in history. This is a story of perseverance, friendship, and the power of the human spirit.

Everyone has a Pacific to cross.

Why I Had to Make This Film: I was alerted to the story of the Coxless Crew in January 2015 only a few short months before they left on their record-setting journey. I couldn't believe what they were setting out to do and furthermore I couldn't believe no one was telling their story. So even though I had no experience rowing, or making such a large scale film with no guarantee of an ending, I couldn't pass up the opportunity to help tell this extraordinary story. And the fact that they happened to be women and were rowing in a pink boat didn't hurt either. It was truly the adventure of-a lifetime to make this film, and I wasn't even on the boat.

Total Run Time: 92 min

Production: April 2015 – January 2016 (9 months)

Completed: February 2017

Total Time to Make the Film: About 2 years

Total Budget: $250,000

Fundraising Route: I put in a good chunk of my own money to get the project started, I brought on investors, I applied for every grant possible and was awarded about $40,000 in grants, I did some crowdfunding (not a formal campaign, but throughout production), and I called in all of the favors I could (i.e. my husband Ryan who is not a cinematographer served as our drone operator one more than one occasion and my Dad jumped in to help shoot more than once as well).

Distribution Strategy: We licensed the film to Netflix worldwide for 3 years (May 2017-May 2020) so it was seen in 190 countries and subtitled in 25 languages. It is also on iTunes and Amazon, we are selling DVDs through our website, and new broadcast and AVOD deals are popping up now that we are no longer on Netflix.

How to Watch Now: iTunes and Amazon

For More Information: losingsightofshore.com

NEVERTHELESS (2020)

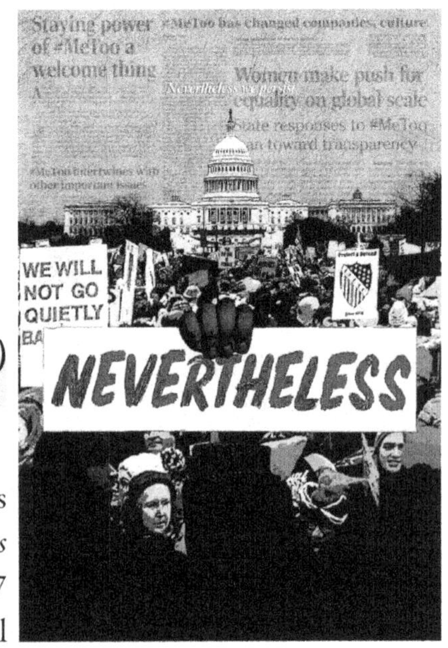

Taking a look behind the headlines of #MeToo and Time's Up, *Nevertheless* follows the intimate stories of 7 individuals who have experienced sexual harassment in the workplace or school context. From a writer's assistant on a top TV show to a Tech CEO and 911 dispatcher, the film shines a light on the ways in which we can shift our culture and rebuild.

Nevertheless we persist.

Why I Had to Make This Film: In 2017 I was 7 months pregnant with my daughter Bryce and as many parents may feel, I wanted to help make the world a safer place for her to exist in. I was also tired of hearing every single one of my female friends share a story of being harassed, assaulted, or violated in the workplace and in the world. I had my own stories as well working in the television industry. I thought, why is this the price we pay as women to be in the workplace? I did the only thing I know how to do in that situation which is pick up the camera and get to work. I started interviewing employment attorneys, diversity and inclusion experts, sexual harassment training consultants, and brave men and women willing to share their stories. It just so happened to coincide with the Harvey Weinstein story breaking in The New York Times and the #MeToo movement unfolding. I didn't know exactly what I was making at first, but as time went on the project evolved, and so did I as a woman and as a mother. I am very proud of what the film turned out to be and I am thrilled to see it being used as a tool for social impact.

Total Run Time: 80 min + 50 min (2 versions)

Production: On and off throughout October 2017 – April 2019

Completed: February 2020

Total Time to Make the Film: a little over 2 years

Total Budget: $225,000

Fundraising Route: I put some of my own money in up front to get the project started, I did a 30-day campaign on Kickstarter to raise $58,521 from 610 backers (while I was breastfeeding my 3 month old daughter), I received grants as well as private donations. No investors or equity in this project.

Distribution Strategy: I am working with educational distributor Indieflix again to distribute *Nevertheless* in to workplaces, schools, groups and organizations worldwide to incorporate this film in to sexual harassment training programs and school curriculum. We have a comprehensive discussion guide that accompanies the film with resources, questions, activities, a glossary of terms, as well as a whole dashboard of materials so that schools and workplaces can take the messages presented in the film ten steps further. Due to covid-19 we have been doing several virtual screenings and events in 2020. Down the road we will pursue streaming platforms, broadcast deals, and transactional video on demand platforms as well.

How to Watch Now: Host a Screening or join in on one of our upcoming virtual screenings on our website.

For More Information: neverthelessfilm.com

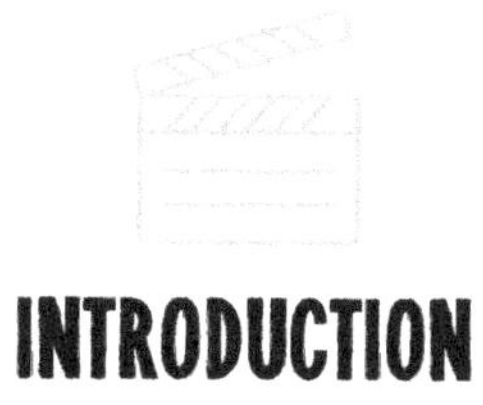

INTRODUCTION

It was truly the best day. One of those days that reminds you how life can be wonderful, and sometimes luck, opportunity, and hard work meet in a delicious trifecta. I was on the South Island of New Zealand taking a much needed vacation with my husband, Ryan, who has cheered me on as a filmmaker since we were in high school. This was December 19th, 2016, and I had recently finished directing, producing, and, let's face it, shouldering the burden of my second feature-length documentary, *Losing Sight of Shore*. I was so unbelievably proud of the film and my journey making it, which spanned almost two years. It wasn't lost on me that in order to even feel proud of finishing the film, a team of six women had to physically row across the entire Pacific Ocean over the course of nine months, setting two world records in the process. I didn't physically row any oceans, but I certainly felt like I had crossed a Pacific of my own to tell their story.

Days earlier I had gotten the official rejection from the Sundance Film Festival, which is apparently harder to get into these days than Harvard. Over the course of those two years, I had spent upwards of $50,000 of my own money to make this film happen. There were countless grant rejections, and after meeting with endless production companies, I had clawed tooth and nail to tell this heroic story largely on my own. I believed in my heart that people would be inspired by the bravery, courage, and perseverance of these rowers. So every day, I woke up and figured out how to keep it moving forward.

Even with all that determination, I was afraid. What if it wasn't a good film? What if no one wanted to watch it? What if I didn't get any distribution deals, and no one ended up seeing it?

I gulped all of that down to enjoy the first full day on our vacation in Queenstown, New Zealand. I needed a mental break. I needed to go out and enjoy nature again, and remember that there was more to me than being a documentary filmmaker. I was also a woman, a wife, a friend, a sister, a daughter, and a human. Ryan and I had decided to splurge on a trip to celebrate and enjoy an incredibly busy, tough, and wonderful year in our lives. We decided to spend our first day in Queenstown exploring Milford Sound by ferry, slowly cruising along the fiord under waterfalls and alongside stunning mountainous rocks, all atop impossible turquoise-blue water. It felt like a dream. My soul needed to be present and not stressed out for a day. I loved the water splashing in my face and the wind blowing in my hair.

At the end of the day, refreshed and rejuvenated by the natural beauty of our Earth, and thrilled to have weeks in front of us to do nothing but explore, we walked back to our rental car. Ryan suggested we find a place to grab a glass of wine before dinner. I turned on my phone for the first time that day to look up a nearby spot. My phone flooded with unread emails and texts from my Mom hoping we were enjoying our trip. I wasn't even planning to check my email at that moment, wanting to stay in vacation mode as long as possible, but one email alert subject line caught my eye. It simply said: **Netflix.**

Ryan started driving back towards the nearest town, assuming I'd shout out directions as soon as I found a place with New Zealand's finest Sauvignon Blanc. (Or let's face it, any wine would do.) I opened the mysterious email, which was from my sales agent. It was written to me and my consulting producer on the film. I started to shake. I knew that my sales agent was planning to send the film to a handful of streaming platforms and broadcasters to see if we could sell or license it, but given that both Sundance and Christmas were around the corner, I had no expectations of hearing back anytime soon. I had never been on this path before, so I could only keep my expectations low.

Suddenly, the world stopped as I read:

Some good news.

Netflix was a fan. They want worldwide svod. I was able to hold on to theatrical non theatrical and tvod. I was also able to get them to pay for all the subtitling for the numerous countries where the film will be on the service. I think this is a big win.

I told Ryan to pull over. We read it again and again and again. We cried. We screamed. I called my editor immediately to share the news. We got all the wine.

Netflix, the largest streaming platform in the world, the one and only home I saw for this film, my dream of all dreams, had come true. They made me an offer to license the film for three years worldwide, and that six-figure deal allowed me to pay back my investors in full, pay myself back in full, and finally pay myself a salary after working for two years without a dollar. And I would still own all the rights to the film. *Losing Sight of Shore* was going to be seen in 190 countries and subtitled in 25 languages. It was the best possible scenario for the film and for this powerful story.

Sometimes, hard work pays off. Sometimes, a good story wins. I didn't have a celebrity executive producer on board, or a production company attached; I didn't get into any big name festivals; there was no DEADLINE article written about me or the project. I didn't win any big awards for this. When I started making this film, I had absolutely no idea how I was going to pull it off. And no one—*no one*—would have hired me to direct this film. I wouldn't have had the "right credits" or the "right experience" to prove I was capable. I proved to myself I was capable. I figured it out piece by piece. I persevered. And you can too.

That's what this book is about.

I'm not special. I'm a hard worker, and I don't give up. If I don't know how to do something, I figure it out, or I hire a talented person to help me.

I'm Sarah Moshman, Evanston, IL born and raised, author of this book, and Emmy Award-winning independent documentary filmmaker. In this book, I want to take you through the entire process of making a documentary—from idea and development, all the way through to distribution and marketing. This book includes practical skills like camera, audio, and lighting basics, as well as more abstract exercises on how to conduct a good interview and what you define as success. I will share my personal stories of making three feature-length documentaries over the past seven years, and I hope you can learn something from all of my triumphs and all of my mistakes.

Think of me as your friend giving you the inside scoop on how things work in the documentary space. If you're looking for more of a high-level, educational, perfectly fact-checked presentation on filmmaking, this might not be your book. This is anecdotal, at times casual, but filled with heart, and practical advice on how to get your projects off the ground. This is everything I didn't learn in film school, but wish that I had.

If you want to know how to get into the top tier film festivals or pitch to the best production companies, you're going to need to ask someone else or buy another book. That hasn't been my path as of yet. I have, however, raised hundreds of thousands of dollars to make films, and I have helped create hundreds of thousands of dollars in revenue from those films, all independently. I give myself the permission to get started on a project, and I don't wait around to be picked. Historically, we have seen that if women wait around for opportunities, they might be waiting forever.

I believe documentary filmmaking can be a viable career path that mixes art, storytelling, activism, and business. It's the greatest career I could have ever hoped for, and I want to share my knowledge with you. I want you to read this and feel empowered to go out there and tell your own stories too.

Shall we begin?

CHAPTER ONE

You and Your Voice Matter

As I've traveled around the world screening my documentaries, there is a common theme that comes up when I speak with young women interested in making their own films. We often feel like we need some kind of permission to get started. As if one day we'll wake up and the universe will send us a sign that we've checked all the boxes and earned a gold star of permission. Instead of automatically thinking we have the intelligence and creativity to dive into something new, we often doubt ourselves and wonder if we have all the pieces in place to get started. And if we don't feel 100% qualified or confident, we may put our dreams aside forever, assuming someone else will be better suited to tell this story. This likely comes from a lifetime of girls being told to be small, to not take up space, and to follow the rules. We are socialized from a young age to please others, not make waves, and follow the status quo. There is something defiant and rebellious in following your heart, and deeply listening to that voice inside your soul that wants to move in a new direction.

Making a film is a wildly personal journey, but it also goes beyond you. It's an important act of change for the issue or story you're wishing to represent. It's not a decision to take lightly, but it's also a path I wish for so many women to take. Filmmaking builds confidence, and forces you to learn skills you might never have learned otherwise. What other profession teaches you about PR, social media, marketing, writing, legal contracts, fundraising, cinematography, interview techniques, sound mixing, editing, music composing, graphic design, animation, distribution, and *so much more*? When I finish a feature-length project, I *feel* like I've gotten a master's degree in the subject I was studying, and sometimes editing a documentary can feel like writing a thesis.

Guess what? YOU DON'T NEED ANYONE'S PERMISSION to explore your creativity and get out there and be a storyteller. We desperately need more stories from the female perspective to create a more equal world. Who tells the story MATTERS. It matters who directs the camera; it matters who chooses the shots in edit; it matters who shapes the story and determines how to present information and emotion to the audience. The filmmaker, especially in documentary films, is creating the world in which the audience is learning about a person or subject. So much of documentary is shaped in the editing room, and you bring your unique experiences and perspective to every choice regarding what to include and what to leave out. I often think about how if 10 filmmakers were given the same hard drive of footage, they would make 10 different films. You make 1,000 tiny decisions each and every day that will add up to the final film. You are the auteur, and we need to see this issue, this character, this story from your eyes—there is no one in the world quite like you.

You don't need to wait to be invited to sit at someone else's table—you can make your own. And you deserve that seat.

What I love about documentary filmmaking is that the barrier to entry is quite low. Unlike narrative filmmaking, you don't need a polished screenplay, a cast of actors, locations, or costumes. All you need is a seed of an idea for a story. You need an intriguing character, or a pressing issue. You need an important event happening right this second, or a long time ago. You just need a spark to get started, to find a camera—any camera—and to start filming. It doesn't have to be perfect; it just needs to be yours. If it's interesting to you, chances are it will be interesting to someone else. There isn't a finite number of spots for documentary filmmakers on the team—the spots are endless.

It's important to remember that no one has all the answers, and taking those first few steps is going to give you the confidence to keep going a little further. Every film is going to present its own journey, its own struggles, its own strategy. No two films are the same to make or distribute. When I embark on a new project, I have very little figured out. I may have an overarching goal or vision in mind of what I think the film could be, but the steps for how to get there aren't clear. It is such a tremendous leap of faith to make a film, but that's where the magic is. The people you will cross paths with, the bonds you will form, the lessons you will learn, the knowledge that you'll share, the immense pride you'll feel—I don't think there's anything quite like it.

If you are reading this and doubting yourself in any way, please stop. I don't care if you went to film school or not, if you've made a film before or not. If you have the passion and enthusiasm to tell a story, then you are right where you need to be.

All I'm saying is: **we need you.**

We need to hear your story.

CHAPTER TWO

Finding Inspiration

So you've decided you're ready to get out there and be a storyteller. Awesome! Now what? How do you decide what you want to create? Where do you find inspiration? These questions are tricky to answer, because each person finds inspiration differently, but here are some things to consider for the wheels to start turning.

I believe it's important to tell stories and create media that matters to you personally. If it doesn't stir up your soul, why would it inspire anyone else? You often hear the advice "write what you know," and this can be a good starting point no matter what you want to convey. You need to find something that consumes you. Something that keeps you up at night because it excites you to wake up the next morning and keep working on it. The truth is, making a documentary can take years of your life to complete, especially when you factor in distribution and marketing. Not only do you need to be excited about this film when you're fundraising, but you need to maintain that enthusiasm all the way through promoting the screenings and doing press. You don't want to lose steam and be frustrated you picked a person, topic, or issue that won't matter much to you in a couple years. A tall order, I know.

Questions to consider:

- *What issues are you passionate about?*
- *What things get you thinking deeper?*
- *What kinds of films do you watch, and what is compelling to you about them?*

Watch Other Films

Take notice of what media you're consuming regularly and how you're responding to it. If you're going to enter the documentary community, it is a good idea to get familiar with the work that's already out there. Watch other documentaries to get inspired and see how other filmmakers kept their audience watching. What's at the core of the films you gravitate towards? Is it an issue, a person, or an event? Consider the genre you're interested in pursuing. Do you like the true crime films, or do you typically watch docs on climate change or extreme sports? Do you like historical documentaries, or more of a real-time political thriller? Do you gravitate towards documentaries that unpack a social issue? You want to add to the landscape, so you need to know what's already out there.

It's hard to find inspiration within the confines of your familiar space. If you can, go outside, take a walk, meet with people who inspire you and ask a lot of questions. Read magazines, newspapers, and books that talk about people and issues you are interested in. **You never know where the inspiration will come from**. What are the issues that are most important in your community, your state, your country, our planet? Not every film has to have an issue at its core, but that could be a path in to telling a story. Let other people know what you're interested in so they can help find stories too.

Find an Interesting Character

In documentaries, we often have the pleasure of meeting someone we would never otherwise meet on screen. Whereas narrative films are populated with celebrities and actors talented at their craft, documentaries present the unique opportunity to bring the audience into a real person's intimate environment. We get to be a fly on the wall in someone's life which is an exciting and rare opportunity.

Questions to Consider:

- *What makes someone a compelling or interesting character to follow?*
- *What is this character doing that no one else is?*
- *Why is this character's perspective unique?*

This character doesn't necessarily need to be a role model; they can be a flawed human working towards redemption, or a person going on a journey and you're going to capture what happens to them along the way. Maybe it's a group of people going through some kind of change or challenge and you have multiple characters to follow. One way to seek out a character is to look within the issue or topic you are interested in spotlighting. If you want to make a film about climate change, who are the people working on the frontlines? If you want to make a film about extreme sports, who are the athletes embarking on an unknown journey and testing their limits? If women's rights is something you are passionate about, who are the leaders in this space? And who are the most vulnerable populations? You might have the whole film revolve around one character, or you might seek out multiple characters to illuminate, depending on the structure of your film.

Access Is Everything

When you embark on making a documentary, one of the first things to think about is **access**. What access do you have to this character, this issue, this story? This is very important because you want to make sure that no one else can come along and make a similar film to yours at the same time. Several filmmakers will make films on climate change, but we're not as likely to see several films specifically featuring climate activist Greta Thunberg. And if we did, chances are they would still be quite different from one another. Carving out your unique lens will become very important for fundraising, as grant organizations and potential investors want to know that you have access to your subjects.

Maybe the main character can't speak for themselves because they've passed on, so you need access to their close family and friends to help paint the picture. Ideally, your character has a great story that can be revealed over the course of the film, like peeling back the layers of an onion.

Securing access may come in the form of exclusive rights, life rights, or simply the unique perspective you'll bring to this story. You might read a story in *The New York Times*, contact the journalist, and find out how to reach out to the subject of the article. Then it's up to you to pitch them your idea for your film, and see if they will sign an agreement with you for the rights to their story.

In the very beginning of making *Losing Sight of Shore,* my film about a team of women who rowed a boat across the Pacific Ocean, getting the exclusive rights to tell their story was incredibly important so that I knew no one else would have access to it. If ESPN was also making a film about this journey, it wouldn't have been worth it for me to pursue raising money and trying to get it distributed because their resources far exceed mine. And there were two layers to consider with this film. There was the journey itself—four women getting in a boat and rowing across the Pacific Ocean, over 8,000 miles. Then there were the characters themselves. It was clear to me that if those four people were not willing to open up along the way—if they weren't compelling characters to watch—this film would fall flat. Characters were everything in this film.

The first thing I did was interview each of the four members of the Coxless Crew on Skype to see what they'd be like on camera, and hear what their motivations were for embarking on this seemingly impossible journey. I asked about their backgrounds, what brought them to this journey, why they would choose to do this, what they thought of each other, and how they might react to an impossible situation of being stuck at sea for months at a time. I essentially asked the basics of who, what, when, where, and why, knowing that we would get far more in depth once I met them in person.

Then, once I could see that they would be compelling characters to watch, each in different ways, we came to an agreement so that I would have exclusive rights to the story of their journey across the Pacific Ocean. Not their individual life rights, but their journey across the ocean, and whatever came of it. You're going to want to work with a lawyer to make sure that agreement encompasses everything you need to move ahead with production.

Access was everything for *Losing Sight of Shore*. That access gave me the confidence to continue. As more and more people heard about their journey and became interested in what they were doing, I knew I wasn't going to lose the opportunity to tell their story. It was indisputably mine. I could tell grant organizations and distributors that I had the exclusive rights, and those rights were more valuable by the day. By the time the Coxless Crew made it across the Pacific Ocean, they set two world records. And I was the only one with the power to tell the story of that journey in a documentary.

When it comes to access, I want you to think about why YOU are the best person to tell this story. Why should these people or this person trust YOU with their story? What point of view are you coming at this with? You need to be able to answer those questions in order to secure the access you need to move forward. I was the best person to tell the Coxless Crew's story because I brought a different lens to the journey. I didn't care much about the rowing aspect – even though that's what the base of the story entailed. I cared deeply about the women taking the risk, I cared about their friendships, their determination to achieve the impossible, and I knew coming from that place would make this unique.

Inspiration Can't Be Forced

These tools and prompts are meant to get you started, but some of the best ideas and stories will come to you when you least expect it. Sometimes it hits you like a ton of bricks, and other times it's a slow burn inside your heart, until you can't ignore it anymore. Sometimes an idea falls in your lap, and if you're not paying attention, you could miss it.

I'll never forget the email I got in January of 2015 from a blogger in the UK named Fiona Tatton. I had recently finished my first feature film, *The Empowerment Project*, and was days away from going on an eight-week, eight-city tour around the US with the film. Needless to say, I was "busy." Fiona was emailing to let me know she had come across four women, known as the Coxless Crew, and they were soon setting off to row across the Pacific Ocean. She wanted to know if I was interested in connecting with them based on my prior work. No pressure, no expectations, just an innocent, "Shall I connect you?"

I was stunned. I had no idea any human ever attempted this, and I was blown away that it was a team of women. Something about this email whispered to me to find out more. I promptly set up a call with two of the rowers the next day, even though I had no idea what I was doing. It all came from an email that I could have let float right on by and no one would have been the wiser. Little did I know, that email—and that call, and the two years that followed—would change my life forever, and launch me into the greatest adventure I could have ever imagined.

CHAPTER THREE

I Have an Idea...Now What?

Ah-ha! The light bulb has finally lit up and you have found the seed of an idea for a documentary. It's a compelling character, or an interesting event, or a social issue that you feel deeply about. Wonderful! Even though there is endless work ahead, now is not the time to lose steam. It is not easy to find an idea, so hooray for the first step! Bask in the glow of feeling inspired, and then let's get to work.

There are three main elements that every documentary project needs to get off the ground: **a treatment or proposal, a sizzle reel or video sample, and a budget**. When you have these three elements, you can start pitching your idea to investors, apply for grants, prepare to crowdfund, and perhaps most importantly, you can articulate what this idea is all about to yourself and to the world. If you don't know why you're making this project, it will be hard to get anyone else on board. Even if you don't know how you're going to fundraise yet (you will learn in subsequent chapters!), trust that these elements are essential to any route you take. It's important to also mention that, early on, these documents are fluid. Things evolve as your project progresses, so it's ok if you don't have all the answers right now. What's vital is that you generally know what you want to make, why you want to make it, and what it might cost. The treatment should answer these questions for the reader: Why you? Why this? And why now? The primary purpose of this document is to secure funding, so you want it to be as compelling as possible.

To be clear, you may be working on these three elements before you even pick up the camera, but that is not always possible. Sometimes you have to start filming to even have something to write in your proposal, and an idea of your budget, and footage to cut in your sizzle. There is no standard order here for the independent filmmaker, but a treatment or proposal, sizzle or video sample and budget are an essential part to the beginning of your journey to make the film. And these three elements will constantly evolve.

First things first, in your treatment or proposal, you will need a logline and a synopsis of your story. Again, it's ok and normal that this will change between day one and when it's time to send these to your distributor for public view. The **logline** is usually one to two sentences of short and sweet information explaining what this film is about. Think of it as the short description you read on iTunes or Netflix that inspires you to watch (or not watch) the film.

An example logline:

Four women set out to row across the Pacific Ocean from America to Australia unsupported. (*Losing Sight of Shore*)

A **synopsis** is a succinct overview of what your story is about, why the story is significant and how you're going to tell it. Give an overview of your story including the main characters and plot points.

An example synopsis:

Losing Sight of Shore follows the extraordinary journey of four brave women known as the Coxless Crew that set out to row the Pacific Ocean from America to Australia unsupported. As they row over 8,000 miles during their nine months at sea, they face extreme mental and physical challenges they must overcome in order to go down in history. This is a story of perseverance, friendship and the power of the human spirit. Everyone has a Pacific to cross.

Now, did I have the synopsis written out like this from the beginning? Not exactly. First of all, I didn't know for sure if they would make it across the ocean. Also, I didn't know it would take nine months, or how many total miles they'd row. So my synopsis would look different from the beginning of their journey to the end. Try writing one for your project, send it to a few friends, get feedback, and keep tweaking it until it feels strong.

Another example synopsis:

Taking a look behind the headlines of #MeToo and Time's Up, *Nevertheless* follows the intimate stories of seven individuals who have experienced sexual harassment in the workplace or school context. From a writer's assistant on a top TV show to a Tech CEO and 911 dispatcher, the film shines a light on the ways in which we can shift our culture and rebuild. Nevertheless we persist.

A treatment or proposal explains the nuts and bolts of the story, the anticipated path at the outset, and what you're hoping to discover and accomplish through the making of the film. Include a synopsis of the story, detailing characters, scenes, and events you anticipate being included. The two documents are slightly different. A proposal will read more like a business plan. A documentary proposal includes a synopsis of the story, but also talks about the distribution strategy and financials so that potential investors can get excited. A proposal is a more holistic view of the whole project, from creative to financial, whereas a treatment is typically rooted mainly in the story and characters.

When writing your treatment or proposal, use definitive language like "The film is..." rather than "This film might be about..." It's also important to include some idea of the visual language of the piece. Film is a visual medium, so including visuals in the treatment is important. Some filmmakers like to create look books to go with their treatments or proposals to give an idea of tone and style for the visual language of the film. Also acknowledge how you're going to shoot the film—what cameras you'll use, and what access you have to the story. Tell us your vision for this project, even if it will change. Tell us why we should trust you with our funding or support through your clarity of vision and confidence in your ability to tell this story.

Questions to consider when writing:

Who are your characters?

What challenges will they face?

What is going to happen in this film?

What themes do you see emerging as you tell this story?

Why should audiences care to watch this?

Why does this matter?

Why are YOU the best person to make this film?

Here is a look at one of my treatments for *Losing Sight of Shore*, and this was written when I had done about two thirds of the filming with the Coxless Crew, they had set off on their journey, but I didn't know how it would end up when I wrote this. I used what information I had so far, and then projected what we hoped would happen for the ending. As the journey progressed, this document was constantly evolving.

Losing Sight of Shore

A documentary by Sarah Moshman

Everyone has a Pacific to cross.

In April of 2015, four women set out to row across the Pacific Ocean—*unsupported*—from America to Australia. If they make it, it will be a world's first. The epic journey across the Pacific will cover 8,446 miles in three stages and take more than nine months to complete. Stops are planned in Hawaii and Samoa.

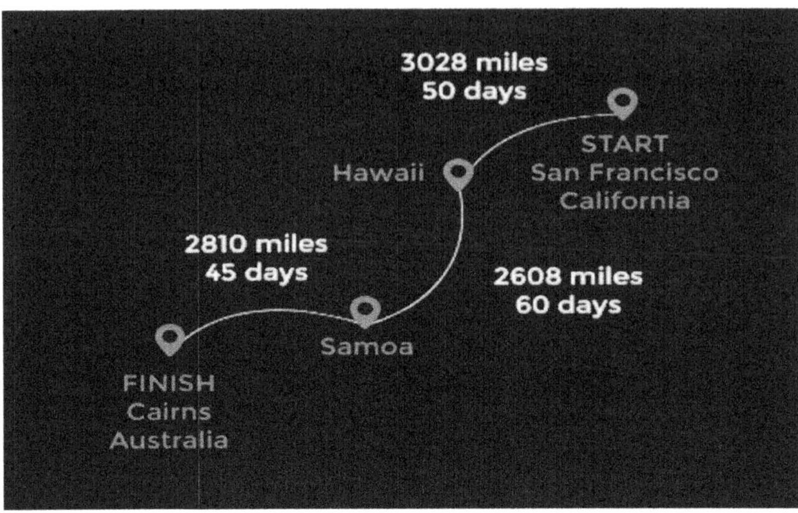

Laura Penhaul, Izzy Burnham, Natalia Cohen, and Emma Mitchell make up the Coxless Crew, hailing from England and South Africa, and are taking this extraordinary journey to not only test their own limits, but to honor women who have faced adversity in their lives.

The expedition supports the work and is raising money for Breast Cancer Care and Walking With The Wounded organizations. By completing this challenge the team wishes to inspire others to reach their own potential and to meet the trials and hardships that life throws at them, however big or small.

We will all have to face our own Pacific Ocean at some point in our lives.

Losing Sight of Shore begins as the fearless crew prepares to travel to the United States from their home country of England. Final workouts, meetings, and packing take place before heading to San Francisco for the big launch. Once in the US, Laura, Emma, Izzy, and Natalia work tirelessly to prepare their 5th team member—*Doris*—their boat and home at sea, for the epic journey ahead.

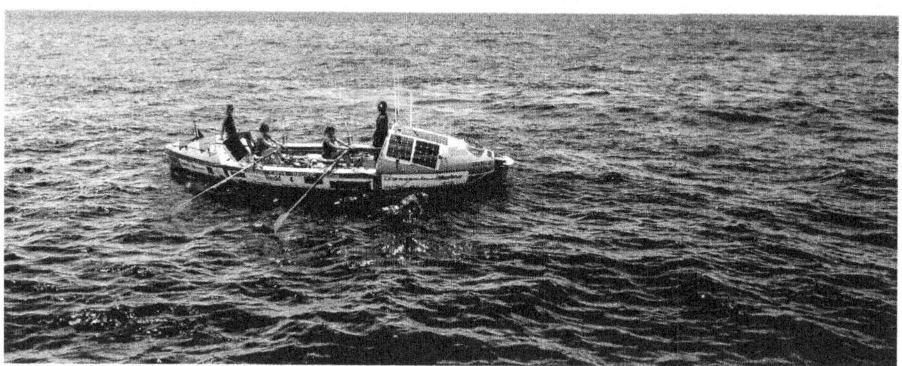

Doris is 29 feet long, seven feet wide, and is fully equipped for any scenario that may come their way. She has solar panels to power their devices, as well as two sleeping compartments complete with all the necessary navigation tools.

These four women come from all different backgrounds and skill sets, but all crave this journey for a similar purpose: to leave their mark on the world.

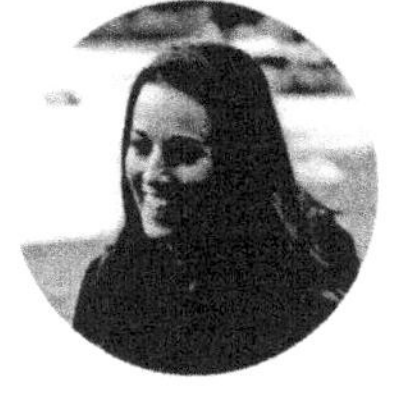

LAURA PENHAUL
TEAM LEAD

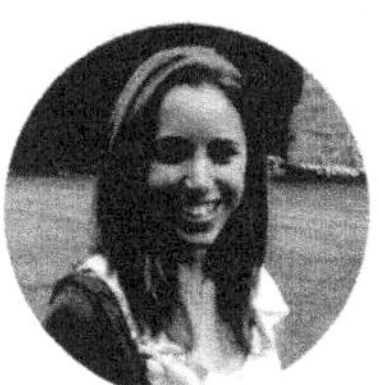

EMMA MITCHELL
TEAM MEMBER

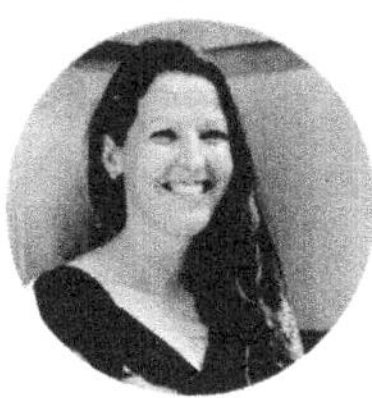

ISABEL BURNHAM
TEAM MEMBER

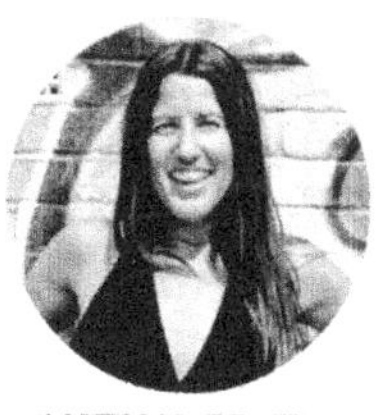

NATALIA COHEN
TEAM MEMBER

Laura Penhaul (32) has been preparing for the trip for the last three years in between working as a Sports Physiologist with Paralympic athletes. Laura has the most at stake in the journey and serves as the leader of the crew. She is evolving her definition of what it means to be a good leader each day at sea and showing her vulnerable side.

Emma Mitchell (30) is the introverted, serious, hard-worker with the most rowing experience since she picked up the sport at the age of 12. Always putting others before herself, Emma is the resident rowing expert.

Izzy Burnham (30) is the practical, organized, lawyer of the group with the most inner turmoil given that her family doesn't want her to take the whole journey for fear of her safety. Izzy must decide if she will row the entire way, or stop once they reach Hawaii.

Natalia Cohen (40) had never rowed before joining the Coxless Crew, and plans to draw on her mental strength and spirituality in tough times. She is the most in touch with her emotions and vows to bring as much fun to the group as she can. She refers to the ocean as the "Almighty Pacific."

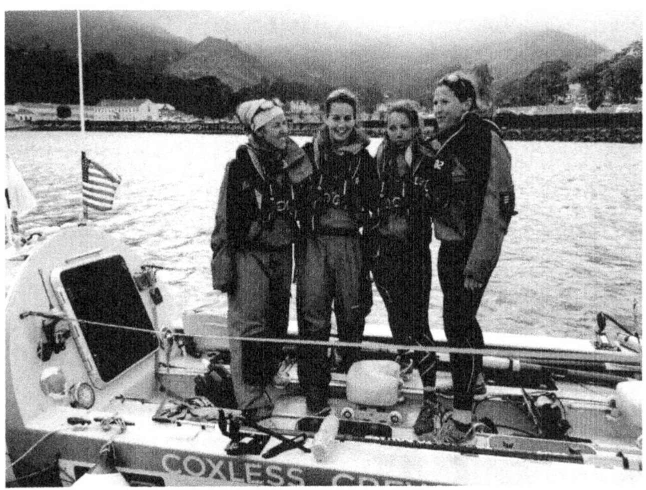

With their worried and tearful parents by their side, the Coxless Crew successfully secures *Doris* into the harbor and embarks on a practice row in the choppy seas of the San Francisco Bay. The overwhelming winds of the Bay foreshadow some rough days ahead at sea. Months of planning and training for their once-in-a-lifetime journey to row across the world's largest ocean has led to this moment. Confident they can handle the turbulent Pacific, the women launch with the midnight tide under the fog shrouded Golden Gate Bridge. "Three cheers for *Doris*! Hip Hip, Hooray...Hip Hip, Hooray...Hip Hip, Hooray!"

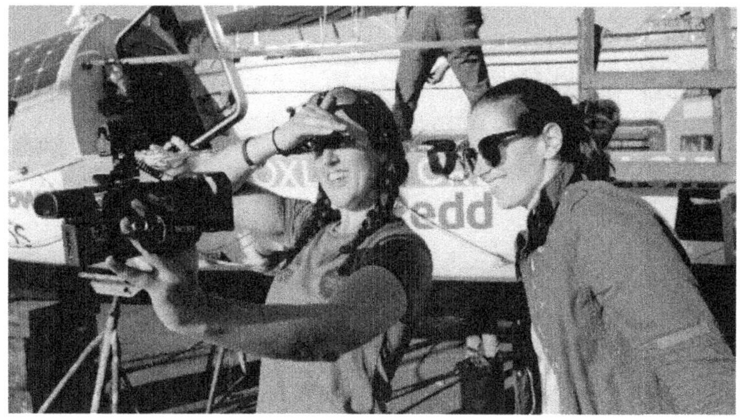

Director Sarah Moshman has empowered the crew to be storytellers and bring the audience into their experiences—the good, the bad, and the ugly. Once at sea, the team tells their own story of determination, bravery, and fearlessness in a way that no one else could. Their tools are weatherproof Go Pros, as well as a Sony 4K camera and a digital audio recorder. **There is always a way to record their story on the boat. No matter what.**

Sixteen days out at sea, *Doris* has a leak and ruins one of their MPPT batteries, disabling them from continuing to charge their devices. Disappointed and discouraged, the team make the tough decision to turn into Santa Barbara and fix *Doris* before continuing on, delaying their trip, and in essence, causing them to start over.

On the boat, the crew faces challenges on a regular basis. From huge waves crashing down on them, to large boats and storms they must avoid, to sleep deprivation, life on the boat is anything but ordinary. They make friends with wildlife as they spot birds, sharks, and whales along their path. Wind is their greatest asset as well as their worst enemy when it comes to staying on track. **The Crew rows 24 hours a day in two-hour shifts, thus only sleeping for two hours at a time, and often in a boiling hot cabin.** The crew must keep each other encouraged and determined through seasickness, scary weather conditions, and extreme exhaustion.

The story continues in Hawaii, now 68 days in, with the Coxless Crew finally able to sleep in a bed, eat hot food, catch up with friends, and of course, shower. The greatest challenge the ladies face at this point is to summon the strength to get back in *Doris* after their week-long hiatus. Tony Humphreys, their on-land supporter and trainer, is there to coach them and help problem solve for the next leg.

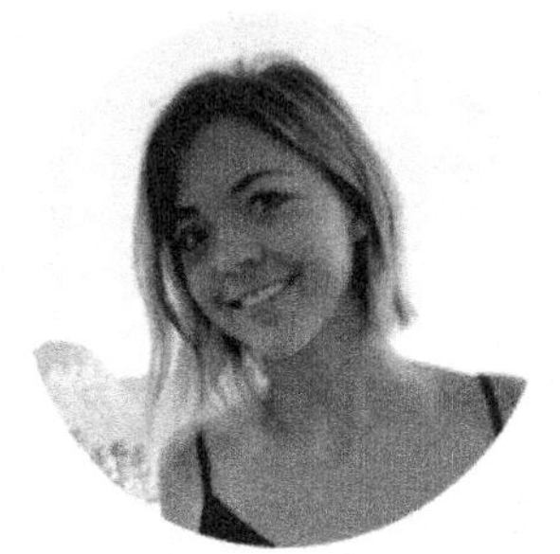

LIZANNE VAN VUUREN
TEAM MEMBER (2ND LEG)

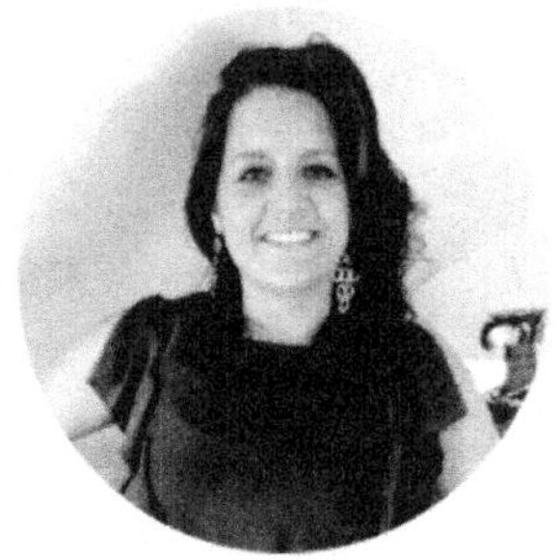

MEG DYOS
TEAM MEMBER (3RD LEG)

Izzy's inner battle to please her worried parents flares up, and she decides to let Lizanne Van Vuuren take her place in the boat and continue on the trip across the Pacific. Even though she may always regret it, Izzy doesn't want to cause a rift in her relationship with her family, so she makes the tough decision to head home instead of continuing on.

Refreshed, re-invigorated, and with a new energy in the boat, the Coxless Crew set off on the second leg of their journey to Samoa. They must cross the equator on this leg and face the dreaded doldrums—an area of the Pacific known for its stagnation of current, trapping boats for days or weeks. **What should have taken 60 days from Hawaii to Samoa is now taking 97 days to complete, and the Coxless Crew must ration their short food supply in order to survive.**

"Imagine if you will being on a roller coaster. Now imagine being on the roller coaster without being strapped in. This is what being aboard Doris is like at the moment."

Emma Mitchell (Day 9 at Sea)

Once on the shores of Samoa, the crew is greeted by the locals and immediately fall in love with the culture. Again they are challenged with getting back in the boat after such a short rest, but this time they have the finish line in their sights. Lizanne swaps out for the sixth member of the Coxless Crew, Meg Dyos, who again brings a new perspective and energy to the team. Emma, Laura, and Nat happily show her the routine of life on *Doris.*

These women have become a unit. Each one's strengths compliment and protect the others' weaknesses. Roles are divided and clear, and they keep each other in check. The emotion of reaching Cairns, Australia is almost too much to bear as the world is watching these brave women achieve their greatest dream—together.

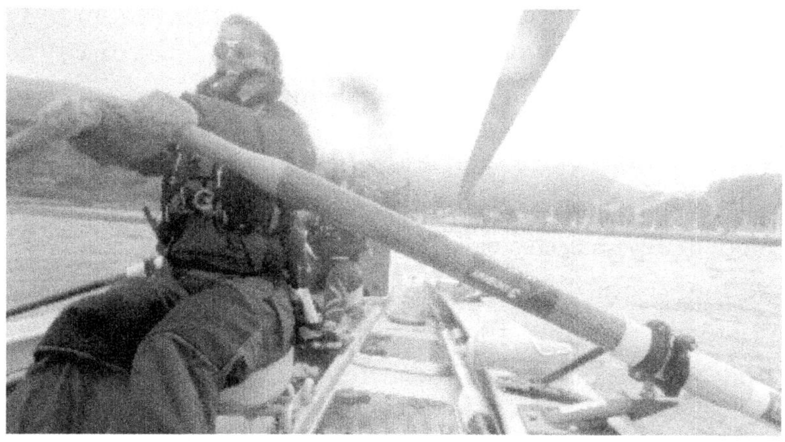

Family and friends greet them on their triumphant arrival, and life will never quite be the same. They have set three world records, but most importantly, they have achieved the extraordinary goal they set for themselves and proven what the human spirit is capable of.

Losing Sight of Shore visuals are a combination of the footage from the boat cameras capturing the raw vérité of the struggle, as well as the film crew documenting of the launch and each of the stops along the way. (Shot on the Sony FS7 in 4K as well as the DJI Phantom drone system.) As the Coxless Crew approaches Cairns, Australia for that final moment of success and fulfillment, a camera boat and aerial drone join the rowers up close, in action, in their last hours coming to shore. The completed film will mix both types of footage to create the unique and captivating cinematic narrative.

Losing Sight of Shore is an international story of friendship, perseverance, and adventure. These women have embarked on a journey of a lifetime to inspire anyone in the world to pursue their wildest aspirations and not let anything stand in their way.

Everyone has a Pacific to cross...what's yours?

***

In the treatment, I include quotes, photos, and I bold the important parts of the story, so that if someone is simply skimming, they can still grasp the concept. I never want to assume someone is going to read my treatment thoroughly. The information is there, but with such a fast-paced world, I want to make it easy for people to read and understand.

A sizzle reel or video sample is as it sounds: a visual representation of the film and the characters. This is your chance to bring the treatment to life. You don't always need a video sample to pitch a project, but it certainly helps to further explain and explore what it is you are making. And if a potential funder is looking at several projects at once, it will set you apart to have a video sample rather than just a written treatment. A sizzle reel is also tremendously important if your film is character-based, as you will want to show how dynamic and interesting your characters are in order to pitch the film properly.

This too will evolve over the course of making the film. At the beginning you might have no money to start the project, or you might have some development funds from yourself, or a grant organization. The good news is your sizzle reel doesn't have to be expensive to be effective. It can be as simple as recorded Skype or Zoom interviews edited together. As you progress in your filming, it will evolve into a polished trailer.

When I was beginning *Losing Sight of Shore*, I didn't have any funding in place, and I was introduced to the women rowing the ocean less than three months before they were set to leave. I wanted to make a sizzle reel, but there wasn't really a way to do it when they were in England and I was in the United States. So I bought Call Recorder for $20 (a recording add-on to Skype), and I arranged video interviews with all four members of the team. I interviewed each of the women for about an hour, and then I cut that together with pictures of the boat from their website, a map of their projected journey, and some music. I ended up with a two- to three-minute piece. It is not something I shared widely, but it did help me understand what story I was telling, who these women were, and why they were taking this journey. I could tell they were going to be good on camera, and I wanted to see more. It's one thing to read about four women getting in a boat and rowing the Pacific Ocean, but to hear directly from them, to understand why they're doing it, and to see the boat put it all in context. It drove home that this was going to be an extraordinary journey.

That first sizzle worked until I could cut a new one with better footage when I got to meet them in person a couple months later. And, fun fact—one of the sound bites I got in the first Skype interview with rower Natalia Cohen ended up as the last line of the film. She said, "I believe everyone has a Pacific to cross." Even though she said that line again in interviews (with better microphones), she never quite said it the same as she did on Skype day one. So record everything, even early on. You never know if you're getting content you can use!

If you do have some funding in place, it might make sense to spend a little bit of money and time to be in the world with your subjects. This can be a great way to begin building your relationship with them, as well as capture some initial footage, which will help the project progress. Think about setting up some interviews with the major characters, perhaps shooting a scene if this story is active and happening right now, and start establishing your access. You will learn so much about your project by picking up the camera and going to shoot some footage. And if you are not an editor yourself, you can hire someone to edit a short reel for your project. It may even be a great way to find the editor for the full film, testing how well you work together.

For my documentary *Nevertheless,* I didn't know where to begin to talk about sexual harassment. I didn't have any inherent characters yet; I just had an issue to dissect, so it could go any number of ways. I began with researching the topic and decided to set up interviews in Los Angeles and San Francisco over the course of two weeks, with six shooting days. I did pre-interviews and exploratory calls with sexual harassment training consultants, employment attorneys, diversity and inclusion managers, and brave women willing to share their story. I interviewed 16 people in those two weeks, so I had a ton of content to use to make my first sizzle. I pulled footage from women's marches, I pulled news clips of this timely issue and #MeToo, and put it all together with an editor to make a three-minute sizzle reel. Since it was so early in the process, I didn't know what the film would ultimately say about sexual harassment, but I could present the problem, the timeliness of the issue, and I could establish the tone of the piece with this first sizzle. I was very happy with it, and we cut down a one-minute version as well for crowdfunding. And truthfully, that sizzle didn't end up being very close to the final film trailer, but that's ok. It was all part of the journey. You can also do what's called a **found footage** sizzle reel. This means you don't go out and shoot a frame, but you still create a sizzle reel for your project by pulling clips from similar projects with a similar tone to show the visual style, and pairing it with great music and effective graphics. This works more often for a television show pitch, especially when a celebrity is involved.

Any route you decide to take, it is a tremendously helpful exercise to create a video sample of some kind, even if it evolves considerably from when you begin, to help articulate your project to yourself, and to the world. This sample will come in handy immediately as you begin fundraising. It may even help you write a stronger treatment, since you will know your subjects and vision that much better. Typically, the sizzle reel can be anywhere from two to seven minutes, depending on what you're making. Try to watch as many other sizzles from films and filmmakers you admire. See how they structured their piece, and allow it to inspire you.

Ok. Now—how much is this going to cost to make?

The budget is essential for fundraising, as well as mapping out what your project needs in order to complete it the way you envision it. The budget is also a living, breathing document that will change as the project progresses. Creating a budget is tricky, as you want to be truthful about what this will cost to create, but you also don't quite know what challenges you will face along the way, which often incur more cost. Especially when it's your first project, there are many line items in the budget you may not know to include that are inherent to every film. But you need to start somewhere.

Questions to consider when it comes to budget:

- *How long will it take to shoot this film? Days/weeks/months?*
- *Where do you need to go to film? Domestic/international?*
- *What kind of equipment is needed? Underwater cameras/drone photography?*
- *How big is your film crew? Cinematographer/Sound/Producer/ Production Assistant?*
- *How long do you think you need to edit the film?*
- *Do you know who you want to hire and what their ideal rate is?*
- *When is your goal for completion?*

These questions are a good starting point when thinking about the costs. You can even break it up phase by phase.

What will **pre-production** cost? This phase may include some research and consulting, making a sizzle reel, but should remain relatively low cost.

What will **production** cost? That completely depends on the scope of the project. How long will it take to shoot, and where does the shoot take place? How big is the crew? For *Losing Sight of Shore*, I had to travel to San Francisco, Santa Barbara, Hawaii, Samoa, and Australia, and equip the rowers with gear so they could film every day. The costs of that film was very different from a one month road trip with five women in *The Empowerment Project*.

Post-production is often overlooked, but you definitely need to budget for it. It's not unusual for post-production to be the most expensive phase. A good editor is worth their weight in gold. So much of the creation of a documentary is made in the edit room. And once the film is cut, you're going to want sound editing, mixing, color correction, an original score, graphics, animation, and more to make it the best it can be.

Then there's **distribution and marketing**, both of which are also overlooked when it comes to a budget. Finishing the film does not mean the costs are done. You need money for errors and omissions insurance, which most distributors require; you need money to create your deliverables, to host screenings of your film, to run an impact campaign, and to market your film to an audience.

Your salary

It's important to note that you, as the director and likely producer of this project, deserve to be paid for your time making it. You should absolutely include a salary for yourself in this budget. Even if you are the last one paid from the money you raise, you need to make sure to pay yourself for this work. We want the career of a documentary filmmaker to be a sustainable one, so if we get in the habit of never paying ourselves, we set a dangerous precedent for other filmmakers. You are going to put your heart and soul into this project, you deserve to be paid for your time. What should your salary be? One place to start is giving yourself 10% of the total budget as your directing fee. But if you are taking on multiple roles, as so many of us do, you can increase that number to reflect your other responsibilities (a producer, a cinematographer, etc.). Consider how much of your time you are spending on making this project, you could allot a monthly fee for yourself instead of a larger flat rate.

Other costs

Make sure you take note of each line item in a budget, and know what cost it refers to. A contingency, for example, is some padding that you're going to want in case something goes wrong and you need more funding. Typically, a contingency is 5-10% of the total budget. Then there's errors and omissions insurance, which can cost anywhere from $3,000-$5,000 for a feature film. That policy helps protect you and your company if anyone files a lawsuit or comes after the project claiming they didn't agree to be in your film, a defamation claim, etc. After your first film, it will be easier to anticipate the budgetary needs of your next project. Don't forget things like building a website, legal fees, hard drive costs, crew meals, and much more. This budget should encompass all of that.

I typically operate with two budgets throughout the course of a project. I have the day-to-day budget that gets updated constantly on Google Docs, and that no one sees but me. Then I have the shiny budget that goes out to potential funders and partners that has a top sheet and line item budget laid out. I do this because one is a projection, and one is reality. When you're starting a project, you need to put together a full budget of what this project would cost without much sacrifice. If you are able to pay everyone their normal/full rates, if you are able to travel to every location, to pay yourself in full, put it all in that shiny budget. You should know the value of the project you're creating, even if you end up spending far less. This is always a tough determination for an independent filmmaker, because almost everything in this process is negotiable, but you need some place to start. A potential funder will ask you what your total budget is to make this project, and you need to be able to give a number without selling yourself short.

If you are really uncomfortable making a budget, or you don't know where to begin, you can consult with a **line producer,** someone who works with budgets all the time. Use a template, or build a budget from someone else's example, and get advice and feedback from people who know what things typically cost for projects like yours.

Here is an example of my day-to-day budget on Google Sheets for Pre-Production/Research on *Nevertheless* which I funded myself:

PRE-PRODUCTION/ RESEARCH AUG 2017 - OCT 2017	
OCTOBER/NOVEMBER 2017 - LA and SF SHOOTS 16 interviews	
DP fee + meal reimbursement	1038.56
VIDCAM gear rental 2 weeks (severely discounted)	880
Plane ticket Southwest LA to SF round trip	212.97
Gas driving up to SF and back	108.73
Rental space for interviews in LA- Peerspace	631.05
Hard drives 2 Lacie 2 TB drives	319.88
Slate	13.89
Crew meals in LA and SF	260.33
Women's March - DP fee	200
Women's March parking	30
Lunch at Stella Barra on march day (crew lunch)	49.5
Transcribing interviews	300
TOTAL 2017 expenses	**4044.91**

And this is the top sheet for the very first full budget I put together for *Nevertheless:*

UNTITLED SEXUAL HARASSMENT PROJECT BUDGET TOP SHEET	**Total**
Producers Unit	**164,000**
Crew	**37,500**
Consultants/Writers	**5,000**
Travel & Location Expenses	**56,400**
Equipment Rental & Supplies	**20,000**
Cards, Drives, Transcripts	**13,500**
Visual Effects	**72,200**
Sound Studio	**5,000**
Editing	**133,600**
Music	**18,000**
Film, Photo, and Music Rights	**30,000**
Research	**2,000**
Finishing (Online, Mix)	**30,270**

Insurance, Legal, Accounting	**33,000**
Marketing and Distribution	**275,000**
Office	**3,900**
Subtotal	**899,370**
Fiscal Sponsor Fee 7%	**62,956**
Contingency 10%	**89,937**
TOTAL BUDGET	**1,052,263**

It may come as no surprise I did not end up raising or spending $1 million on the film, but it was a good exercise for me to see what the film would cost if I was able to dream big and pay everyone what they're worth. This did also include marketing and distribution costs, which as we will discuss are a whole other phase of the project to consider. There are some great sample budgets on documentary.org. You can also ask colleagues and peers to share their budgets with the project names and personal names removed for privacy.

For *The Empowerment Project* we made that film for about $50,000, which in hindsight was nothing, but at the same felt like just enough to do what we wanted to do. Dana Cook, the producer of the film, and I were not able to take a salary while making the film because the budget was so low.

For *Losing Sight of Shore*, I ended up budgeting and spending right around $250,000 to make that film, which was much lower than what it should have cost considering the scope of the story. But I didn't have the funds to spend more. I spent what I could raise, piece by piece. Had I worked with a production company or brought on a celebrity executive producer my budget would have been much higher to account for those entities. I was not able to take a salary during the making of the film.

My total budget for *Nevertheless* was more in the $200k to $225k range, without all marketing expenses accounted for, which I'm still in the midst of. But this time, I was able to pay myself a modest salary as I was making the film, which was a huge step forward.*

Each of these were feature documentaries in the 80-100 minute range, and that's with me taking on multiple roles to get them across the finish line.

A doc-series is going to cost more, as you are likely creating more content than a feature, just as a short would likely cost less.

Once you have a treatment, sizzle, and budget, you are in a great place to start truly moving down the path to getting this film made.

*A note here to say when I wasn't able to take a salary on my first two films, I hustled to work other jobs to sustain a living. I worked in television as a producer on short-term gigs, started consulting and doing speaking engagements. Also when I was making *Losing Sight of Shore*, I was finally getting revenue from *The Empowerment Project* which helped me pay my bills. I don't like it when we aren't transparent with each other as filmmakers about how we make a living, it can make this profession seem so privileged and unattainable.

CHAPTER FOUR

THE LEGAL SIDE

I am not a lawyer. This is not formal legal advice. Please consult with an attorney before following any of these guidelines.

Before you begin any project, it's important for you to know and have a basic understanding of the legal side of documentary filmmaking. I know, this part can get a little dry and boring, but I promise this is essential to your success and safety for the future of your career. Please make sure you work with or consult with a lawyer at several junctions of your project to ensure that you are set up for distribution and long-term revenue. I have learned a ton in this arena by asking a lot of questions, making a lot of mistakes, and getting burned a bit, so I'm happy to share with you what to look out for.

A good lawyer is going to cost anywhere from $300-$500/hour, but in the long run they will save you hundreds if not thousands of dollars, not to mention headaches. Make sure to build them into your budget! The truth is, you don't know what you don't know. Lawyers are going to point out the red flags you didn't even see, and save you from sticky situations. Seek out an entertainment specific attorney; or better yet, one that has worked in documentaries before. Once you find a lawyer you like, build rapport and develop a relationship. If it all goes well, you will want to keep working with them on future projects. Lawyers are here to help you! Let's break their role down by project phases, and see what kind of legal support you might need.

Setting up an S Corp or LLC

Before you truly begin a new project and raise money, you likely need to set up either an S Corp or an LLC. The primary reason is protection against liability. You want to protect yourself as an individual should anyone file a lawsuit or claim against your project, and an LLC provides a layer of protection.

Additionally, for tax purposes in the United States, when you raise money, you don't want it to appear as income on your tax return. You want the project to be a completely separate entity, and organized as such. This is particularly important for the distribution phase of the project when revenue starts coming in. You can set up your business entity on your own using a service like Legal Zoom, or you can work with your lawyer. They will ask questions about the structure of the project and of the team. Are you bringing on investors? Do you have a partner in this venture? All of that will be important to know before you spend the time and money setting up an LLC. Depending on the state you live in in the US, the annual LLC fee will vary. California is one of the more expensive states at $800/year.

Partnership Agreements

This brings us to working with a partner—or partners—on a project, and what agreement you might need in place to secure that partnership, especially if you're starting an LLC together. It's always hard for people to talk about the legality of partnerships. Especially at the start of a partnership, when everyone is excited and there's a lot of energy to get started, the last thing you want to do is talk about contingencies should things go wrong. But if there's ever an important time to map out the relationship, it's now. You want to be clear about everyone's roles, ownership rights, what salary each partner should get if/when there is a budget to pay a salary, and the revenue share of the film from distribution.

It is very important to include in your partnership agreement what happens if one of you needs to exit the project. Films are often passion projects that can take years to complete, with many life changes running parallel to the project. It's natural if, over time, one of you isn't able to dedicate as much time to this endeavor as you did before. But what then? Are you still credited as a producer? Do you still get a piece of the revenue from the film, or that salary pro-rated? Are you still an owner of the LLC? It's tough to figure all of this out, but it's important to protect yourself and your hard work. And this is where lawyers come in handy. An educated entertainment lawyer will know all of the right questions to ask, and contingencies to plan for. It's a little like creating a pre-nuptial at the start of a marriage—the last thing you want to be thinking about is divorce, and yet the process can ultimately help you protect the things you care about.

I've had my own tough experiences with partnerships. I've been burned many times, working on something I cared deeply about with someone I really admired. In one example, we created a partnership agreement a year into working together, and then six months later, I had to exit the project. It was very emotional and personal, even with an agreement in place. So often we dive into these independent projects not thinking about the money side, because we believe so deeply in the mission or the story. But you need to protect yourself, protect your time, and protect your career. It's ok if things change. Don't be afraid to admit that the contract you had at the beginning of the project no longer serves you. You can always re-evaluate when you get closer to distribution and say that your roles were not as you planned. Maybe you ended up putting in a lot more time and energy than you imagined. Or you made strategic introductions for the project and feel like you deserve a higher credit. A lawyer can help you work through all of this.

Talent or Subject Agreements

A talent or subject agreement is a special one to flag. You might need an agreement with the subjects of your project if they are doing a lot of the filming themselves, or if they are giving or licensing the use of their personal footage to you for your project. Part of this is an **exclusivity agreement**, where you ask for the exclusive right to tell this person's story in your film. The exclusivity agreement can cover exclusive use of their personal footage, which is one way to secure unique access to this person and story. Access is everything in documentary, so your ability to say to a production company or distributor that you are the only one who has access to this never-before-seen footage, or journey, or person is very important when you're selling the project.

When I was making *Losing Sight of Shore*, the Coxless Crew were going to be filming every day while at sea. Now, I wouldn't have a film without their footage at sea, so we had to come up with an agreement to determine what rights I had to that footage, given that it was shot on the cameras I provided. If they turned around and sold all that footage to a sports network, I would lose the special access I had to the story, and I would be unable to make a film. It was an agreement that established my exclusivity to tell their story, our shared ownership of the footage, and what project profit share they would receive in return. This is a special case where the subjects of a documentary were included in the profit stage of the film. That's not typically how it works. You don't want to pay your subjects for taking part in a documentary. There are many dialogues about ethics when it comes to paying your subjects, and in this case it was more about including these rowers in the profit stage of the project, given that they had worked hard to capture so much of the footage in the film, which was important to me, and to them.

Pre-Production

In pre-production, you need to make sure you have all of your proper releases set up before you start shooting. These forms ensure that you have the proper permission to be filming these people, or this location, or this material. If you don't have the right documents in place, or the right wording, then you can't use that footage, and you'll have to reshoot everything once a new release form is created.

There are different kinds of releases, like appearance release, materials release, location release, and area release. You can find templates online for each type of release, or you can ask a friend in the industry for their standard release forms. A lawyer can help you tweak the language of a template to make sure it fits your project. It's really important you get the language of this document right the first time.

Appearance release or personal release is what you ask your talent, or on-camera interview subjects, to sign. This allows you to use their image and likeness in your film, and to edit and distribute the content worldwide, in perpetuity. There are a lot of templates available online for this document, but it's still a good idea to make sure all of the language used agrees with your project. Make sure the appearance release names your company as possessing the rights to this content, and not you as an individual. You should be operating under an LLC or S Corp by now, so at the top of the form it should state your LLC as the producer of the project, not you as an individual.

If possible, get the appearance release signed before you begin filming so that if in the middle of the interview emotions run high and they have second thoughts or get self-conscious, you already have the release form signed. Even simply following up with someone post-interview can be challenging, so you want to make sure you get all the paperwork done on the day, if you can. You don't want to manipulate anyone into being in your film, but you also need to get your paperwork in order so that you are free and clear to distribute the film in whatever way you see fit once it's done. If the person is under 18 years old, they will need a parent or guardian to sign with them, so leave time and space for that as well.

Celebrities and public figures can be a different story. You may need to send the release form to their attorneys to get their approval on the language used, which may take time and some extra money for your lawyer and their lawyers to come to an agreement. Typically a lawyer or public figure will not sign an appearance release outright, so do what you can to send it ahead of time to their team. If you can, get it settled before the interview. If you don't and the interview goes really well, you won't fully feel like you captured it until that release is signed.

A celebrity or public figure will have more concerns about how it's going to be distributed, and they may ask to see a cut of the film before it's done. That's up to you, but make sure you ultimately have final cut of the film, so that even if they give feedback, you decide what to do with that feedback. A celebrity or public figure may also have issues with how the film will be promoted, and may ask to see any trailers or posters. They don't want to be exploited or hoisted up as endorsing this film when they haven't even seen it. These are all valid concerns. Chances are they don't know you, and they don't know your intentions, or what you plan to do with this film once it's done. They're going to sit down with you for an hour, and then you're going to choose a few minutes of sound bites that shape the way they look and sound, so it's important they know they're in good hands. You want them to feel well represented.

Materials release. This release is for when you as the producer want to use someone's personal property in the film. Typically this is for artwork or family photographs, you will list out the items you need permission to use and then the owner of the artwork or photographs will sign a release stating it's ok for you to use those items in the film. This could also be someone's personal diary or journal. If you do an interview with someone in their home and a painting is behind them, you need to make sure you can get a materials release for the artwork in the background or have it blurred or out of focus enough that it's not possible to see distinctively what it is.

Location release. A location release is similar to an appearance release but is used when shooting different locations, including private property, some public property, or a private event. These releases will need to be signed by the property owner or a legal representative of the property. Shooting public or government property, like public streets and public sidewalks, or government buildings, do not generally require a location release. But be aware that a permit may be required if your production causes any disruption to the normal traffic flow of people or vehicles. If there is a large crew, a need for cleanup, security, or closing down streets or sidewalks, you'll need a permit. Without a permit, you may get shut down in the middle of your shoot and not get what you need.

Shooting on public property where a private business sign is clearly visible to the public will not generally require a location release from the business, just as you don't need a talent release from someone walking down the street. With regards to property, also make sure that the right person is signing. A random employee may not have the legal right to give you permission for shooting or release. Make sure that the signer is the actual property owner or a legal representative of the property. Just like with appearance releases, when in doubt, go ahead and get a signed release form.

Area release. An area release is used for an area in which you are filming, so that people coming in and out of the shot will know they are being filmed. It's always better to get an appearance release, but not always practical. No one will have to sign this document. Instead, it's enlarged to put on a poster and placed in several locations at your shoot location. The sign needs to be big enough for people to notice and read. An example of this would be at a conference or concert, where people are coming into an enclosed area and may not know they are being filmed. Print several of these releases with large, bold print, and put them around the venue. Also, make sure you get a photo or video of the posted release and its relationship to the environment, just in case you need proof that you had it.

The language generally states:

By entering this area you are agreeing to be filmed and/or photographed for a project currently titled "________________" and if you do not agree, please do not enter this area.

When starting a project, you want to get all four of these releases ready to go under your LLC or S Corp, so that as shoots come up, you're ready. You also want to stay very organized with these forms and save them all together in a physical or digital folder. An organized filing system will come in handy if a problem ever arises. It will also be helpful if your distributor and insurance company want proof of your releases before giving you a policy.

Hiring Crew or an Independent Contractor Agreement

As a filmmaker/entrepreneur, you will likely need to hire crew members with the budget you raise. You should treat those people with the respect of a boss hiring an employee at any larger company. You need to be clear with the scope of work, the day rate, weekly rate, or flat rate you can pay them, and the terms of when you can pay them. You also need to include in your terms—and have in writing—that the footage you pay them to shoot as a cinematographer, or the music they create in an original score, is solely for the film and material that you/your LLC owns. That way, no one can come back and claim it's their film. Your company is the only entity that has all of the rights to this film once it's done. This is called an independent contractor agreement, and below is a sample of that kind of document:

PROJECT NAME - INDEPENDENT CONTRACTOR AGREEMENT * _________________ LLC *

AGREEMENT OVERVIEW: The following will confirm our understanding of the terms agreed upon between you and ______________________ **LLC.** This Agreement, made this DAY OF MONTH, YEAR between ____(“Contractor”) with an address of ________________________________ _______________ and ___________________ with an address of ______________________________, sets forth the entire understanding of the parties with respect to the services to be provided by Contractor to LLC for the documentary project currently titled **“PROJECT TITLE”.**

DATES: Commencing (DATE) and ending by (DATE) as an independent contractor until completion of all services required by LLC. Services include: (SCOPE OF WORK)

COMPENSATION: For the services of CINEMATOGRAPHER, Contractor is to be paid **$**_________. Payment for services will be made once the work is complete unless otherwise requested.

CONTRACTOR'S RELATIONSHIP TO LLC: Contractor's services are provided as an independent contractor and this Agreement creates no obligation for LLC to provide any employment benefits. Contractor shall be responsible for all tax obligations out of this Agreement.

RIGHTS AND OWNERSHIP: LLC shall own all work produced by Contractor related to Production, but Contractor can re-use art pieces with prior permission from FILMMAKER. Contractor irrevocably waives all rights to all of the results and proceeds of Contractor's services in conjunction with Production. Contractor agrees that these rights shall reside solely with LLC in perpetuity, and that this grant of rights shall survive the termination of this Agreement. Contractor acknowledgment that LLC may, in its sole discretion, assign the rights (in whole or in part) set forth in this Agreement.

LLC reserves the right to terminate this agreement at any time. I agree, as shown by my signature, to accept and abide by all company policies and procedures in this Agreement, and all other posted or publicized, written or verbal Company policies and procedures.

AGREED AND ACCEPTED, BY:

FOR LLC

____

CONTRACTOR

____

You will also need to collect a W9 tax document from each person you hire so that when it's time to send out 1099 forms, you have all the information you need of where to send it, and the contractor's social security number (or if they want to be paid through their LLC, their LLC's EIN number). Depending on the state in which your LLC is registered, you may need to pay your crew as employees and put them on payroll. These are all important questions to ask an accountant or lawyer before you begin. Consult with your state and country's tax laws, or a lawyer or accountant before moving forward.

Investor Agreements

If you bring investors onto your film during the fundraising phase, you will absolutely need a contract with those investors. First, you will establish the budget of the film, which becomes the valuation of the project. Your LLC needs to be in alignment with this agreement, so any partners you have in your LLC need to be part of the investor agreement. Then, based on your budget and the amount of money the investor is offering, your lawyer will help you determine what share of equity your investor is entitled to. This is just one way investor agreements are structured. There are other ways to do it, and we'll talk more about investor scenarios in the Fundraising 101 chapter. Lawyers will be indispensable in this process, but you still want to be involved and understand what's happening. A good way to test your knowledge of investor agreements is to correctly explain your investment structure to your lawyer. Don't be afraid to ask questions—it's imperative that you know what you're agreeing when signing investors.

Questions for you to consider:

- *Who owns the rights to the film?*
- *Do I as the director have final cut of the project?*
- *For every dollar that comes into the project once revenue begins, how is that dollar distributed to me and to the investors? (also known as the "waterfall")*
- *What is my creative and fiduciary responsibility to these investors?*
- *What happens if they don't get their money back? What credit will they receive for investing this money?*

Fair Use

This one is a doozy if you are working on a film that leans heavily on archival footage. Fair use is quite a process to endure, and you're going to want to work with an attorney that specializes in Fair Use Law for this phase, which will come in to play when you are nearing the end of post-production.

Basically, let's say you are using 100 archival clips (news clips, newspaper images, copyrighted clips from a television show, etc.) to effectively tell your story. But of course, you don't own the rights to any of those 100 clips. You could opt to pay to license all 100 clips, but your budget likely doesn't allow for that. Plus, some clips may fall under the Fair Use Doctrine, and you might not have to pay to use them in your film. Fair Use, in its simplest form, falls under four pillars of qualifications:

- The **purpose** and character of your use

- The **nature** of the copyrighted work
- The **amount** and substantiality of the portion taken
- The effect of the use upon the potential **market**

During post-production, you and your editor need to keep track of every single clip that isn't yours, and keep track of them in a clip log. In that clip log you should have a link or description of the original source of the clip, the timecodes of when you are using it, the timecodes of the original source ("I'm using 10 seconds of this 60 minute clip"), and the description of that clip. That way, when you have a rough cut of your film, you can submit both the film and your clip log to a Fair Use Attorney. They will help you determine which of those clips makes a case for Fair Use, and which don't. For the ones that might not fall under Fair Use, your choices are to reach out to the owner of the clip and license it, replace or change the clip, or take on the risk of potentially being sued down the road for using copyrighted work. This is quite a back and forth process that can take months, depending on how many clips are in question. Typically you submit your rough or fine cut of the film with the clip log, the attorney reviews all clips along with the film, sends you notes, and you work one by one to update their recommendation to Fair Use. It can be brutal, trust me. In *Nevertheless,* I remember shedding a few tears when I got my Fair Use review back because it meant I had a lot more time I needed to spend on changing, swapping and adjusting clips (that I loved) and a lot more money to spend on licensing some clips, and coming up with creative solutions for others. Long story short, if you have a lot of clips you are hoping to claim as Fair Use, give yourself more than enough time to make adjustments, and pad the budget more than you'd like to for licensing clips, working with the attorney, and potentially even bringing on a Clearance Coordinator, someone who is a master at towing this delicate balance. It will be worth the money!

Once you have 100% completed your Fair Use review and all clips have been cleared, the attorney will give you an official letter stating that they believe all of the clips in the film fall under the Fair Use Doctrine, and you will take that clip log and that letter and submit to your errors and omissions insurance company, and potentially your distributor, in order to sell or license the film. If you don't have any clips requiring a Fair Use case—like a few news clips—then you don't have to go through this process. But if you do need a Fair Use review, it is essential that you find a great attorney to work with. It totally depends on the attorney you work with for the Fair Use review, I have heard some of the top firms charge $5,000/month retainer, but there are some independent film friendly non-profit organizations that are great like **New Media Rights**, and I paid closer to $2000 for the whole review of *Nevertheless.*

Sales Agent Agreements

When you're looking to have someone represent your film and help you sell it to one of the major streaming platforms or broadcasters, you might want to work with a sales agent. It totally depends on your film and your goals. For me, working with a sales agent has only made sense for one of my films so far—*Losing Sight of Shore.* I needed to pitch to Netflix, and I wanted to give myself the best chance at making the best possible sale. I signed with a sales agent for a two year period to see if they could help me sell the film. The terms were that they were paid nothing up front, but if a sale was made, the first $10,000 would go to the sales agent as his fee, and then he would earn 15% of the total sale. If our revenue reached a certain point, then the percentage would increase to 17.5%, and then 20% which is sometimes called a **step deal**.

I have heard of sales agents charging filmmakers money up front, but that's not the norm. Typically, you want your sales agent to be incentivized to sell your film, and the only way they make money is if you're making money too. With that said, a sales agent won't take on your film unless they see financial potential. Not every sales agent will want to represent every film because they know the marketplace, and they know what networks are buying based on what they've already sold, or based on market trends. At the end of the day, even though sales agents might be great film-lovers, they care less about the art of making films and more about the business of selling them.

Questions to consider:

- *What happens if no sale is made during the contractual time period with a sales agent?*
- *What happens if the sale is less than their minimum fee? Do I make no money?*
- *What happens if I bring a distribution deal to the table, does the sales agent still take a cut?*
- *How quickly will they process payment once a sale is made?*
- *What platforms and distributors does this sales agent have contacts with?*
- *Where does this sales agent advise I take the film to make a sale?*
- *What rights is the sales agent representing? All rights, or can I carve out rights that are important to me (i.e. educational rights)?*
- *Does the sales agent get to claim any expenses in the securing of a deal? Is there an expenses cap, and if not, can I set one?*

Distribution Contracts

Perhaps the last stop with your lawyer when it comes to filmmaking will be the distribution contracts. At this point, the film is done, and you are seeking companies to work with. This process might go through a sales agent, but oftentimes your LLC is responsible for signing with a distributor or aggregator. These contracts are incredibly important because this will determine the future of your film and how revenue will make its way to you.

Things to take note of in a distribution contract are: **The term** — The longevity of the contract. A lot of distribution contracts are 5-10 years! If your contract is for a long period of time, it's particularly important to feel comfortable with everything you are agreeing to. You want to know if they are offering you an upfront payment for your film, called a **minimum guarantee**. Just like it sounds, it's a guaranteed minimum amount of money you will make by working with them. Keep in mind that if you are offered an

"MG," that amount of money has to be recouped on their side before you will see an additional dollar. An MG operates like a forward to the filmmaker, and the distributor hopes to make that money back through the film's revenue, and then some. This is very similar to a book advance. Most authors that work with publishers get some kind of book advance, and then that has to be recouped in sales before they see additional profit.

The rights — What rights to your film does this distributor want? Usually, a distributor will begin with an **all rights deal worldwide**—that's everything. If they are asking for all rights worldwide, that means you are not able to sign with any other distributor for your film during the term. For example, if Netflix is offering you an all rights deal, that means you would be a "Netflix Original." If that's what you want, wonderful! Hopefully it comes with a large price tag to go with it. If that isn't want you want, and you want to pursue other avenues with your film—like educational screenings—then you need to **carve out** those rights from this distribution contract.

There's also the **territory.** You can also carve out parts of the world in this contract. If you know you can sign with an international distributor, then maybe it's better if you assign just the United States and Canada to this distributor, or just the North American rights. That leaves you with the rest of the world to chop up and sell to on your own, or with another distributor.

And finally, what's the profit percentage breakdown? What is the **split** between what they get, and what you get? I have seen 70%/30%, 60%/40%, 50%/50% and 30%/70%, depending on the distributor and the deal. As the filmmaker, if you can keep 70% or more of the revenue, that's ideal.

In addition to the term, the rights, and the territory, you also want to know what kind of marketing this distributor plans to do for your film, if any. If they plan to market, how much are they allowed to spend on marketing if it ultimately comes from your revenue? That is called an **expenses cap.** Without an expenses cap, a distributor could claim that they needed to spend a lot of money to market your film and there isn't any profit left to split between the two of you. Typically, marketing costs come "off the top" meaning they are deducted from the gross revenue before your split with the distributor is factored in. That means, if the distributor racks up significant marketing expenses, you might see very little to no return on your quarterly statements of revenue.

Here's another big red flag I've learned through friends in recent years: find out what happens if the distributor you're signing with dissolves or closes down during your term. Do the rights revert back to you? If this distributor is sold to another company, what happens to your film and your revenue? Under what circumstances would you get the rights to your film back? I have heard many horror stories of filmmakers being disappointed with their distribution deals, and ultimately being cheated out of money they earned. Be educated, work with a lawyer, and protect yourself and your project.

Questions to consider:

- *How long do I want the term to be? Can we negotiate a shorter term?*
- *What rights am I willing to give to this distributor?*
- *Are there any rights I want to carve out for later use?*
- *What is the territory of the agreement?*
- *Is there a minimum guarantee?*
- *What is the revenue split?*
- *How often do they pay, and do they pay on time?*
- *What happens if I want out of this contract before it's up?*
- *What is the expenses cap for marketing?*
- *What marketing does this distributor plan to do for my film?*
- *What happens to my film if this company gets bought, sold, or dissolves?*

As you can see, there are many junctions at which working with a lawyer will save you time, money, and heartbreak, as there are so many things to consider when making a film over the course of several years. Don't hesitate to call up a lawyer and get some advice, and leave room in your budget for these legal fees. It's very important for the life of your film and your future.

CHAPTER FIVE

Fundraising 101

As your ideas grow, you will inevitably need funding to get your project to the next level. Asking for money and fundraising is really hard. I won't lie to you. But the truth is, whether you need to raise $500 or $500,000, you will learn so much about yourself and your project as you go through the process. In this chapter, we will talk about how you can work towards raising money for your project. Here's where your budget turns practical, and it will help you get to the next phase of filmmaking.

Raising money is no doubt one of the hardest parts of this process. I find that it is also one of the most overlooked. Independent filmmaking is parallel with entrepreneurship in that you have to raise money to get your product, your company, your idea off the ground. Financial backing helps you ultimately share your story with the masses, hopefully create meaningful impact and revenue. I think about my time in film school, and how little we focused on raising money. And yet, like it or not, it is a massive part of what filmmakers do. In my opinion, film schools are making a mistake by not empowering students to fundraise for their projects. This requirement would equip students with valuable tools for their careers. Like any other aspect of filmmaking, fundraising is a skill that needs to be learned.

You might be thinking, "Well, I'm the director, so I'll leave fundraising to my producers." That's a possibility, and it happens for some established filmmakers. At the start of your journey, most of the responsibility will fall on you. But don't worry, I'm going to do my best to help you. There is a LOT of information in this chapter, so bear with me and I promise we will get through it. You can do this!

To be honest, for a lot of aspiring filmmakers, this is the phase where they want to give up. They think it's too difficult. Please don't stop now! I promise that all of this helps you become a stronger person, artist, businessperson, and filmmaker. There is a tendency to see fundraising as completely separate from being a filmmaker, as if it requires no creativity. I would argue differently. Even fundraising can be a creative act. I love how it combines left brain/right brain usage, and forces you to think differently. After making three feature documentaries and raising hundreds of thousands of dollars from multiple sources, I'm excited to share what I've learned in hopes that it will demystify the process and empower you to find the right path, for both you and your project.

Beyond this resource, ask others how they fundraised. Research films you like and uncover their methodology. Did they crowdfund? Did they have private donors? Did they do fundraising events, and were they successful? Did they bring on investors? Were those investors paid back? What worked about their fundraising strategy, and what didn't? I want you to be a sponge when it comes to this whole journey of making a film. Knowledge is power, and the more we share with each other as filmmakers, the more we can build sustainable careers in this business.

Keep in mind, you likely don't need to raise your entire budget to start your project; you can raise money in phases. For my three feature docs, I've never had my full budget from the start. I've always raised enough money to get to the next significant phase of production, used that footage to better my pitching materials, and then done another round of fundraising to get through post-production. Yes, I'd like to have my full budget from the start, but documentary filmmaking involves so many unknowns and so much risk that funders often want to see how things progress before giving you money to continue. I like to think of filmmaking as a moving train. No one wants to get on the train when it's just you aboard, waiting to leave. But when the train starts moving, and you begin heading to your destination, no matter what, people are more interested in jumping on board. That attitude of "I'm doing this no matter what, you should want to join me" is very powerful when it comes to fundraising. Desperation is never a good look for investors. Be confident in yourself, your idea, and your path, and people will be more inclined to feel the same.

I'm going to briefly introduce the different routes you can pursue when determining your fundraising strategy, and then I will do a deep dive into each one. Now, you might only need one of these strategies—maybe you find a private donor to fund your entire project, or you bring on investors that believe in the story and in you and they bring all the capital you need—but it's likely you will utilize a combination of all these methods to get to the finish line.

With three films under my belt, I have a fair bit to say about fundraising (as you'll soon read). I want to take a moment to recognize the inherent privilege in my experience as a filmmaker. I am a white, cisgender, heterosexual, college-educated woman in the US. That means, the people in my immediate circles and networks might be more inclined to have disposable income or money to donate to my crowdfunding campaigns or as private donors. What I hope to provide here is guidelines and inspiration to successfully fundraise for your films no matter what your background is.

Fundraising is hard no matter where you come from and what I hope to do here is break down some of those barriers to entry. The documentary film industry has inherent biases. I am still working to understand what opportunities are afforded to me and not others, and to do my part to rectify that. I believe in a film industry that supports filmmakers equally. Everyone's stories and perspectives are important. I hope we can work towards that future together, so that we aren't only watching films from those who are privileged enough to make them.

Crowdfunding

By now, you likely know all about this, but keep in mind these platforms are relatively recent in our landscape. Being able to crowdfund is an incredible tool that filmmakers 10 years ago did not have! That's amazing.

Crowdfunding is the act of setting a financial goal on a platform, setting a timeframe, and getting people excited enough about your project to donate money. This money is donation based, so you do not owe it back to anyone. There are many platforms today— Kickstarter, Indiegogo, Seed & Spark, GoFundMe, etc.—and the typical fundraising timeframe is 30-45 days. Depending on the platform, you either need to meet your financial goal to receive any of the money, or you keep any donation that's made (some platforms, like Kickstarter, are "all or nothing," whereas GoFundMe is more of a rolling payment). Some platforms are incentives-based (you give things to the funders), whereas others are pure donations.

Pros: You will learn a ton about social media, marketing, PR, and how to rally people around your idea to raise money.

Cons: It takes a tremendous amount of energy and time to pull off a successful campaign, and fulfilling the promised rewards can be a pain. It's hard to ask friends and family for money.

Grants

There are several film-specific grants to apply for throughout the year, each with different guidelines and mandates. The funder of the grant can be the government, a private funder, a foundation, or a non-profit. Typically in this context, it's a person or organization passionate about film, and they want a methodical process to support filmmakers from marginalized communities, or films about a certain topic, like climate change. There is a lot of competition when it comes to grants, and no guarantee that your work will pay off, but it's important to apply to as many as possible so that you have a chance. It can feel daunting at the start, but once you get through a couple applications, the process gets easier. You will submit your proposal, often a video sample, and an application to apply for a grant.

Pros: It's free money, and an honor to get a grant. The best grants are the ones that include mentorship, or a meet-up with other filmmakers. Best yet, a pitch forum so you can meet industry professionals to advance your project (for example Tribeca Film Institute).

Cons: It is quite time consuming and tedious to apply for several grants, and you won't hear back for months. Then, if you are accepted, you have to wait to receive the money. It's not the easiest to plan around grants. Apply for several through the year. You might get rejected by 10 grants before you get your first one.

Private Donors

Private donors are individual people interested in donating money to a documentary project. They may be passionate about the social issue you are addressing, or they like you and believe in your work and want to support you. These people may come from your own network—like a family member or old friend—or they could come along your journey when you least expect it. Unfortunately there is not a list of private donors to give you. They are a little harder to come by, but they are very cherished resources. If you're lucky enough to work with private donors, you want to keep them happy, so that you have a long-term relationship with the potential to collaborate on future projects. You might gather these people by hosting a fundraising event, or through other smaller donors. My private donors have all originated in crowdfunding—they donated a small amount through the platform, kept up with my progress, and then reached out to talk with me about how things were going. From that relationship, they eventually donated larger amounts of money to help me make it to the next phase.

Pros: You will hopefully have great private donors that see your vision and give money right when you need it the most, and you don't have to pay them back. They will likely want some kind of executive producer credit for their donation.

Cons: Cons would only come if there are expectations not met somehow, or if your private donors feel like they want some kind of creative control (which they don't have the right to).

Related to private donors, you're going to want to set up a **fiscal sponsorship** at the beginning of your fundraising journey. A fiscal sponsorship means you team up with a non-profit, a 501(c)3 organization, so that private donors or grants can write their donation check to a 501(c)3 and not to you, or your LLC (Limited Liability Company). This allows them to have tax benefits from the donation. To do this, bring on a fiscal sponsor for your project in the form of a non-profit organization, like IDA (International Documentary Association), Fractured Atlas, Women Make Movies, etc. They take anywhere from 5-8% of the donation to process payments, and you get the rest.

For example, say a private donor you met on Kickstarter wants to donate $50,000 to your project so that you can get through post-production. The private donor writes the check to your fiscal sponsor, Fractured Atlas, for $50,000. Fractured Atlas cashes the check, takes 5%, and then writes you or your LLC a check for the remaining $47,500. In a sense, everyone wins. The donor gets the tax benefit, the fiscal sponsor gets $2,500 for the paperwork, and you get a donation of $47,500 for your project. And yes, this is totally legal. I would set up your fiscal sponsor at the beginning of your project so that you're ready for this scenario, instead of having to scramble to get one when you need it the most. It may cost a small application fee and some time to fill out their paperwork, but it's a relatively easy process. I would keep in mind that YOU are doing all the work to secure this funding. Don't expect your fiscal sponsor to work to help you raise money. They may feature you on their website which could yield some attention, but don't expect them to help you raise any money. This is also something you'll need to set up for each project. What you're looking for here is an organization that is transparent, pays on time, and is aligned with your project.

Pros: You are able to receive donations from private individuals and foundations so that they can get the tax benefit.

Cons: Giving up 5-8% of your donation even though you did the legwork to secure the donation and you can really use every dollar.

Investors

The main difference between a donation and an investment is an important distinction to make. A donation is your money to keep, with no expectation that it will be returned. An investment is money put in to a project based on the total budget and valuation, with the expectation of financial returns. You're going to want to be very careful when determining the terms of an investment. It will completely change the structure of your company and project. Often, investors own a piece of your company and profits, in perpetuity. When you bring on investors, you will need to work with a lawyer to make sure the contract in place serves all parties and protects you and your assets.

It's important to note here that any dollar of your own money that you put into your project should be treated as an investment as well. Keep track of all your personal expenses to get the project off the ground, and hold yourself accountable to get that money paid back as well. If you don't fight for yourself, no one else will. Especially if you bring on investors for $50,000 and you've put in $10,000 of your own money, make sure you mention that to your lawyer so that you are included in the structure of the deal.

Pros: You are truly an entrepreneur bringing on investors and starting a business. You have some breathing room to make your film with the money you need.

Cons: The added pressure to bring in enough revenue once the film is done to pay back your investors. You're exhausted when finishing a film, and now every dollar that comes in a portion of (or all of, depending on your deal) will go to your investors until they are paid back, plus interest. This will influence your distribution path, as you need to create revenue. Investors also might have a lot of notes on the film before it's done, and you'll have to balance keeping them happy and maintaining the integrity of the project you envisioned.

Now, let's do a deeper dive into each of these fundraising methods: crowdfunding, grant writing, private donors, and investors. I want you to know and understand what tools are available to you so that you can make an informed decision about how best to move forward.

CROWDFUNDING

How do I crowdfund effectively?

First things first: when considering crowdfunding, know that it is a big, time consuming strategy. This is not something you can phone in or pawn off on someone else. If you aren't ready to dedicate months of your time to managing a campaign, I would skip ahead to another option now. Crowdfunding is a FULL TIME effort, not only during the campaign itself, but in preparation for the campaign (which could be anywhere from 30-60 days, or longer), and after the campaign (you may need to fulfill rewards and follow up with donors). Very few people throw up a campaign and watch the donations flood in. That kind of effortlessness is typically reserved for a well-known celebrity, or a project that has a built-in audience. That kind of success is the exception, not the rule. Most of us will work tirelessly to raise every single dollar of that campaign, and swear to never crowdfund again... until the next project comes along.

So why put yourself through this?

I know, I'm making it sound awful, but I just want to be realistic with you and not sugarcoat how difficult it can be. I will also highlight how wonderful and educational crowdfunding can be! I have learned SO MUCH from running two successful campaigns for two different films, have met amazing people, and have even raised more money outside of the platform as a direct result of the campaign. I have learned firsthand about PR, social media, marketing, and perhaps most importantly, presenting myself effectively to people I've never met. I have learned how to build an audience for a film that doesn't even exist yet. I have learned how to persevere past self-doubt and exhaustion, I have learned how to get incredibly creative when things aren't going my way, and I've learned about the endless kindness of strangers. But the real answer to consider crowdfunding? It's a way to make your project and your dream come true with full creative control! You're just going to have to earn it every step of the way.

Pick a platform, a time frame, and a financial goal

There are many crowdfunding platforms out there now, so you need to start by exploring the options available to you. Investigate which platform will be the most user-friendly for your donors and you. Things to consider are: What other projects exist on this platform? Is it all film and TV projects (Seed & Spark), or will I be alongside all different kinds of projects (Kickstarter, Indiegogo, GoFundMe)? What are this platform's parameters? Kickstarter is an all-or-nothing platform, meaning you set a goal and timeframe, and if you don't reach that goal or higher by the end of your campaign, you get nothing. Nada. It all goes away. So in essence, people are pledging money to your cause and are only charged if you hit 100% funded or more. If you end up with $49,990 with 0 seconds to spare, and your goal was $50,000, you will end up with no funding at all. Harsh, I know. But what I like about that model is that your back is against the wall. You are incentivized to reach your goal fully, not compromise or settle for less. There is a sense of urgency like none other. Maybe I'm a bit masochistic in that way, but I liked those stakes, and they drove me through two campaigns on Kickstarter—one for $25,000 in 60 days from 404 people in 2013 for *The Empowerment Project*, and the other for $50,000 in 30 days from 610 people in 2018 for *Nevertheless.*

Indiegogo, on the other hand, has a flexible funding option. You can set your goal at $50,000 in 30 days, and even if you only raise $10,000, you can still keep it. Seed & Spark has a feature called the "Green Light," which grants you access to the money once you achieve 80% of the goal. For that same $50,000 campaign, once you raise $40,000 (80%), you get the green light, and won't go home with less than $40,000. You still work towards 100% funded and beyond, but it's a lower threshold for success. GoFundMe—which is often used for campaigns for disaster relief, medical bills, and more personal causes—collects donations as they come in. You still set a goal, but as people donate each day, you receive payment right away, no matter how much you raise.

You'll also want to consider the cost of running a crowdfunding campaign. Each platform takes a platform fee as well as the credit card processing fee. For example, Kickstarter takes a 5% platform fee, but the payment processing fee is an additional 3-5% on top of that. If you choose to work with Kickstarter, you need to factor in up to 8-10% of what you raise will not go to you as the creator. If you need a net of $50,000 for your project, you actually need to raise about 10% more than that on Kickstarter to ultimately hit your full goal.

A quick overview of the four main platforms for film crowdfunding:

Kickstarter – All or nothing/fixed campaigns, many different kinds of projects present on the platform, 5% platform fee, it's a bigger company so it can be tough to get a hold of someone to help.

Seed & Spark – 80% Green light, only film and television projects, highest success rate for independent films, 2% platform fee, and your backers can opt in to cover any additional credit card fees. More personal attention for projects, as it's a smaller company. Special focus on diversity and inclusion, many opportunities for your film outside of crowdfunding through distribution, film festival perks, and much more.

Indiegogo – Flexible Funding option as well as fixed, all kinds of projects featured, 5% platform fee, harder to get personal feedback on your campaign.

GoFundMe – Raise money as you go, no fees taken out, special focus on personal causes on the platform, less film projects present.

There are others to consider as well, like Women You Should Fund, Fundly, and film financing platforms where you seek investment or equity, like Crowdfunder, Slated, or Junction. There are new platforms emerging everyday, do your research on what works for you.

Whatever platform you choose, make sure you live and breathe that platform before you launch your campaign. You should be an expert in how it works. You will be the primary contact to help your donors navigate the platform. Research successful projects on the platform, and the ones that failed. What rewards did they offer? What was their time frame? What tactics did they use? How many people donated? What was the main pledge amount they received? Better yet, if you can find someone who has run a successful campaign on that platform, try to get them on the phone for some advice before you launch. Chances are they will have some great hacks to pass along. I would also advise you to donate to a few projects to see what the process is like for the user. Even if it's $1 to three projects you admire, what email did you receive upon donating? Were you motivated to share on social media after that? Why or why not? The more you can understand the user experience on that site, the better you can motivate your backers to go through it too.

How long should my campaign be?

For your timeframe, you need to be realistic regarding your bandwidth. What you can handle? Research shows the sweet spot for campaigns is 30-45 days, with a heavy preference on 30 days. Sixty days is an eternity when you're crowdfunding, let me tell you. However, I'm glad we had 60 days that first time around in 2013, as I had no idea what I was doing and needed time to understand how crowdfunding works. Additionally, crowdfunding was a relatively new concept, so part of our campaign was educating people on how crowdfunding works, and that it was ok to trust these sites with your credit card information. My second Kickstarter campaign was in 2018. I spent the month before prepping, so that I could run an efficient 30 day campaign. You definitely need to build in prep time so that you aren't scrambling to send out emails and market. When choosing your timeframe, think about you're going to create urgency and motivate your backers to act now, instead of waiting a month to donate.

How much should I aim to raise?

This is a tough one to answer without knowing the specifics of *your* project and *your* network. In general, if you're going to put in all of this effort to crowdfund, the amount should be significant enough to tangibly move your project forward. On the flip side, you don't want to aim so high that your network can't get you there. Some people do end up running a second or even third campaign for the same project. You can break the project up into stages, with a production crowdfunding campaign, and a post-production crowdfunding campaign. Ideally this campaign will get you to the next rung of the project. For example: $30,000 will help us finish production, or $20,000 will get us to a rough cut of the film in edit. People need to know what their money is helping to contribute to. And don't forget, you can always exceed your goal, but on a platform like Kickstarter, set that number wisely, as you have to meet your goal to get anything.

Questions to consider when deciding how much to raise:

- *How big is your network (social media, email lists, a blog, YouTube channel, etc.)?*
- *How active are you on social media already?*
- *Will anyone be helping you with this campaign?*
- *Can you tap into their networks as well?*
- *Do you have any influencer-like friends who can help amplify your message during the campaign?*
- *Do you have any larger donors in your network on whom you can call to help?*
- *Is there a built-in audience for this subject matter?*
- *Are any well-known people or causes involved?*

I'll tell you straight up, if you are not very active on social media as of today, if you don't have a big following, don't have any kind of email list or press contacts, and you're doing this alone...it's going to be a tough road. If you are reading that and feeling personally attacked, I apologize, but use that as fuel. Build your social media following now before you launch; consult with other crowdfunding successes; start an email list; find some press contacts; consider teaming up with someone who does have those things to help you run the campaign. Prove me wrong! In some ways, crowdfunding can feel like a huge detour from the actual making of the movie, but I promise all of this hard work can also help you when you get to distribution and marketing the film once it's done.

In summary, look at your projected budget, and choose a goal that will significantly move the project forward so you can deliver on the promises you've made during the campaign. Be realistic about your bandwidth and your network. Only you can truly decide what that number should be.

Ok, I've got my platform, timeframe and goal—what should be on the actual campaign page?

Spend time on your title and tagline

First things first—what will be the title for your campaign? Seems simple, as you might assume you would just list the name of the project, but more often than not, the title of your project doesn't fully explain to an audience what the project is about (especially those that don't know you or your work). Peoples' attention spans are so short that you need to make sure you spell out for people what this is, and quick. You only get a small number of characters for your title and tagline, so leave yourself plenty of time to play with this.

My two campaigns were:

The Empowerment Project: a docu-series about women

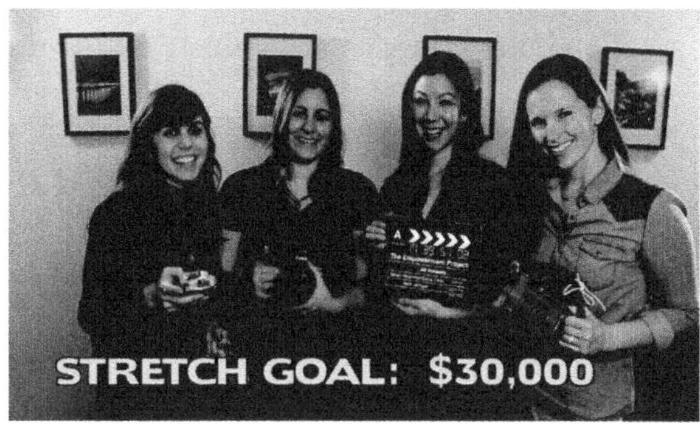

With an all female crew, we want to interview inspirational women across the US to create positive role models for women everywhere

Created by

Sarah Moshman & Dana Michelle Cook

404 backers pledged $28,590 to help bring this project to life.

Last updated March 3, 2018

NEVERTHELESS: Documentary Aims To End Sexual Harassment

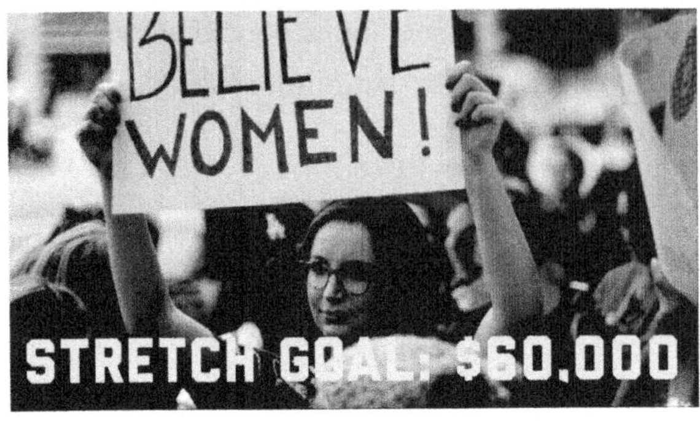

Social, legal, and masculinity sides of the sexual harassment crisis interwoven with personal stories and calls to action for change.

Created by
Sarah Moshman

610 backers pledged $57,821 to help bring this project to life.

Last updated January 21, 2020

These are by no means perfect, but I played with them a lot and landed on options that ensured the intention of the project was clear from the very top of the page. Keep in mind: **The title, short description, financial goal, and timeframe DO NOT CHANGE once you launch your campaign**. Almost everything else can be adjusted.

Then there's the image you choose to represent the project. That you can change from time to time, but you want to choose a striking, great image that helps to further explain or reiterate what the project is about; something you couldn't fit into the tagline and the title. Most people will only see your image, the title, and tagline before deciding whether or not to click and potentially donate, so these elements are very important. This will also serve as the thumbnail image whenever you link to the campaign across the internet.

Here's an example of the power of these variables: A filmmaker was having trouble reaching her goal on Indiegogo, and I was asked to take a look at the campaign to see if anything popped out that wasn't working. I quickly noticed that their title gave absolutely no insight into how awesome the project was! The title of the campaign was "The Bird Chapters," which must have been the title of the project, but when I read further, I learned how the film crew was all women, and they had this awesome concept for a narrative series. None of that was easy to find. In my opinion, they could have had a much better title and description for their campaign so that people like me (their ideal donor!) would quickly see why supporting them was important.

Make it as easy as possible for people to fall in love with you and your idea. The title and description are the first step.

Make an amazing video

Sounds obvious, but you'd be surprised that projects about films—like moving pictures, television shows, documentaries, narrative films, anything with a video or film camera—don't always have the best videos. Hmm. Why should I support a video project when you couldn't even get together a good video for the campaign? I don't mean you need to spend lots of money and use visual effects and shoot on the RED camera in order for it to be good, but there is a certain expectation of quality. People want to trust that you know what you're doing. It needs to sound great and look great, even if it's shot on an iPhone. If it's a film with heavy amounts of animation, then I would expect to see either some sample animations, or at least drawings, in your video. For my first campaign, we did a whole pilot interview for the Kickstarter video, which was tremendously valuable in showing our audience what the project would look like, feel like, and what kinds of knowledge and wisdom these women would impart. We used a section of that interview in our video, and I'm so glad we did. Don't just tell us what the film is about—show us. Introduce yourself so we know the person behind this campaign, and tell us why this matters to you. And get creative! What is the theme of your project? How can you stay in line with that theme in your video instead of doing the same things as everyone else? Watch as many videos of successful campaigns as you can stomach. Identify what works, and when you lose interest.

Keep it succinct. My video for the first campaign was over four minutes long, and I made the mistake of giving my passionate pitch at the end of the video, only to learn that a measly 33% of people actually watched the video to the end. (These platforms give you great statistics on the back end, use them!) The second time around, my video was two minutes 21 seconds, and I made sure to include captions this time. Many people don't turn on their audio when watching a video. Captions help communicate the gist of the video, and are accommodating for the hard of hearing. I would also advise you to make a one minute or less version of your video for Facebook and Instagram posts and ads, also with captions. You can make additional videos for your page of course, but I would hold additional content until your campaign has started so that you don't release it all on day one. You need things to announce and release throughout the 30 days, so don't be afraid to spread out your additional content. It's too much for one person to absorb it all on day one.

Have solid rewards that people actually want

Oh rewards, how I dislike thee so. Rewards or incentives are important, necessary, and oh so frustrating and tedious. Rewards are what you offer your backers in exchange for their donation. Depending on the level of money they donate, they will receive multiple rewards, and it's up to you to decide what these are. Rewards for a film campaign are tough because the product you are creating might not be done for a year, or much longer. Giving a "sneak peek" to watch the film before anyone else only gets you so far, and it should be reserved for donors at the $25 level. What do you do for the other reward levels? Study other film campaigns, and observe what they offer for rewards. They might inspire you.

Any way you slice it, this is the least glamorous part of crowdfunding. Because once your campaign is done and successful (yay!), you still have to fulfill rewards, which can take money, resources, time, and energy when you're exhausted and just want to go make your film already! You might find yourself sitting on your floor stuffing padded envelopes with crappy t-shirts and handwriting hundreds of addresses wondering how you ended up being a t-shirt distributor instead of a filmmaker.

A few tips I picked up after two campaigns and lots of rewards:

1. Spend as little money as possible to create and ship your rewards. That money is meant for the film.

2. If you offer your film as a reward, make it a digital download or password protected link, not a physical DVD or Blu-ray, as you will save money and a huge headache getting addresses.

3. For the love of God, avoid offering t-shirts. Unless you are already a t-shirt distributor, you will be in t-shirt hell trying to order the right

sizes and ship them out when people will not respond to your sizing survey for months, if ever, and then you will be following up with your friend from high school a year later for their new address. It sucks.

4. Always offer a small reward level, like $1 or $5. Some people just want to support you, but don't have a lot to give, so you want to make sure you have something for everyone. They have to choose a reward level on most platforms. Those levels are often "virtual hi fives!" or "social media shout out!" Please value every donation, as they could up their pledge before the end of the campaign, and truly every dollar helps.

5. It helped me to work backwards. For your higher donation amounts on a film project, it's often a producer credit of some kind. See what you're comfortable with, but I have done $10,000 as a co-executive producer credit, $5,000 as co-producer, and $2,500 as associate producer, and that felt about right. It's like these people are getting in on the ground floor, even if later an executive producer is more at the $50,000+ level when you do additional fundraising.

6. If it makes sense for your project, add a name that's on theme with your campaign to each reward level. For *Nevertheless,* each reward level was named for a feminist hero of the #MeToo movement. YOU ARE A PIONEER LIKE ROSIE THE RIVETER $15, YOU ARE GROUNDBREAKING LIKE ANITA HILL $25, YOU ARE A LEADER LIKE TARANA BURKE $50.

7. Popular film rewards at other levels are: tickets to the premiere, a private screening of the film (make sure you clarify travel not included), a spot on a panel discussion, consulting sessions, their name in the credits, swag with the film branding on it from notebooks to posters to t-shirts, and more.

8. You can always add more rewards during the campaign, so if you have a super rare signed poster for your film, but only three are available, you could set that reward just a bit higher than your average pledge

amount and see if you can motivate people to increase their pledges for that reward. Once someone has claimed a reward, you can't change the rewards at that level, but you can add rewards throughout. You don't need to have everything up at the beginning.

Give yourself time to work on rewards and make them exciting enough that it gives people the extra push to donate. Also, look beyond your own campaign. Do your fellow filmmakers a solid, and when it comes time to donate to their project, click "No Reward" and save them the trouble. And if you donate to a campaign and somehow don't receive your reward, understand that they are doing their best and somehow it slipped through the cracks. A gentle reminder will suffice, or let it slide. We didn't get into this business to sell t-shirts, after all.

Use your preview link

Before you officially launch your campaign, you will be able to send out a private preview link to the page. Use this to get feedback while you can still make changes. Give your VIPs early access to whatever you are cooking up for rewards, and make sure it is the best it can be before launch.

By the way, launching doesn't happen in an instant

At least on Kickstarter, you have to get approval from the site before you can officially launch. Yes, pressing the launch button is instantaneous, but before you can even do that, Kickstarter has to make sure your page is up to their standards and doesn't violate any rules or regulations. Do yourself a favor—if you have a set launch day planned (which you ideally do), make sure you go through the approvals process a few days beforehand, in case there are any problems. Especially with larger platforms like Kickstarter, it can take 24-48 hours to get a response. If there is a problem, you have to fix it and resubmit. Fixing the problem could mean replacing a reward, changing some type, or something more involved, like re-uploading your video. I've seen filmmakers in tight spots on their launch day, and it's stressful.

Copy all that. But how do I actually run a successful campaign?

Here we go. I get asked this question a lot, so I've boiled down one piece of advice for running a successful crowdfunding campaign. I'll share it, then explain what I mean and give you real world examples.

Ready? Here is the key:

How are you going to present the same information in a different and compelling way each day?

You've got a 30 day campaign, guess what? You cannot expect to post that same crowdfunding link every day and garner donations until you reach your goal. You are going to have to get WAY MORE creative than that. Your goal is essentially the same each day of the campaign, right? Inspire people to take time out of their day to open up their hearts and wallets and donate to your project. Some of those people will know you, and some of those will be strangers if you do this right. It's up to you to figure out how to inspire people to want to donate to your project, and it won't happen by re-posting the same link to your campaign on Facebook and saying: DONATE NOW PLEASE. That will get lost so fast. That might not even get you very far on day one, honestly. This is where you need to get super creative and put on your marketing hat to get people to notice what you're trying to do. The old marketing adage is they say people have to see something seven times before they take action. That's a lot of exposure you have to fight for over the course of 30-45 days before your audience is taking action.

Here are some examples and ways to achieve this:

Day one of your campaign, you need donations coming through the door to get the train moving. Who in your immediate friends and family can you lean on? Give them a heads up to that you need donations on day one. Even if they aren't large donations, your potential backers are going to be impressed to see multiple donors ready to go on day one. And then, each donation that comes in, or after a group of donations come in, you can celebrate and use that as a way to post again on social media.

10% FUNDED on DAY ONE?!?! Thank you to Ryan, Bryce, Diane, and Harvey for all donating to my campaign on day one!

Also, on day one of your campaign, **you need emails ready to be sent out**. You don't want to be scrambling to write a mass email or individual emails to your networks when your campaign is already live. You can write that the night before, or even the week before, and "Schedule Send" so that it goes out minutes after your campaign launches. You can use an email marketing software like Mailchimp or Constant Contact, or you can use your own email service to distribute messages effectively and efficiently. As people donate, try to keep up with thanking them individually or as a group at the end of the day. Keep track of who of your friends and family is donating so that you don't hit them up for funding twice. That doesn't feel great if you donate to someone's campaign and then two days later, they ask you for money again, as if they didn't even bother to notice that you chipped in.

You're going to want **some kind of website as a landing page** to promote your campaign easily. That way, if you someone posts about your campaign, or you're handing out business cards, it isn't too clunky for people to click through to the website. It should be as easy as possible to find. Instead of telling people to go to Kickstarter and search "Nevertheless," I referred people to neverthelessfilm.com, and I had the website set to automatically redirect to my Kickstarter campaign. Simple and effective. Even a basic template on Squarespace, Wix, or Wordpress will do the trick. You want to make this as easy as possible. If your potential backers encounter any sort of hurdle, they will scroll on. Our attention spans are too short.

Design and implement social media materials to use throughout the campaign before and after you launch. What are the best materials that go with your campaign? If you have a social impact documentary—let's say it's about the environment—you could share facts and stats about your cause while also promoting your campaign. If you've shot some footage already, you can share screen grabs from the film as a way to promote. If it's a documentary, you can share a screen grab with a quote from one of your interview subjects and post that with a link to the campaign in the post, or in the comments. **A great app for this content is Canva.** They have a free version as well as a paid version, but there is so much you can do with limited graphic design skills on Canva to make your posts look clean and professional. If you're great with Adobe Photoshop and Illustrator, even better.

Speaking of graphic design, one amazing strategy I have seen some crowdfunders utilize is thanking their most recent donors with an almost immediate personalized graphic for social media. For example, in the crowdfunding campaign for a documentary about Miss America, the filmmakers would pull a photo of their donor off Facebook or Instagram, digitally add in a sash (as if they were a beauty queen) that said "I SUPPORTED MISS AMERICA" and sent it to them as a thank you. More often than not, the person who donated was delighted to see this photo of themselves, and would immediately post it, saying, "I supported this campaign, and you should too!" Not only do they feel good for giving their money, but they also get to show off to their friends in a fun way that they supported the cause. If you or someone on your team has this skillset, use it!

More marketing ideas:

Can you **create videos** from footage you've shot already as a sneak peek? Or can you **share behind the scenes photos** from your latest shoot? These are all ways to present the same information—that you're raising money to finish this film or make this film—in a different and compelling way, each day. But you need to take the time to think about and gather these materials, ideally prior to the campaign beginning, so you can spread them out and plan when to use them. Tell us about yourself as a filmmaker—what is your prior work? **Why does this film mean so much to you, especially right now**? If you can answer that question, it can help guide a lot of these materials. Share photos of you holding a camera as a teenager, or you on the debate team arguing about climate change long before it was cool. Show off your creativity as you promote. That way, the process of asking people for money doesn't feel so heavy handed. Near the end of my first campaign,

I started holding up signs that said "4 DAYS LEFT" at different LA landmarks. The mystery of "4 Days left till what?" drove people to pay attention to the photo and the link. I even made a red t-shirt that said, "ASK

ME ABOUT MY KICKSTARTER CAMPAIGN," and I wore to work all the time. I cringe at the thought of that shirt. But hey, try all the things!

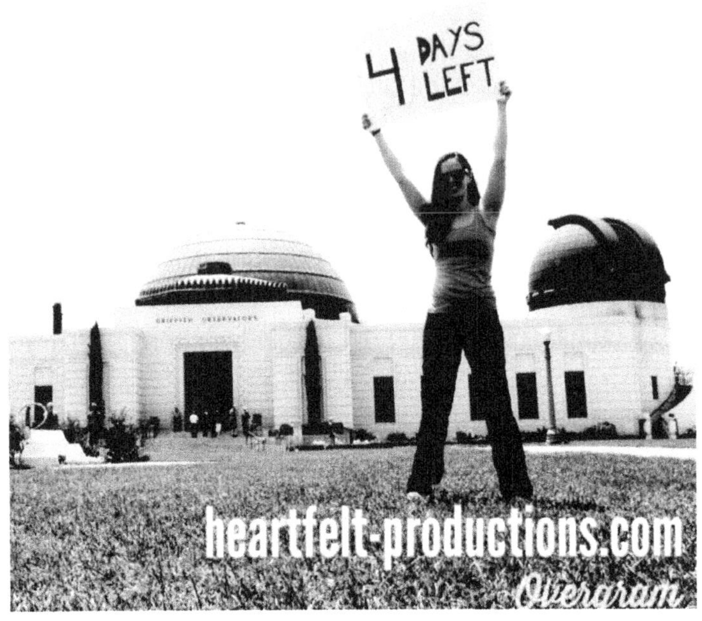

Promoting Your Campaign

PRESS is a great way to gather attention for your crowdfunding campaign. Press can be harder to come by these days. There is such a saturation of crowdfunding campaigns that it's not really newsworthy. It's up to you to find an angle for a journalist or reporter to get excited about. Knowing who is involved in the project might be a reason to write about it. Maybe you're making it in a unique way, or the social impact at the core of the project is timely and worth covering. You can write your own press release, or consult with a publicist to get a solid pitch written for reaching out to journalists.

I remember writing to at least 30 different reporters at the *Chicago Tribune* (I'm from the Chicago area, so I thought I'd start there) about my campaign in 2013 for *The Empowerment Project*. Not knowing much about what I was doing, I wrote to every single reporter I could get an email address for, and I wasn't getting any responses. Then I started doing research into the *Chicago Tribune* reporters who had previously written about female empowerment, feminism, or women's rights, and I found a writer named Ellen Jean Hirst. I emailed her my homemade press release about the film we wanted to make and the campaign, and I'll never forget she called me a couple days later saying they wanted to do a story on us. We ended up with a half page spread in the Lifestyle section of the Sunday paper. They even took our picture and interviewed us in person. I have it framed above my desk, and I'm looking at it right now. It reminds me to persevere and never give up. That article led to hundreds of dollars in donations to the campaign in our second half. It also gave us a credibility and prestige for having been featured in the *Chicago Tribune* as a timely, important project that was being made.

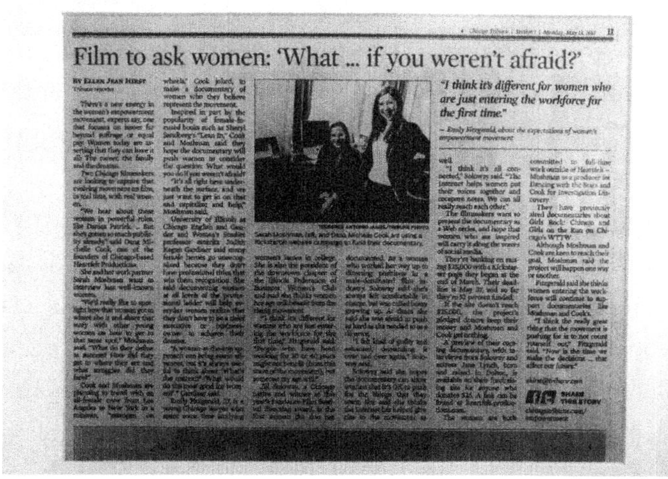

Film to ask women: 'What ... if you weren't afraid?'

By Ellen Jean Hirst

"I think it's different for women who are just entering the workforce for the first time."

In terms of press, use the resources you have, use your network, and use the subject matter of your project to guide you. Press might not come in the form of magazines or newspapers. **It may come in the form of a blog post**, which could be incredibly effective. Make a list of 30 blogs that you can reach out to on day one of your campaign (or sooner) and see if they would be interested in interviewing you about your project or subject matter. Or better yet, ask if they would let you do a guest post so you can control the narrative of what is posted. Then they can distribute the blog to their subscribers and you can share as well, hopefully yielding donations.

I wrote a guest post for the "Good Men Project" blog about "Why Having a Daughter Changes Everything" during my 2018 *Nevertheless* campaign. I wrote a personal essay about what it was like to find out I would be having a daughter after an extremely vulgar and sexist comment from my neighbor at the time. It related to the subject matter of the campaign—sexual harassment—and it allowed me to tell the story of why I was making the film, all while organically promoting the campaign at the same time. That blog was shared over 1,000 times because of the content, but also their subscriber base. It led to many donations, and of course, more content for me to post that wasn't just the campaign link. That was excellent, but it takes time to write those blog posts, so the sooner you can start that outreach, the more time you can have to craft a post or do an interview that can be shared in the right timeframe.

Team Up with Influencers Who Can Amplify Your Content

This one is great, but doesn't often happen quickly. A home run would be if someone on your team (or you!) has a larger social media following; bonus points if it's already in the space in which you want to promote. If your film is about feminism in some form, and you or your partner is already building up quite an army of loyal followers in the feminist/activist space on social media, that will work well for you when promoting this campaign. If you're like most of us who have a more modest but mighty social media following, you are going to want to seek out other people and organizations to help you amplify this message. But why would they do that? They might believe in your project and simply want to support it, which is great, but rare (not because they don't care, but because they have a lot of people vying for their time). To help nudge them along, try creating such strong content that they want to share it on their page or feed because it's so good. Maybe you have a killer trailer they could re-post, or an impactful image that aligns with their brand. Maybe you have a really strong statistic or quote that speaks to them and they want to re-post it, and it tags back to your campaign.

It's up to you to figure out a way to engage with influencers in this space and get them excited about supporting you. It isn't a sure thing, but chances are you're going to be exposed to more people on their page then on just your social media. It's worth trying. Just like with your donors, you want to make it as easy as possible for them to help you, so don't make them go searching for the right link or social media handle. Write a "cheat tweet," or a sample post, so they can literally copy and paste.

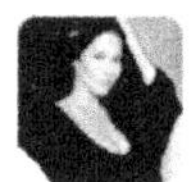

Brooke Burke-Charvet @brookeburke

@SarahMosh pleasure! Good luck. I hope your goals are met.

Retweeted by Sarah Moshman

View conversation

I remember working on my 10th and final season as a field producer on *Dancing with the Stars* as I was running my 2013 Kickstarter campaign for *The Empowerment Project*. Brooke Burke was one of the hosts of the show—she's a celebrity host, model, fitness spokeswoman, and more. I finally got up the courage to tell her about my project at work one day, and she agreed to tweet about the campaign! She had over three million followers at the time!

I thought: *this is it*. My campaign will be funded at the click of a button. (I should mention, my co-worker had run a successful Kickstarter campaign the month before, and he told me a story about Seth Green tweeting about his project, and he was literally funded overnight after that one tweet.) I wrote up a tweet which included a link to the campaign, and she tweeted it that night. After all this work, finally things were clicking into place. *But nothing happened.* I don't think I got one single donation from that tweet! And I realized quickly how fickle this all is, but that also the people who follow Brooke Burke weren't also the people who were donating to crowdfunding campaigns, and don't normally hear from her in this manner. She tweeted mostly about health and fitness, life as a mom, sponsored posts for brands, etc. Seth Green, on the other hand, is likely followed by an army of fan boys and comic book nerds, and the film he tweeted about? It was all about comic strip *Calvin and Hobbes*. So it was right on target for his demographic. That was a tough pill to swallow, but I kept on moving. You have to try 100 things and see what sticks. Nothing is guaranteed with crowdfunding. I ended up asking all of the professional dancers on the show to tweet about the project (my pre-written tweet), and a lot of them did! Keep going. You never know what will work.

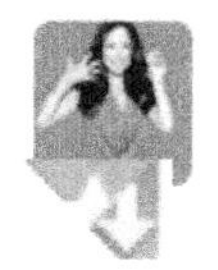

Cheryl Burke @CherylBurke

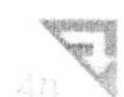

Hey guys check out my friend @sarahmosh and her new project about female empowerment! Donate and share kck.st/WUDWax

View media

Try to become a "Staff Pick" or highlighted project by the platform itself

Depending on how big the platform is, do everything you can to get their attention and have them help highlight your work. On Kickstarter it's called a "Staff Pick" or "Project We Love," and you need to get a hold of the person who runs that category on the platform and see if they will help you. Why? For people that don't know you personally and need to discover you on the platform, this is a great way for the website's algorithm to work in your favor. It's basically the platform saying, "Hey, we think this project is cool, check it out." And remember, you are doing all of the heavy lifting to make this a successful campaign, and the platform will make money off of it, so don't be afraid to fight for some extra exposure. It could really help.

Use the Data They Give You.

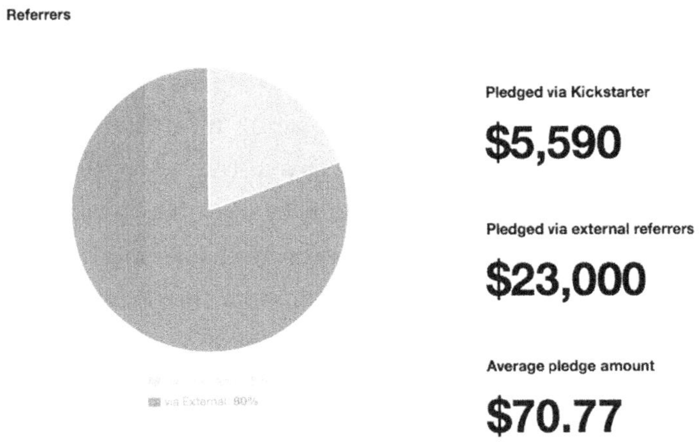

As you move through your campaign it's not a secret where the donations are coming from. At any time you can see on your creator dashboard where the majority of your donations originate from, all the way down to your least engaging route of discovery. This data can help you refocus your efforts as your campaign is running. If you are putting a lot of time and money into Twitter and you see that no donations are coming from that path, you might want to put that time and money towards a more effective channel. You can also see what your average pledge amount is, and you can even add a new reward around that same level to get more people excited. You don't have to fly blind here. Use this important information to make informed decisions, and be flexible during your campaign so you can respond to what's working and what's not.

The algorithms will get ya

I'm going to sound like I have some inside scoop to the back end of the internet here, but I don't. I know so little about coding and how websites actually work. But I want you to pay attention to how these social media sites work, as well as user behavior. When we're campaigning, we have to think like marketers. I can tell you firsthand that in the five year gap between my crowdfunding campaigns, the internet changed completely. All the things that worked well for me in 2013 were no longer possible in 2018. The social media algorithms, especially on Facebook, are designed to keep you on there. They don't want you clicking away to another webpage, no matter how cool or meaningful it is. Facebook even has their own donate feature for non-profits! That means, when you post a link to another site, like Kickstarter, Seed & Spark, or Indiegogo, Facebook buries it because the last thing they want you to do is take your data and user behavior elsewhere.

The quote that sticks with me about these "free" social media platforms is that, "If something is free on the internet, *you* are the product." That means our data is being monitored, distributed, bought, and sold constantly, thanks to all the information we pump into these sites on a daily basis. If you're Facebook, you don't want your user to click on a link and leave. This was especially apparent to me on day one of my second campaign, in 2018. I must have had 50 or more close friends donate on day one of my *Nevertheless* campaign, and then share the campaign link to Facebook and say something incredibly thoughtful and kind about the project or me, encouraging others to donate. But every. single. post. went completely unseen and got exactly one "like" on it—from me. Whereas in 2013, a huge way people found out about my campaign was through their friends sharing, or getting "likes" on our Facebook page. The organic exposure played a huge role. It was maddening thinking I had a plan going into my second campaign, and then finding out I wouldn't be able to use those tools again. So be prepared to get creative, and adjust when necessary!

Save some budget for paid marketing tools that are actually worth it

I found a couple of paid services to be incredibly helpful for my campaign the second time around, and I want to share what those were. **Green Inbox** is a really great service (I'm sure there are many others like it) where you can pay to send individual messages or emails to your network. Just go to greeninbox.com, sign into your Facebook account, for example, and then you write a short message that can apply for all of your friends to receive information about the campaign. It needs to sound general enough to work for everyone, and yet personalized enough to make it seem like you wrote it to just them. Green Inbox will fill in their first name, and when the person receives the message, it will appear as though you spent hours writing each of your Facebook friends a personal message telling them about your campaign. This message will land in their email inboxes with the email address they used to register for Facebook.

Something like:

Hi <FIRST NAME>,

How are you? Hope 2018 is treating you well so far.

I'm writing to tell you about a crowdfunding campaign I'm running right now for a new project about sexual harassment called Nevertheless. *If you can donate and share, I would really appreciate it!*

<LINK>

Thank you,

Sarah

Each message costs about six cents to send. You can also use a service like this for direct messaging all of your Twitter followers, LinkedIn contacts, and more. Yes, the cost will add up, but the results are well worth it, including the time saved. It would be impossible for you to do these individual messages on each of these platforms efficiently. It would take the whole campaign! I spent about $300-$500 on Green Inbox for my *Nevertheless* campaign, and it led to thousands of dollars in donations, and other opportunities too, including job offers! It was a great way to ping everyone and let them know what I was up to.

If you do go this route, try to initiate it towards the beginning of your campaign, as it takes a little while to get going (48-72 hours). Additionally, they can only send a certain number of messages per day, so if you have a ton of followers, it may take several days to get all the messages out. If Green Inbox isn't for you, there are similar services you can seek out. The functionality is a lot like Mailchimp or Constant Contact, where you write one mass message, import your contacts, send the email, and then each person feels like you wrote them a personal email. This is a way to tap into your entire social network at the click of a few buttons, and save hours of your precious time.

Facebook and Instagram Ads

Social media ads are a tremendous tool at your disposal for crowdfunding. We will talk more about this in the Marketing chapter in relation to distribution, but the concept is the same. Spend a little bit of money to market your crowdfunding campaign directly to the people who would want to see it. Social media advertisements have a lot of power these days to specifically select the people who will see your ad based on other variables (remember the data I mentioned these platforms collect? This is how it comes in handy). You can target your ad to a specific group of people based on their interests, age, where they life, social issues they support, and so much more. This laser focus saves you time and money. Instead of blasting a message to everyone you've ever met, you target the intended audience for your film.

When creating these ads, experiment with the one minute version of your video with captions, spend $10 over a few days, and target a group of people who like similar content and might really want to see this. It can be simple, like targeting the Facebook ad to the people who already like your film's Facebook page, but if you don't have much of a following there yet, you need to consider the characteristics of your intended audience, and what kinds of content they might like. That way, you can target the ad to, let's say, women in the United States ages 20-65 who went to the Women's March. Even that's quite broad, and you can create a more specific target. The great thing about this tool is you can run a few tests and see what's getting traction, and then go further in that direction.

Create a post or an ad that's engaging and not just about you and your campaign. What makes it a shareable piece of content? Why would someone share your video if they've never met you? These are all things to think about so that you don't waste time and money on ads that don't work. Set aside some budget for these paid marketing tools that can make your life easier. Fun fact, I met one of my best friends via a Facebook ad that I paid for in 2013 for *The Empowerment Project*! My friend Asha Dahya reached out to me after seeing one of my ads, we met up at my fundraiser, and have been besties ever since! That proves these campaigns go way beyond the funding itself.

In person events are great too!

Between my two crowdfunding campaigns, I not only met amazing people I wouldn't have otherwise met, but I also developed skills as a public speaker. In March of 2013, I found myself hosting in person events, which is something I had never really done before. After doing so much to push my 2013 campaign forward online, I knew I also needed to take this fundraising in person. I was still working on *Dancing with the Stars* at the time. The studio where we shot in was right next to The Grove in Hollywood. The Grove is a beautiful outdoor shopping center with lots of restaurants and bars. On Monday nights, the cast and crew would go to a place called Mixology after the show wrapped. Knowing that would be a great way to gather a lot of the people with whom I worked, I contacted the owner of Mixology and told her about my Kickstarter campaign. I asked if one Monday night could be dedicated to supporting this film, and I could charge a cover of $10 and have iPads out for people to donate more. She said yes! It was awesome. We had a special drink for sale called "The Kickstart," and one of my co-workers sang a song she had written for the film. Another co-worker served as DJ, and there was dancing. We even showed the crowdfunding video at the event on all the TV screens. We raised about $1,300 cash in one night, which I immediately deposited and put towards the campaign.

It was incredible, and the timing was perfect. I was close to the end of my 60 days, and I was exhausted. Although crowdfunding is about community and connection, it can sometimes feel like you're shouting into a void, and lacking personal connection. I needed that in person energy to make it across the finish line. Even though so much of your campaign is online, make sure you put your phone down and interact with people in person. What resources are available to you for an in person event? The less you spend to put on the event, the more money goes to the campaign. What talented friends of yours can help lend their creativity for the night to help you raise money? Or is there another event happening you can team up with? Perhaps you show your video clip prior to a movie screening of another film, and a portion of ticket sales go to the campaign. Maybe you put on a silent auction, or sit atop a dunk tank. Let your mind wander with the possibility of bringing your community together around this project.

Believe in the magic

As I wind down the crowdfunding section of this epic chapter, the sentiment I want to leave you with is the possibility of magic, if you open yourself up to it. It's so powerful to plant your feet firmly on the ground and say, "Hey universe, I'm Sarah, this is my dream, I'm going to do whatever it takes to make it happen, and I need your help to do it." All of this hard work will add up to something amazing. Both times I crowdfunded, I had a moment where I felt so overwhelmed by the kindness of strangers, and so grateful that I had put myself out there. It's no small thing to share your dreams with the world and ask others to support you. When they do, there's nothing like it.

In 2013, about halfway through my campaign for *The Empowerment Project*, I got a message through the platform from a woman named Lynn. I had no idea who she was, and her message could have totally been spam. She said she was impressed with the project, would donate, but wanted to know if I had a fiscal sponsor because she was interested in giving $25,000 outside of the campaign. What?! I didn't even know what a fiscal sponsor was at that time, so I quickly Googled it, thought it seemed doable, and responded right away that I would love to talk with her and learn more. She fulfilled her promise, donated $2,500 to the campaign, and then a couple months later processed payment for $25,000 through our fiscal sponsor, Women Make Movies. Our budget literally doubled overnight. In exchange, Lynn was an executive producer on the film, and only a few months after that we met her in person in San Francisco while on our road trip to make the film. In a beautifully serendipitous fashion, she introduced us to a person who would become incredibly influential in my life: Scilla Andreen, the CEO of Indieflix, who not only became the distributor for *The Empowerment Project*, but has been my mentor and friend for the past six years, AND is the distributor for *Nevertheless*. It's absolutely amazing when you go back and connect the dots of your life like that.

Fast forward to 2018—I have 11 days to go in my 30-day campaign for *Nevertheless*, with a goal of $50,000. My daughter, Bryce, is three months old, I'm breastfeeding around the clock, overwhelmed, and worried that we aren't going to make our goal. We're stuck at 69% funded. I go to bed feeling depressed, I wake up, and I do a double take. I'm suddenly 89% funded! A wonderful family in Germany found my campaign and donated $10,000 while I was asleep. I messaged this guy, Ralph, to make sure it was real, and to say thank you!

He was so kind and said that he and his wife donate money to causes that impact women every year. They were very impressed with *Nevertheless*, so they donated the maximum amount! I was speechless. And once we got to 89% funded, the momentum was strong, and we were fully funded just a few days later. I even ended up exceeding my goal, raising $57,821 from 610 backers in 30 days. Later that year, my husband, Ryan, and I decided to take a trip to Germany, and we actually met (and stayed with!) that same wonderful German family outside Munich. I was able to thank them in person, and get to know them better. None of that would have happened without crowdfunding. None of it. Those are just two stories of two people who found me through crowdfunding and changed my life with their kindness. Between the two campaigns, over 1,000 people saw what I was doing, thought it had merit, and gave some of their hard-earned money to help me fulfill a dream. That's magical.

I hope that helped you see crowdfunding in a different, more accessible light. Yes, it's hard, but you can do this!

GRANT WRITING

"If you don't apply, some other idiot will."
— My grant writing workshop teacher.

Switching gears a bit, let's talk more in-depth about applying for grants. Like crowdfunding, one of the benefits of grants is you don't have to pay the money back. What are grants? In this context, grants are funding for documentary projects that foundations, non-profits, and organizations set aside to support a certain number of films and filmmakers every year.

Some grant organizations are focused on specific missions, like supporting women in film, or specific issues, like racial justice. There are grants for every stage of the filmmaking process—from development grants, to production grants, post-production grants or finishing funds, to impact campaign grants. There are tons of grants to seek out and apply for from a variety of sources. Some are incredibly competitive to get; some pick out of a smaller pool of applicants. Some are micro grants, like $500, and there are some very large grants, like $100,000 from IDA (International Documentary Association). I've even heard of a grant that can fund an entire film at $400,000 from ITVS (Independent Television Service). No matter what grant you apply for, you will need to fill out a lengthy application where you articulate who you are, and what your vision is for the project. It's likely that you will be asked to provide some kind of video sample to go with it. If you've followed the process I've shared so far in this book, including the materials to create early on, you'll be prepared for any grant. Your treatment, your budget, and your sizzle will help you show the foundation what you're up to and why they should support you. All of the questions they ask on the application should be things you're thinking about anyway, so at the very least, it's a great exercise in eloquently explaining the main three questions: **Why you, Why this, Why now?**

I have applied for upwards of 30 grants between three feature docs, and as of now, I have received five grants, totaling about $60,000. They came from the Rogovy Foundation, the Tribeca Film Institute, and the Influence Film Foundation. Grants are great if you're lucky enough to be awarded one. But many filmmakers feel lost and helpless when applying for grants; it's like their applications are sent into a black hole that spits out rejections. Trust me, I've been there. So here are some basic principles I've learned over the years when applying for grants. I hope this will ease the process for you a bit, and make grants less intimidating.

Find out when all the grant applications are due

There isn't necessarily a grant applying season, so I would encourage you to dig in and do some research about which grants you'd like to apply for, and put those deadlines on your calendar now. That way, you can set aside time to apply, and not miss the cycle for the season or the year. For *Nevertheless*, I set aside most Friday nights as my grant applying time. (Watch out, huge party animal over here!) Some grant orgs announce winners once a year, and for others, it can be two or three times a year. It all depends on their funding schedule. **A helpful resource is Documentary.org → For Creators → Grants Directory.** This database is a collection of all the grants available, categorized by due date, amount of funding given, and much more. You don't even have to search around the internet endlessly for every grant available! Which is for sure what I did before I found this directory.

Read the instructions

This may sound beyond obvious, but it's so easy to overlook: make sure your project aligns with the mission of the grant organization before you bother applying. If a foundation is focused on projects about climate change and the environment this year, and your project is not about that at all, don't waste your time (or theirs) by applying. Also, if there is a word count requirement for a response, make sure you don't exceed that amount. Also, choose the most appropriate phase of the project to be applying. If you are in production and also in post-production, you will need to decide which phase of the project you list it as. Keep in mind that, if you say you're in post-production, the grant organization may ask you for a rough cut. If you don't have it yet, don't apply for post-production. Whatever phase you apply for, you'll be in competition with other films in that phase. If their films are mostly done, and yours isn't yet, choose production instead.

Fully read their FAQs before you begin, and contact them directly if you have questions. Basic mistakes like not following instructions can get your application thrown out. Approach this process from the perspective of a judge. They have tons of applications to sift through, so they're looking for any reason to make their workload lighter. When you don't follow instructions, they likely won't even read your full application. It's a frustrating way to be disqualified, especially because you might never know that the reason wasn't related to your film—it was simply because you didn't follow instructions.

It's less about who you know, and more about the project

One thing I have come to really like about grant writing is that, unlike film festivals and most part of the filmmaking process, applying for grants is less about who you know. Of course, the more people you know in the film industry, the better off you are when applying to programs and labs. With grants, I have found that the funding is distributed more based on the merit of the project, the filmmaker behind it, and the story they are trying to tell. It's a more even playing field. And if you ever make something with the focus on diversity and inclusion, there's usually a special prioritization given to those stories.

Of course, if you can get an "in" to a grant organization and find someone who can help you get the application to the top of the pile, wonderful, but the project still has to be great. For all the grants I received, I was applying blind, not knowing anyone on the other end of the judging table. Also, a lot of these grant orgs want to give money to new talent, emerging filmmakers, and people who deserve a shot.

It's a numbers game for sure

Real talk: you need to apply for every single grant that is applicable to your project. You do not know which one you will get, if any, so it's a good idea to increase your chances by applying to as many as possible. It's also good to keep the timeframe in mind as you plan your budget. It can take anywhere from two to nine months to hear back about your application, depending on how big the foundation is. And then, if you are lucky enough to get one of the grants, it might be another one to three months to process the payment. Know that, with a grant, your timeline might be anywhere from three months to a year before you receive the money.

Remember when we talked about processing payments through fiscal sponsors? You'll want to know if the grants to which you're applying require one. Some nonprofits can only donate money to other nonprofits. If you get to choose how payments are processed, go through your LLC or S Corp so you don't have to pay the 5-8% fee for the fiscal sponsor.

In short, applying for grants is not a fast process. Unlike in crowdfunding where you could have money in hand within one to two months, there are no guarantees with grants. The best strategy is to apply apply apply, and then forget about it and wait to hear back as you continue with your project as best you can. And who knows? You might get an email on a gloomy Tuesday in January saying you're going to receive $20,000 when you need it the most, and you cry. A lot. *Oh, just me?*

See if you can connect with past winners

Look at who won this grant the past couple cycles, and see what sorts of projects this organization tends to fund. Is it all social issue driven? Is it all doc features and not shorts? Is it all BIPOC filmmakers? If it applies to you, see if you can reach out to one of the filmmakers who won the grant in the past. Ask if they're willing to talk with you and give any tips. Bonus points if you can get a copy of their winning application to reference. Your project is completely different, so it's not like cheating on a test. It's like seeing an example of an A+ paper that was awarded $10,000. I have shared my winning applications with other filmmakers, and it's been helpful for them to reference. They may even help you out by sending an email to the person who runs the grant organization and let them know you will be applying. Couldn't hurt!

OK. OK. What the heck does this lengthy application ask of me?

Here's the great news. In recent years, many grant organizations got together to form the almighty CORE APPLICATION. This is huge. Remember the Common Application for college? You filled out one application and then sent that to multiple colleges with ease? It's just like that. Thankfully, there is now a core application for grants, so you won't have to fill out 10 wildly different applications for 10 different grants. Some grants deviate slightly from the core application, but all in all, you will generally be asked these same questions. Hooray! Here is the latest core application. I would encourage you to go to documentary.org and download this so you can start to work on these responses sooner than later. That way, you will be prepared for almost any application that comes your way.

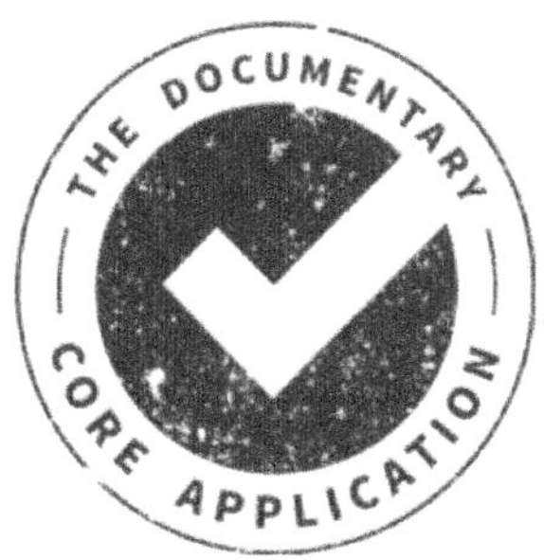

The Documentary Core Application Proposal Checklist from Documentary.org

1. Project Description

    a. Logline - Provide a brief, catchy summary of your story.

    b. Story Summary/Synopsis - What is your story and structure? Give an overview of your story.

    c. Topic Summary - Describe why this topic is important, timely or relevant. Why are you the best person to make a film about this?

    d. Artistic Approach - How are you going to tell this story?

    e. Project Stage and Timeline - Explain the current status of the project.

2. Audience and Distribution
    a. Distribution and Marketing Strategy - Specify plans for festival, theatrical, community screenings as well as plans for securing distribution.
    b. Intended Audience - Describe the anticipated audience for your project, how do you plan to reach them?
    c. Audience Engagement and Social Impact - Do you have partnerships lined up?
3. Key Creative Personnel
    a. Bios of Key Creative Personnel
4. Fundraising Strategy
    a. Fundraising Strategy - Describe the strategy for raising additional funds necessary to complete the project.
    b. Funding to Date - Provide a list of all sources and amounts raised to date.
    c. Amount Requested/Grant Impact - Should you receive a grant, how would you spend the money and how would that help the project?
5. Budget
    a. Comprehensive Line Item Expense Budget
6. Work Sample
    a. Director's Prior Work, if applicable
    b. Current Sample/Rough Cut, if applicable
7. Supplemental Questions - If applicable

Whew! That brings back many memories of late nights writing. I know, it's a lot. But the good news is, once you fill this out, you will be way ahead of every other application that comes after.

Don't feel like you have to have it all perfectly mapped out in order to apply

These grant organizations inherently understand that these projects are evolving constantly. Documentaries are living, breathing organisms that change by the day. They get it. Do your best to lay out what you anticipate the story and the vision to be, as well as your hopes for distribution, but know that it's ok if you don't have all the answers. None of us do. Resist the impostor syndrome, and simply tell them your intentions.

Always ask for the maximum amount of money

This is an important tip. Some of these applications say they are giving out grants that span a range of money, like between $10,000 and $25,000, and then ask you how much you need to get to the next phase of your project. Say $25,000. Cause guess what? You need that much and more for a plethora of things to make this film the best it can be, and get it out to the world. It's not greedy, it's smart. Let them decide to give you less. You may say you need $25,000, and they may give you $10,000. Always err on the higher side of your request. If you ask for $10,000, there is zero chance they will give you more than that. Everyone else is asking for the maximum amount; you should too, and leave it up to them.

Include a salary for yourself in your budget

This came as a surprise to me when attending a webinar from a well-known grant organization, so I'm passing this along to you. The documentary community is invested in making sure this is a viable career path for filmmakers. No one wants to see you working for free for years and years. For a grant organization to take you seriously—and more importantly, to take your budget seriously—they want to see that you've allotted to pay yourself a salary of some kind to complete this film. Your instinct might be to show them you're tirelessly working on this film for no money, but I have heard the opposite. This film would not exist without you, so pay yourself something if you can. At the very least, include yourself as a line item when submitting your budget to these grant organizations.

Reapply!

If you don't get the grant, apply again if they encourage it. Make sure your project has advanced in some tangible way so that you can demonstrate progress to them, but don't be afraid to apply again. Some organizations will explicitly say they don't want you to reapply, so look out for that, but more often than not, reapplying shows perseverance and determination. Most of the time you won't get feedback about why your project did not make it to the final round. See if someone else you know can look over your responses and give you feedback some other way. Reapply for a new project as well, if it makes sense.

If you've been awarded a grant from this organization before, they may or may not be open to giving you another. Some grant organizations encourage applicants to apply again with new projects and want to keep supporting you, assuming it went well the last time. Others are more excited about supporting as many filmmakers as possible, so they wouldn't consider you for the same grant twice. If you get a grant, you have an in with them, and can ask directly what they prefer.

Be open to programs and labs that don't necessarily provide funding

I know funding is the main goal here, but there are also a lot of programs, labs, fellowships, and mentorships that could be incredible launching pads for your project as well. When I received the Tribeca All Access Grant in 2016 for *Losing Sight of Shore*, they gave me $10,000, but what was honestly even better than that was the 30 meetings they set up for me during the Tribeca Film Market, where I was able to meet with distributors, film financiers, film festival programmers, post-production houses, grant organizations, and much more. It was a three-day program, and it was like speed dating for distribution! I learned so much, and those meetings ultimately led to more funding, and my sales agent for the film, which ultimately led to Netflix. Sometimes the money is not the prize, it's the access. Check out the Sundance Institute, Tribeca Film Institute, IFP, Good Pitch, Women in Film Financing Intensive, and Film Independent for a ton of amazing programs and resources.

At the end of the day, think about this from their perspective

I try to think about what these grant organizations want. They want to support filmmakers who have missions and projects that align with theirs. They want to go back to their funders and their board and say, "Hey, look at all these great films we helped fund this year, and look what they went on to do! They changed the world!" That way, they can get more funding for the next year, keep their jobs, and support more filmmakers. Show them how you are creative, innovative, trustworthy, and that you will make them proud.

Why you, why this, why now.

PRIVATE DONORS

Next let's talk more about Private Donors. Now, this always sounded to me like a secret group of wealthy people you could somehow tap into and get your project funded, and I suppose it can feel that way, but private donors are essentially just as it sounds. Someone you meet or come across that is interested in donating a large sum of money to your project in exchange for a Producing credit of some kind—usually executive producer. This money can come from a few places, but I have found that it usually comes from their own personal wealth, a family foundation set up for this exact purpose, or they might have access to funds within larger foundation, with influence over its allocation. A private donor is typically some kind of advocate or philanthropist for specific causes, and your film project might fall into one of the buckets they want to support.

Typically, private donors help a variety of individuals and organizations outside of the film industry. It's possible that in funding your film, they're dipping their toe into something different or new. I want to share what I've learned about working with private donors, and what a tremendous privilege it is to find people who want to support your film in this way. I'll also share how these relationships came about in case it inspires you to find private donors in your networks.

They want to give money through a fiscal sponsor

This is really where your fiscal sponsor will come in to play. A private donor is going to want the tax benefit of donating money to a cause, so they are going to want to write the check to a non-profit 501(c)3 organization. All of my private donors have processed our finances through my fiscal sponsor. That way, they get the tax benefit, you get funding that you don't have to pay back, and the fiscal sponsor gets 5-8% of the donation. Everyone wins.

They shouldn't have any creative say in how your film turns out

I thankfully haven't had an issue with this, but I have heard about filmmakers working with private donors who had a lot of opinions about how a film should turn out. Because they have provided funding, they felt they were entitled to participation in the creative vision. You want to make sure before you take anyone's money that you have some kind of agreement, or at least an understanding, that you as the filmmaker have final cut of the film. Although you might go to them for feedback or notes, you are in control of the final narrative. In that agreement, also clearly state that this is a donation and not an investment. There should be no expectation of them getting any piece of this money back, and you are able to use it at your discretion. They may ask for executive producer credit in exchange for the funds; you might negotiate that they get co-executive producer credit, if you happen to have a larger donor that wants to be the sole EP. Either way, that does not mean they get creative control of the film.

Crowdfunding is a great way to get in front of them

I mentioned a couple of magical stories in the previous section where I formed a relationship with a private donor through my crowdfunding campaigns. I have been contacted a handful of times through crowdfunding from people who wanted to support the project in a larger way. It's an ideal scenario. If someone is willing to be a donor outside of the platform, that means you don't have to pay the processing fee, and you can offer different and more special credits or rewards. But these folks might never have known you existed without crowdfunding, so these two things often go hand in hand.

Here's another story of how crowdfunding connected me to a private donor: a backer generously gave $2,500 to my *Nevertheless* campaign in 2018. I kept my backers updated on my progress throughout the year that followed. About a year after the campaign—the following March of 2019—I was hosting an in person fundraising event for the film, as we were in post-production. This private donor, who didn't even live in the same city as me, saw that I was hosting this event and asked how the film was coming along. We got on the phone a couple days later and I shared our progress from the past year. He asked me how much money I was looking to raise at this upcoming event. I told him that, if I was dreaming big to get through the end of post-production, I would want to raise $50,000. I had no idea if this person was interested in giving further funding, or if he and his wife were simply interested in hearing about my progress. Just a few days later, they contacted me again and said they wanted to donate an additional $50,000. I was shocked. And honored. And humbled. They believed in what I was doing; they saw the progress I was making, and that I had a solid plan for distribution, and so they wanted to help me cross the finish line. It's insane that I spent 30 days running a Kickstarter—plus all of the prep that came with it—to raise about the same amount of money I raised within one phone call with this amazing couple. Sometimes you feel like you have to push a boulder up a mountain, and other days it can finally feel lighter and more effortless. Also, there is certainly a lesson in here about aiming high and dreaming big, and being clear. Is it no accident that they chose $50,000—that's the number I said I needed. You have to go for it. Just like with grant applications, private donors can always give less, but they likely won't give more than you ask for.

At the fundraising event a couple weeks later in L.A., I raised about $3,000, which wasn't close to my goal, but by simply promoting the event, and stating my needs out loud, this magical domino effect unfolded, and I got the money I needed. It began with crowdfunding, and a year later it resulted in a large donation that got me across the finish line. Private donors could already be in your network, you just need to keep people informed about what you're doing and what you need.

Fundraising Events

Another good way to get in front of private donors is through fundraising events. In the typical format you bring some kind of value to the evening, like exclusive clips to watch, or someone from the film is present to give a talk or perform, or something that feels extra special for the attendees. I have hosted a couple of these now, and none have yielded huge results at the event itself, but they've all been valuable in their own way.

I've learned a couple of things about how to create a success fundraising event. First things first, you need to spend as little money as humanly possible to make this work. That means you need to find a venue that is either free or donated, or costs very little. A friend of mine hosted a fundraising event at a fabulous home in the Hollywood Hills that someone lent her for the night, which made the whole event seem expensive and fabulous, despite not costing anything.

Not all of us have friends with houses in the Hollywood Hills, but use whatever resources you have, or ask to use a venue on an off night, and share your email list with the venue so they could potentially bring in new customers. Search for the win-win situations. In terms of food and drink, try to get those things donated as well so that any money from donations or the cover charge goes to the project and not the expenses of the night.

For my March 2019 fundraiser for *Nevertheless*, the donated venue was a multi-purpose room at a West Hollywood hotel (a huge connection from a friend who had a friend there), but we had to pay for appetizers, and the drinks were an extra cost to guests. Then we found out the valet was charging $20 per car, since it was West Hollywood. I charged $15 as a ticket price with the promise of seeing exclusive clips from the film, and a panel discussion on the topic of sexual harassment. I had a packed house of friends and new friends, but when I think of this event from the perspective of an attendee, they paid $15 for a ticket, $20 for valet, and if they wanted a drink, they spent at least $10 more. Before I've even asked them for money, they have spent $35-45 dollars. It was a great event, and I got a lot of support for the project that I needed, but if I did it again, I would make sure the people attending had spent as little as possible before I ask for donations. I would also try to get more people in the room that I didn't know, that perhaps were of greater means financially.

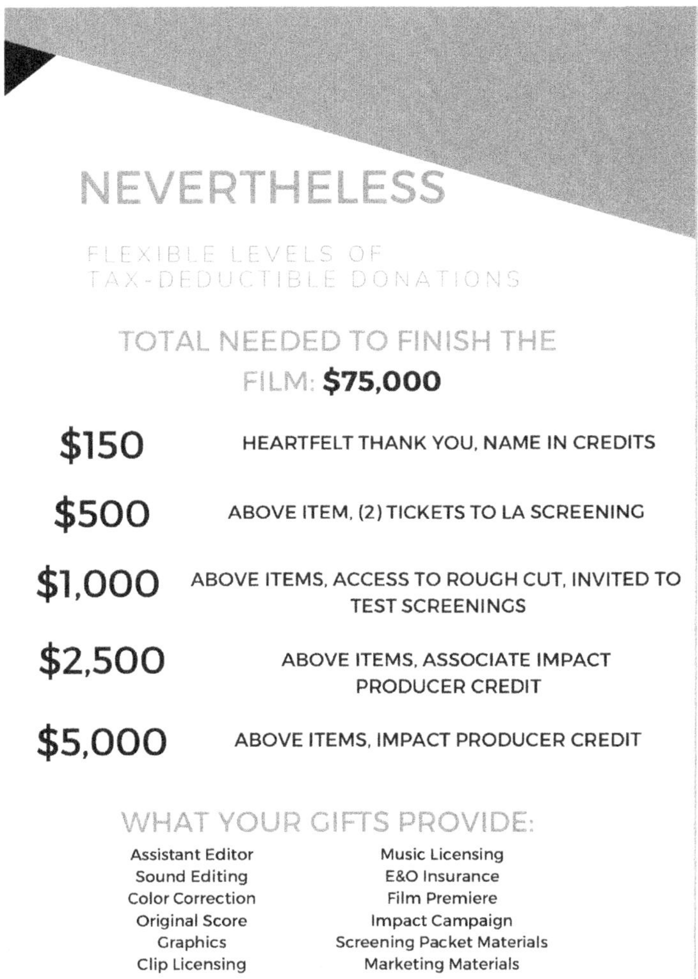

It doesn't feel great to ask your friends for money over and over again when they have projects that need funding too. Raising $3,000 in one night is great, and I am so grateful to everyone who came, but I have seen peers raise $10,000 or $20,000 in one night, and spent far less. If you're going to do an event, make sure it's worthwhile.

In my experience, finding private donors doesn't have a clear path, but when you come across one, they are a very important special relationship to foster, as they could help fund your next project as well. And ultimately, when you're making an independent documentary film, your fundraising strategy is going to be a combination of all of these avenues.

INVESTORS

"Truthfully, we didn't bet on the race, we bet on the horse."
—My investors talking about me at a screening of "Losing Sight of Shore" in April 2017. (I am the horse)

Last up in Fundraising 101 is bringing on investors. I saved this for last because it is not to be taken lightly. Investment changes the structure of your project completely. I often hear filmmakers use the words "donation" and "investment" interchangeably, but that is a mistake, and honestly will make you sound like more of an amateur when you are a professional. Also, that distinction is extremely important when talking with people who might give you funding. To review, a **donation** is money you *do not* have to pay back (like crowdfunding and grants and private donors) and an **investment** is given with the expectation and hope that you will do everything in your power to *get that money back* to the investor, usually with interest, and with an additional share of equity or profits to go with it (*Shark Tank* anyone?).

Of course, there is no guarantee an investor will get their money back, but that is the expectation, and that becomes one of your priorities. Taking on investors is akin to being an entrepreneur and launching a start-up. And like any start-up, you need to treat your project like a business that will become profitable, which will ultimately dictate how you distribute the film to pay back your investors. Trust me, this changes a lot for the filmmaking process, and adds an extra layer of pressure and expectations.

Any accountant or lawyer will tell your potential investors that films are historically bad investments, and let's be honest, it's true. Very few independent documentary films are going to actually recoup their investors' money. So when you bring on investors, make your distribution plan as clear as possible (demonstrating that you're going to do everything you can to repay their investment), but that the landscape is changing constantly and there is no guarantee they'll get their money back. This could come in the form of preparing a business plan.

So why would any investor do this? There is still a cool factor when it comes to investing in films. Some people are itching to be executive producers on an awesome project, whether or not it makes money. Maybe your film aligns with their mission and ethos in life. Maybe they have money to spare, and maybe best of all, they believe in YOU.

How do you find investors?

This is a similar sentiment to how do you find private donors—you need to get in front of potential investors. That could be through crowdfunding, including equity crowdfunding, meaning you run a crowdfunding campaign to seek out equity financing, not donations. Platforms like Crowdfunder, Local Stake, and WeFunder all allow you to put your project or company up and see if investors are interested. Another way you can get in front of potential investors is through one of the grant or lab programs I mentioned in the grants section. For example, the Women in Film Financing Intensive can get you in front of potential investors. When I participated in the Tribeca Film Institute Market there were potential investors present, as well as the Sundance Institute.

In addition to these formal routes, you might know someone in your extended network who's interested in investing in a film or a cause. You first need to decide if that's something you want. You don't want to take investments out of desperation, but because it's the right thing for the project and your career at that time.

What if someone says they want to invest in my film, what do I do?

The first thing you're going to want to do is contact an entertainment lawyer. Please don't make the mistake I made, which is to start promising a part or percentage of your project or company when you don't know how these deals are typically structured. You want to make sure you consult with a lawyer and speak from an informed place. Find out how much the investor is thinking of putting into the film ($50,000? $100,000?), then work with your lawyer to determine how much equity that would equate. Even if the investor doesn't have a number in mind yet, I would still consult with a lawyer and find out how much each point or percentage is worth. For reference, my investor agreement for *Losing Sight of Shore* was 42 pages long. This is not a casual document, and it will take weeks, if not months, to iron out. Bringing on investors is not a fast option. Know that going in.

Please note: Everything I am sharing in this section (and let's face it, the whole book) is anecdotal from my own experience with investors and lawyers, and is not formal legal advice. Please consult with a lawyer before making any decisions for your project, as I am not a lawyer.

First, your lawyer is going to ask about your total project budget. This is very important, as it will essentially become the valuation for the project, and the basis for equity shares. This budget should realistically reflect what the project costs to make, while also including a healthy salary for you. This is not the time to skimp on your salary, even if you haven't been paid a dime yet. Why? That budget is going to become a part of the investor agreement, and if possible, you are going to want to make sure your lawyer accounts for your salary being paid to you BEFORE the investors get any of their money back. Your salary is part of the cost of making this project happen. Without you, there is no project to sell. Just as you need money for a sound editor and a cinematographer and a colorist in order to finish the film, your time is incredibly important in making sure this project gets completed, and you deserve a salary, dammit!

How are these deals structured?

I will share the structure of working with investors that I utilized, but please note there are other ways to structure working with investors in film. This is where it really feels like being an entrepreneur or start-up founder more than a filmmaker, but there is so much to learn if you go down this path.

I was in production on *Losing Sight of Shore* in 2015, and had no idea how I was going to raise money to make this project happen. I didn't want to crowdfund, as I had just done that, and I was applying for grants, but they weren't reliable enough and took too long to hear back. I started investing my own money, but I knew that wasn't sustainable for the whole project. I had no time to fundraise through events or private donors, because I was always preparing for the next shoot, which happened to be in the middle of the ocean. Suffice to say, I was getting worried.

In the process of pitching to potential production companies, I ended up connecting with a lovely couple who was interested in getting into the doc space. They offered to invest in the film in exchange for executive producer credits. They had worked in the television world and wanted to diversify their portfolio of projects by including film. They had seen my sizzle reel, treatment, and heard my pitch, but never asked for a formal business plan. They loved the story and they believed in me, which was the most important part. When they told me they wanted to invest, I was excited and nervous to find out what that could actually look like. I had never worked with investors before and wanted to make sure I did everything right. I contacted my lawyer right away, and we began the several-month process of ironing out the investor agreement. Finally, I received the money and was able to get through the rest of production. At this point, Netflix was a distant dream—I hadn't even made contact with them yet.

Here's how the investor structure was created: I submitted my current budget of $250,000 to my lawyer, which included a salary for me built into it as a cost of production. My investors wanted to put in $50,000. Based on those numbers, my lawyer determined that 50% of the project was for Producer Shares or Class A shares (that's me), and 50% of the project was for Investor Shares or Class B shares. Each investor share (or Class B shares) cost $5,000 for 1% of the project, up to 50%. Thus, this investment of $50,000 was equal to 10% of the project. In addition to that 10%, we offered them an additional 5% (of Class A shares) because they were the first investors that signed on to the project.

In summary, my total budget was to be $250,000, and their $50,000 investment terms were that they were to recoup their $50,000, plus 10% interest (so $55,000 total), and THEN they would also be entitled to 15% of profits in perpetuity after that based on our deal. Apparently interest on an investment can be 10% but it can also be up to 20% depending on where the deal is made.

Here is an illustration of my investment structure to help make it clearer:

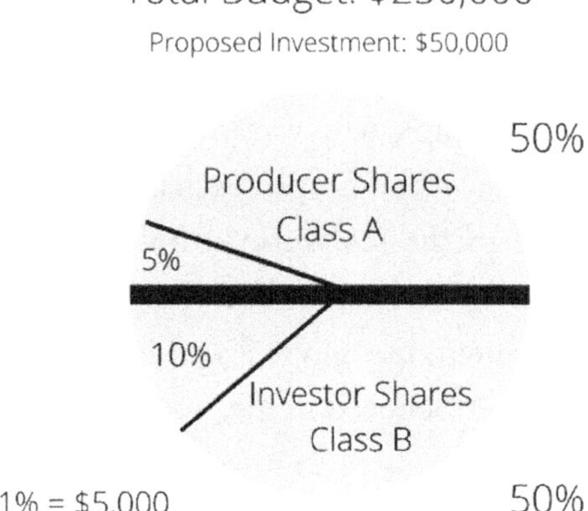

It's important to note that I am also an investor in *Losing Sight of Shore*. It's vital that you keep track of any money you invest in your own film, as you should recoup that money alongside any other investor. As part of this lengthy agreement, I was also stated as an investor (Class B shares) based on how much I put in. That way, every dollar that came into the project in the form of net revenue was split between investors (them as a couple, and me). I wasn't sure if I would need to bring on more investors down the road at this point (which I ultimately didn't), but I wanted to make sure that I was credited as an investor as well, and would be repaid as such.

Fast forward to the Netflix deal two years later—every dollar that came in from the licensing deal (**gross revenue**) first went to my sales agent (15%) and consulting producer (10%) and then the **net revenue** was split 50/50 between myself and my investors until we were all paid back, plus interest of 10%. Once that was done, then we moved into the profit stage where my investors received 15% of every dollar that came in (net revenue), and the remaining 85% of the net revenue was split between myself, and everyone else with whom I had a profit-shares agreement: the Coxless Crew, and any deferred payments owed, etc. (this concept of how the money is distributed is often referred to as a **waterfall** and this agreement continues for as long as the film makes money). I know this may seem quite complicated, but this is typical for a documentary that brings on investors. Through grants and private donors, I was able to finish the project, and thankfully didn't have to allot more profit shares to other investors.

In terms of profit sharing outside of investors, that will be dependent on your team and your project. I had to bring on a sales agent in order to license the film to Netflix, and I had a wonderful consulting producer that helped me throughout the life of making the film that wasn't paid a salary and deserved a piece of profits for all of his help to make this project happen. In addition, I set up deferred payments to key players that I didn't have the funding up front to pay. In this case I also included the subjects of the film the Coxless Crew in to the profit participation of this film, which is unique to this film. That is not normally something that documentary filmmakers do, but in this scenario, my subjects were integral to the collection of footage and we had a specific agreement in place that honored all of our roles in the making of the documentary. All in all, there were a lot of factors and players that came together to make this film possible, so all of that is honored in this structure, and it worked for us. Looking back, I have no regrets about bringing on investors for that project. It went well! We all got paid back, and then some, which is rare. But I do see how much pressure investors can add to a film project. There is a specific focus on commercial success with your film because you have investors on board. If you're OK with that and you see the potential for a return on your film, this could be the best way to go. Make sure you go in to this with your eyes wide open and so do your investors.

When I was making *Nevertheless,* I wanted to do everything I could to avoid investors. I received a few offers to pitch to investors, and I kindly turned them down. I vowed to raise 100% of the funds through donations, which I ultimately did through crowdfunding, grants, and private donors. I was even able to pay myself a salary while making the film, which was a first for me. Working with investors might not be for everyone, but my experience was really smooth, all things considered, and everyone was happy with how it all turned out.

It's important to know what you want to get out of your fundraising process for each project. Each film will each have different needs. Hopefully with all of this information (I know, it was a lot!), you feel equipped to make those assessments. I didn't know ANY of this when I was in film school, or when I started making my own projects. If I can figure this out piece by piece, so can you.

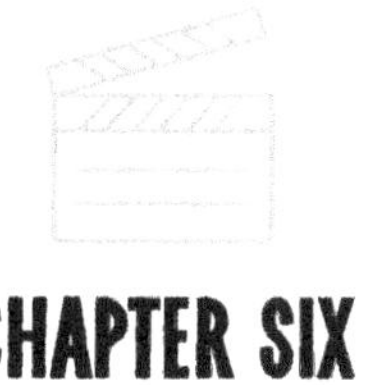

CHAPTER SIX

PRE - PRODUCTION

Pre-production is an important phase of the filmmaking process, and can last anywhere from one day to several months, depending on the scope of your project. Pre-production is everything that happens before you grab your camera and start shooting the film. What preparation do you need to do in order to begin?

This is where you put on your producer hat on and think about putting out fires before they start. This is where you educate yourself on the history of the issue or person you are exploring. This is also where you take the necessary measures to protect yourself and your crew before filming (including what we previously discussed with release forms).

Pre-production often happens in conjunction with fundraising, and even production. You may come back to pre-production several times throughout your process, or you may progress sequentially. We've touched on a lot of what this phase can entail from the legal side, getting your contracts in order, starting an LLC, and creating a budget. Let's explore some of the areas of pre-production we haven't touched on.

Research and Development

Even before you reach pre-production, you might need some time to dive in and research the person or subject you will be filming. This may require phone calls, Skype or Zoom interviews, books or articles on the subject—anything that helps you feel ready. There will be a lot to discover in the filming process, but you need a basis of knowledge so that you can hold a conversation with people in this arena. If it's a social issue film, ask yourself: Who are the experts in this space? What different perspectives do you want to include to make a well-rounded film? What is the history of the issue?

If it's a personal, story-based film, ask yourself: Who in this person's life would help paint the picture of the main character's story? Where might you need to travel in order to tell this story fully? What kinds of archival footage are available on this person? Does the family own it, or is it publicly available? Start to gather that now. Fortunately, a lot of research and development can be done from your computer. Read articles, watch interviews, and watch other films, especially if there are any in this same genre. Start to lay out emergent themes or pieces of the story on note cards. This technique helped me so much when I was researching for *Nevertheless.* Where do you even begin when telling the stories of people who were sexually harassed? And what was I trying to say about the issue overall? Notecards helped me make sense of the bigger picture. I wrote down the themes I saw emerging while researching, and while conducting early interviews. This all shape my future interview questions, too. It was as if the story built on itself.

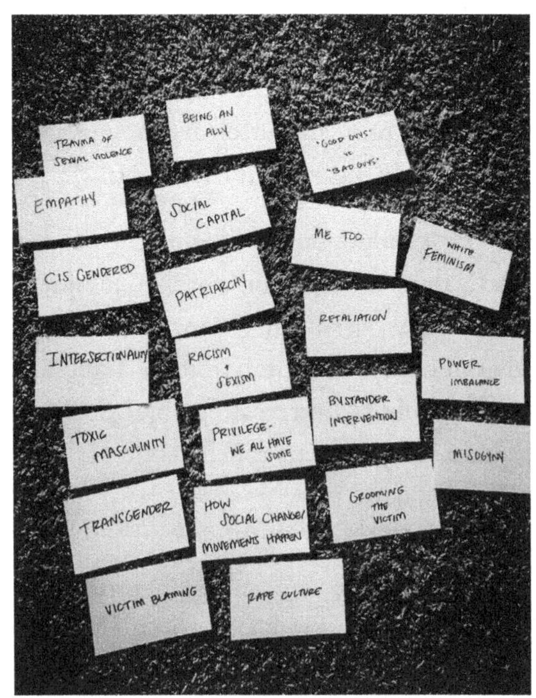

I wrote down themes like INTERSECTIONALLITY, SOCIAL CAPITAL, BEING AN ALLY, WHITE FEMINISM, PRIVILEGE, RETALIATION, EMPATHY and more. These words were circling in my mind throughout the entire project, and they became the main themes in the final edit.

What is your film about? What is the A story, and what could be the B story or C story? There is a lot of time and ground to cover in a feature-length documentary, so it can't just be an interesting person or important cause. What is going to happen to that person? What journey are they going on internally or externally? For the issue-based film, information is great, but how are you going to bring this issue to life? Who are the characters you will spotlight or follow, and what will their stories help amplify?

Pre-interviews

Getting some footage of your main subject on camera before you formally start shooting is a great way to ease into the project and understand some of your story pieces. You could do this over Zoom or Skype and record the interview, you can do it over the phone, or even in person, with or without cameras rolling. The idea here is to see what your subjects are like on camera, to get the basic idea of the depth of the story, and to start building rapport with your subjects. If you have the budget, getting out and shooting some footage with your characters, or doing some sit-down interviews with experts in your field, is a great way to get started as well.

After a few months of research, I did 16 on camera interviews for *Nevertheless* in October of 2017 in Los Angeles and San Francisco. These were with employment attorneys, sexual harassment training prevention specialists, diversity and inclusion managers, brave women willing to share their stories, and more. It was so unbelievably helpful to get out there and start asking questions when I was still distilling what I wanted to say in that film. I used a few of those interviews in the final film, but I see a lot of that time and work as an extension of the research process. I took the information I learned from that first round of interviews, and I not only used it to cut my sizzle reel and write my treatment, but I used it as a jumping off point to understand what I needed out of the next round of interviews. Off camera, I was constantly on the phone with experts in the field to better understand the nature of #MeToo, and what was happening in the United States at that time. In pre-production, be a sponge gathering insight and asking people about their point of view. It will help shape your own.

Spending time with your subjects

This is an often overlooked part of documentary filmmaking—you need to have a good connection with the people you are showcasing. They need to trust you, and be willing to open up to you when things get tough. Don't be afraid to be vulnerable as well. A great way to form a strong bond is to share part of your life, if appropriate. You want your characters to feel at ease with you behind the camera, because there will be moments when they are unsure or want to quit. Your connection with them can save the project.

The way in which you spend time is up to you. You could go out to coffee or dinner with the person or people you are going to be filming; you could exchange phone calls or emails. It depends on the situation, your distance, and the person. Tell them who you are and why telling this story is important to you. Show them your prior work if it's appropriate and will help them understand where you're coming from as a filmmaker.

I remember showing the rowers of the Coxless Crew my first feature, *The Empowerment Project,* before we committed to working together on their journey across the Pacific. That helped me garner their trust and admiration, as they could see the mission and message of my work—to empower women and showcase strong female role models on screen. If my work hadn't reflected those things, it would have been harder for them to trust me with their story. If you don't have related prior work, it'll be up to you to demonstrate why you're the right person to tell this person's story. Share who you are as a person, the experiences that have shaped you, and why this project is important to you personally. The relationships you form with your characters might last years, depending on how long the project takes. If your instinct tells you this person or group may be difficult to work with, listen to it. Incompatible dynamics only intensify on film projects. By the way, it's also ok to get to this phase and decide this relationship—or project—might not be the right fit. It's ok to put in time and work, and then ultimately determine now isn't the right time for you to tell this story, or work with these people. You might need more time, or maybe the project needs to evolve a bit before you truly get started. It's ok to listen to your gut at this stage, and truly any stage.

Insurance

A much less fun and interesting—but still important—part of pre-production includes getting insurance for your production. Anytime you're going to be renting equipment, hiring a crew, and going out to shoot something, you will need insurance to make sure you are covered in the that event something happens. What if a camera you rented gets damaged? What if a crew member gets hurt on your set? Will they receive worker's compensation? It's not fun to think about, but you need to protect yourself and your LLC as much as you can going into your shoot. If you have an LLC that is managing multiple productions at once, you might have an annual insurance policy that covers all of your staff and crew. Otherwise, you need to seek out a policy to insure your gear and crew, whether your shoot lasts a day or a year.

There are a number of ways to go about this: you can contact a specific insurance company, you can work with an insurance broker who will help you find the right company and policy, or you can compare policies based on the scope of your shoot. The insurer will want to know about: 1. Your LLC, which will become the insured party; 2. The value of the gear you are renting; 3. Where and when you're shooting, and for how long; and 4. How many crew members will be on set. An international policy will be more expensive than a domestic policy.

You may have a special scenario for your shoot that requires extra coverage. For example, if you're going to be bringing the cameras over water or on a boat, you need extra coverage for your shoot. I learned this firsthand on *Losing Sight of Shore*, and ultimately decided that the cameras I supplied the rowers with were cheap enough that if they dropped one into the ocean (which they did), I would replace it myself rather than insure it for nine months, which would have cost a lot more. I also rented camera gear to use when we were filming on the boats, and for drone photography. In these instances, I had separate coverage.

Make sure you know what your policy includes and what the deductible is. Ask: What happens if I break a camera, how much would I have to pay to replace it based on this policy? Equipment rental houses will require a certificate of insurance, or a **COI**, before letting you rent their gear. You will need to list the equipment rental house's name and address on the COI. Once you have your policy, these forms are easy to fill out. If you are renting a location, you will also need a COI for your shoot. Best case scenario is that you spend money on an insurance policy for your production and you never have to use it. Hopefully, it feels like you paid for nothing but peace of mind.

Production Schedule

Pre-production is the ideal time to lay out your intended production schedule, and even think ahead to post-production. Start by working backwards to fully understand the scope of this project. You can pick a festival deadline, or time of year you'd like to finish the film, and then build in about 6-8 months for post-production. Then determine when production needs to be complete to meet that deadline.

Or you can build the schedule in chronological order based on the events happening in your character's life and story. Is there a culminating event that will likely be the end of the film? For *Losing Sight of Shore*, I was told the Coxless Crew would row the ocean in about six months, but as they got started it became clear that timeline was way off. They ended up rowing the ocean in nine months, so my timeline shifted back three months. But once they had made it to Australia, I knew I had the entire film shot and could move on to post-production confident that I had captured it all. It's easier to create a production schedule when the journey is linear and has a built-in ending.

For an issue-based film like *Nevertheless*, it was harder to determine the timeline. I gave myself all of 2018 to be in and out of production and research, so that going into 2019, I was focused on the edit. Having a timeline mapped out for yourself will help keep your brain organized, and it will also be valuable for grant applications and funders! Even if it changes, at least you'll know what's supposed to come next.

Pre-production is also when you write interview questions, create shot lists, and more, which we will talk about in the coming chapters.

CHAPTER SEVEN

PRODUCTION

At this stage you've come up with an idea, you may have raised some money to get it off the ground, and you're ready to shoot! That is no small feat. This is where the magic starts to happen as you go out into the world and find your story. My dad, who is also a filmmaker and TV producer, always told me: "If you make the film you set out to make, you did it wrong." That simply means things will evolve and change as you turn on the camera and see what there is to capture about this person, this event, this issue. It's your job as the director to trust your eye and find what is most captivating about the story. Maybe there is a character you didn't anticipate; maybe there is a change in the course of the story you didn't expect; maybe the content is much richer and more complex than you could have imagined. Whatever the change is, embrace it. This is the process.

This is where documentary film and narrative film truly differ. In narrative filmmaking, you have a script written by a screenwriter, with characters and some amount of instructions that describe the world you are to create. Then you cast actors, hire a crew, secure locations, source wardrobe and set design, all so you can bring the script to life. Many things can and will change as you go, but the final film will resemble the script you originally read. In documentary filmmaking, that couldn't be further from the process. You start with some inspiration, a seed of an idea, and then you go out and discover what the story truly is. In the edit process the film truly takes shape and is given a structure. We have no script in documentary filmmaking; we only have our gut instincts, and a passion to see a story through to the end.

I like to think of production as gathering information and story so that I can bring it all back to the edit room and shape it. The more story you capture, the more options you have in the edit room. Especially if you're covering a social issue, it's also important to accumulate as much knowledge as you can throughout the process. You want to represent this issue well, both in filming and editing, and that expertise will help you make intelligent decisions about your film.

When I set out to make *Nevertheless,* those initial 16 interviews captured in October 2017 helped me cut a sizzle reel (which I needed for fundraising), and more importantly, gave me some clarity about how to move forward. I didn't do more interviews until May of 2018 because I had to focus on my Kickstarter campaign—oh, and I had a baby(!)—but by the time we were ready to shoot again, I had some budget raised and a lot more clarity about who to talk to next. I also knew with certainty we needed individual stories to anchor the film in empathy. I didn't just want 50 interviews with intelligent people giving facts. I needed real men and women who had personal stories to share that would add intimacy and emotion. So my next task was to find five to eight stories that would populate the film. I ended up with seven. Production for *Nevertheless* lasted from October 2017 to April 2019, with many breaks in between interviews to fundraise or edit, or both. I needed production to last that long so that I could interview people, come back and digest the information, digest the footage, and create a plan to move ahead.

For *The Empowerment Project*, production lasted exactly one month. We set out to drive across the US to interview inspirational women with an all-female film crew, and we drove from LA to NYC in 31 days. It was all self-contained, and once we got back, production was done and post-production could begin. It was very clean in that sense—we raised money, then we shot, then we edited.

For *Losing Sight of Shore,* production lasted nine months—from when the Coxless Crew rowed away from San Francisco to when they arrived in

Cairns, Australia. I had toyed with the idea of filming with the rowing crew after they returned home to the UK, but once I saw the ending unfold in Australia, I knew that was the end of the movie. This was a unique situation where I wasn't physically shooting for nine months, but the rowers were. They were filming every day on the boat, so they were constantly in production, and I met them on land along the way in California, Hawaii, Samoa, and Australia. I didn't know production would last nine months—we all thought it would be about six months—but it was actually a great situation (in hindsight). When production was in process, I could fundraise and edit in between my time with them on land. If I had been on a boat with them for nine months, the project would have taken much longer to finish.

Just with my three feature docs, production took anywhere from one month to a year and a half, and all for good reasons. Your project is yours to shape, and it's up to you to figure out how much content you need to fully tell this story, and how long it will take to capture it properly.

Let's talk about the components of production in documentary filmmaking.

Interviews

Interviews are often the best place to start production, as the interviews usually serve as the backbone of the story. Even if you end up never seeing the visual of an interview, it can be the narration of the story. One example of this is the Oscar-winning documentary *AMY* about the infamous singer Amy Winehouse. The entire film is made up of sound bites from her friends and family, and yet you never see their faces. Instead, you see home videos of Amy in her life, and clips from her career. It's clear that is the filmmaker's artistic choice, but he still had to capture all of those interviews, and then made that choice.

You might need to do multiple interviews with your main subjects. You might want to break up a very long interview process, or see them in a new setting, or you realize once you get into edit that you need more coverage of the story. You might want to see them as they progress in life—getting older, getting sicker, or changing their physical appearance somehow.

It's up to your cinematographer and you to make that interview visually interesting as well. What can we learn about your subject through the background of the setting? How can you make the frame pleasing to the eye so that people will listen and take in what the person is saying? This is where you want to work with your cinematographer to come up with some visual language for the film. Early on you could decide you want all interview subjects to be filmed slightly from below, so they all seem larger than life. Or, if a story is about the ocean, you want all interview frames to incorporate water somehow. This is where you can start to think about the cohesion of the visual language of the story.

Interviews are often the most important aspect of production. Once you have the bulk of your interviews captured, you can get started in post-production.

Vérité Shooting

This term refers to realism or naturalism, being a "fly on the wall" as you shoot. Part of production often involves spending a "day in the life" with your subjects. Here you have an opportunity to paint the picture of a person without needing interviews to explain things. You will certainly pair those things together in edit, but right now you want to capture your subject in their natural existence, as if you weren't there. What do they do all day? What are their interactions like with the people around them? What do they do alone at home?

Depending on the nature of the story, you will know what to capture or look for when filming vérité. Some documentaries are made up entirely of vérité, which means production could last for years. The purpose of vérité is to capture life as it happens, rather than shape it. This kind of filming lends itself to a very small camera crew of one to three people, as you are trying to blend into the surroundings and let your subject forget you are there. You can learn a lot about a person by observing them in their daily life. Some good examples of films vérité shooting: *Gaga Five Foot Two, Whose Streets, Citizenfour.*

B-roll

In a general sense, b-roll is what you shoot to supplement the main interviews, providing supporting shots or scenes for what was said. B-roll enables you to cut away from the interviews to help paint more of the picture of the story. B-roll can come in many forms, and can include vérité. An establishing shot of a school or a house that the characters frequent is b-roll. An insert shot of someone holding an important photo can be b-roll. Watching someone get up and get ready for school and walk out the door can be b-roll. B-roll is anything that supports the main interviews so that you're not just staring at a talking head for two hours. I often come to a shoot with some b-roll planned, but then once I'm in the environment, I will shift the plan based on what's right in front of me, or what I've learned about the person by being with them.

I was shooting in Chicago with an auto plant worker named Tonya for *Nevertheless*. After we did the interview, I wanted to get some footage of her getting ready for work in the morning, since she talked about how stressed she gets preparing to leave for the day. We filmed each piece of her morning routine—putting on her uniform, turning on her walkie talkie, looking in the mirror and praying, gathering her belongings, and walking out the door to her car. Then we got in the car with her and she drove her normal route to work so we could get b-roll of her face looking out the window, her hands on the steering wheel and turning on the radio, and footage outside the windshield of the world passing by. All of those shots are a useful sequence to use as a transition, and during her interview to help paint the picture of her daily routine.

THE MORE B-ROLL THE BETTER

There is nothing worse than only having a couple shots to choose from in edit. You need to capture far more than you'll use so that you have options and plenty of room to play. In fact, with Tonya in Chicago, I didn't capture quite enough b-roll on that one day. When we were editing, I realized there was a gap that required more footage. I ended up hiring a local Chicago camera operator to go back and film more with Tonya, this time at her local church. In her interview she talked about praying and how important God was to get her through tough times. Seeing her in church felt like the only logical way to tell that story. Had I known prior to the shoot that Tonya would discuss praying, I might have arranged to go to church with her, but it was something we went back and got later. And it turned out beautifully—we used many of those shots in the church of Tonya nodding along and closing her eyes praying to help further paint the picture of her life.

Archival Materials

If you can help it, I would recommend gathering archival material in production rather than pushing it off to post-production. Archival includes: pictures, videos, audio recordings, newspaper clippings, and anything else from the past that will help tell the story. You might need a rare piece of footage that is hard to come by and will take time to source, so you want to begin this process sooner rather than later. If you have a budget, you might want to hire someone to help you in this arena, as it is truly a skill to be able to locate and organize archival elements. Not to mention staying on top of licensing or organizing your clip log for fair use is a lot of work. Archival footage is so vital to helping us understand what pieces of the past link us to the present. Some films are made up almost exclusively of archival footage, especially historical documentaries. This footage might be in the public domain, or it might be considered fair use, or it could be something you need to pay to license.

Re-enactments

Once you've filmed all of your interviews and whatever b-roll you can gather, it may be an interesting addition to bring in some narrative re-enactments to the story. I don't mean super cheesy re-enactments that you might think of from Investigation Discovery, but highly stylized, seamless re-enactments when you don't have b-roll to cover and you want to fully immerse the viewer in the story. The HBO doc series *McMillion$* did an unbelievable job with stylized b-roll/re-enactments. You really felt like you were watching these events unfold in real time.

The only time I've used this technique was in *Nevertheless.* Two of the seven stories were really rooted in the past, and there wasn't good enough b-roll to bridge the gap. We needed to show more to truly understand the impact of what they were sharing. One story in particular was about a 911 Dispatcher named Patricia who was sexually assaulted by her supervisor when they were working late one night in the 1990's. How do you tell that story when of course there wasn't footage from that night? All I had was one or two pictures of Patricia during that time. So, I went for the re-enactments, and I'm so glad I did. I worked with a casting director to help me find a woman that looked like Patricia from about 20 years before, I rented a police station set in Los Angeles, I sourced and rented props that would have existed in the 90's—including things like the computers, phones, and walkie-talkies—and I rented costumes and encouraged my actors to bring wardrobe as well. I hired a narrative cinematographer and gaffer to help with lighting, and we shot all of the scenes in one day. It was so fun to use a different part of my creative brain and see this story come to life. We had complete control over the whole environment, and I prepared a shot list ahead of time so that we came in and got each shot on our list, and then some. If you're going to use re-enactment, it's important to weave the shots effortlessly into the narrative. It should carry your story forward and enhance what's already there.

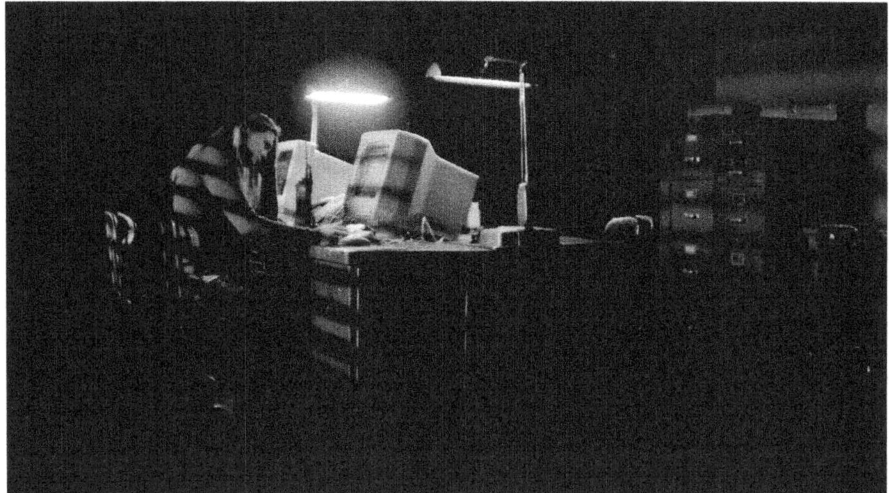

Downloading Footage in the Field

When you're in the field, you will likely need to download your footage during the shoot or at the end of the day to make sure it's safely and securely on hard drives. Filmmakers no longer have to haul around boxes of tape. Nowadays we shoot on memory cards specific to the cameras we're using. You can rent multiple memory cards from the equipment house, but at some stage you're going to have to delete and reformat what's on a card. You want to ensure the footage is safe on hard drives before you can feel confident enough to do so. The techniques I'm going to share are what I use on set to make sure my footage is safe and secure. And yes, no matter if I hire crew or not, I always find myself downloading footage late into the night after a long day on set. It's too important to me to pass off to someone else when, ultimately, it's my project. On a larger crew or on a show, the AC (assistant camera) person or the media manager would handle this, but when it's small and scrappy, you are in charge.

The first thing I do is check the footage on the camera itself to look back at what we shot today and make sure it is looking good and sounding good. I may even take some shoot notes from the day so I can remind myself later what was done if it's a series of days. That way, when I get to post-production, I'm not totally lost on what is where.

Simple notes like:

CHICAGO

DAY ONE

SONY FS7 - CARD 001

Master Interview - Tonya A CAM, Tonya lav Ch.1 Tonya boom Ch. 2

B-roll Tonya at home

B-roll Tonya driving

Exterior shots of house

Establishing shots of Chicago

Once I can see that the footage looks good and is working properly, I will safely eject the memory card from the camera—usually there is a green light that appears to indicate the camera is ready to eject the card. Red light means it is still in use, and not to be removed. DO NOT FORMAT THE CARD YET, you have not downloaded the footage.

Next, I will plug the memory card reader into my computer, typically using a USB port, and I will also plug in two hard drives using the USB port and/or the Thunderbolt port on my laptop or desktop. I wish I could have my desktop with me on the road so I can take this one step further and make sure the footage plays in Adobe Premiere before formatting, but that's not always possible. My laptop is quite slow; if you can download Adobe Premiere or the editing software you prefer, that's great. Now, I have two hard drives plugged in to the laptop as well as the memory card reader. I can now place the memory card within the reader, which should load quickly and pop up the footage you shot. Depending on the brand of camera you are using, that folder will look different. For the Sony FS7 for example, that folder is typically labeled XDROOT. If you double click on that you will see your individual files in the extension of MXF. Canon file extensions are typically MOV. The larger files will be the interview, and the clips that were more than a few minutes long.

Open up each of your hard drives separately now, and begin your process of organization the clips into folders. If you're using brand new hard drives, make sure they are formatted and ready to accept footage using your Disk Utility, or the set-up function when you plug the hard drive in for the first time. I often use the ExFat formatting for a hard drive so that it can be used on Macs and PCs. MS-DOS is only for PCs, and MAC-OS is for Apple computers. In my mind, I don't know who will need to open up these drives in post-production, and if someone with a PC needs to access these files, they need to be in an accessible format. To test that the hard drive is working on my computer, I usually drag over a file that's larger than 1GB file. If you are working with multiple drives, make sure all of the hard drives are formatted to be the same—ExFat, MS-DOS, MAC-OS, etc.

First, make a folder that can hold the other folders on your hard drive. This is hard to explain without knowing the scope of your project, so I will give a few examples congruent with the notes I listed above.

HARD DRIVE NAME: NTL_01 (Nevertheless is too long, so I abbreviate the title of the project)

Folder: CHICAGO

Inside that folder: DAY_ONE

Inside that folder: SONY_FS7

Inside that folder: CARD_001

The CARD_001 folder is where the footage from that memory card should be dragged. Now, this is important—you want to make **two unique copies** of the footage from the original card. That means you want to drag the footage from the card individually to each hard drive. You don't want to copy a copy. Don't drag the footage to Hard Drive 1 and then copy that same footage to Hard Drive 2. The reason for that is if there is any corrupted file that transfers to Hard Drive 1, it will absolutely transfer to Hard Drive 2. If you make two unique copies from the original, you have a better chance of not copying a corrupt file.

At this point, a dialogue box should pop up saying how long it will take to copy to each hard drive. Depending on how much you've shot, that can be a few minutes to a few hours. Using thunderbolt as your connection often speeds up the process beyond the USB connection. If time is an issue, you could transfer these one by one, otherwise you can set it and wait for both copies to be done. Take note of the total file size being copied. On a Mac, you can right click or control click and go to "Get Info" on the memory card to find out how much footage you shot. If it says 64.38 GB, then you want to make sure 64.38 GB transfers to each hard drive successfully.

Once the hard drives are done copying all the files from the memory card, you can go to "Get Info" by right clicking or control clicking each hard drive and make sure it says 64.38 GB as well. If it doesn't, something may not have transferred, and you'll need to figure out what's missing. I typically safely eject the memory card at this point. On a Mac, you safely eject a device by dragging it to the trash or clicking the eject button next to its name in the Finder Window. With the memory card ejected from the computer, you now have two unique copies of the footage on each of the two hard drives. If you can, click on one of your clips and open it up to make sure it plays the audio and video properly. You can use Quicktime, VLC, Adobe Premiere, Final Cut Pro, Preview, etc., depending on the computer and depending on the footage. If you see any issue with the footage you're watching back, you can put the memory card back in the camera and see if the issue is on the original or if it was a problem in the transfer. You may need to transfer the footage again if it seems like the problem is only with the copy and not the original. **DO NOT FORMAT THE MEMORY CARD UNTIL YOU KNOW YOUR FOOTAGE IS SAFE.**

If you feel confident that you have at least two copies of the footage you shot on your hard drives, that the files are working and opening properly, and that all of the data transferred and the numbers line up, you can put that memory card back in the camera now and format it for more shooting. If you don't need to format it, then I suggest you don't. If you can keep that footage on the card until you absolutely need the room, that's ideal, in case you are worried that it didn't work for some reason. Check and double check. When you're 100% ready, you will go into the camera menu and choose "Format Media." It will ask you if you're sure, and you will say "Yes" or "Delete" or "Execute" or some variation of that. Once your card is formatted, it's ready to be shot on again. Rinse, repeat. This is the workflow of working in the field and having to download footage again and again.

Two copies of your footage is the bare minimum to feel secure, three copies is even better. Trust me. I have had two copies of footage, and somehow both versions decided not to work, and I had to pay to have a hard drive recovered to save some of the footage that was lost. You will not regret having more copies! In fact, when traveling back home from an out of town shoot, I often place my two copies of the footage in two different places, just in case. One might go in a carry on, one might go in checked luggage. One might go with me, and one with my cinematographer. You could even take one on the plane and ship the other back to you. Whatever you want to do to feel secure that the footage is safe. It sounds like a lot of effort, but when it comes down to it, your entire film exists in this memory card and on these hard drives, so it's incredibly important that you take this seriously.

When you get back to your office or home base, you could purchase a master hard drive that can hold all of the footage for the whole film, and you can copy your footage to that for a third copy when you return. That will likely be the hard drive that goes to your editor. You may also wait to do this until you have all of the footage collected, i.e. the end of production.

Organizing footage on a hard drive gets more complicated when there are multiple cameras used in one day, and then multiple interviews and locations over time. Come up with an organizational set up that works for you and that you can effectively communicate to your editor or assistant editor when the time comes. If you don't know where the footage is, it's going to slow you down and frustrate you and your post team. That's why shoot notes are so helpful too, so you can reference something quickly down the road when you're too tired to remember what was what.

No matter how long or short production is for your project—a day, a week, a month, a year, 10 years—it is a marathon, not a sprint. I hope you can stop to appreciate your progress at this stage, the fact that you had an idea, you had the passion and drive to follow through on that idea, raise some money, and start to see it come to life on camera. That is amazing. The story is taking shape in front of your eyes. I always love the feeling of being in production, when there is so much possibility in front of you, and a successful day with great content captured is immensely satisfying.

Go forth and make it happen!

CHAPTER EIGHT

Camera Basics

Being able to use the camera has been one of the greatest skills at my disposal in my career. I am not a classically trained cinematographer, but I have a deep admiration and curiosity for the way the camera works and what results it can provide. I find myself asking other filmmakers what cameras they used to achieve certain looks, what lenses yielded a beautiful frame, and what accessories were there to accompany the package. For me, cameras were a part of my life since I was very young. My dad is a TV producer and documentary filmmaker as well—the apple definitely doesn't fall far from the tree. He had a whole cabinet full of old photography cameras and a darkroom in our basement, so learning how to take, frame, and develop a great photo was a big part of my adolescence. I can still smell the photography chemicals!

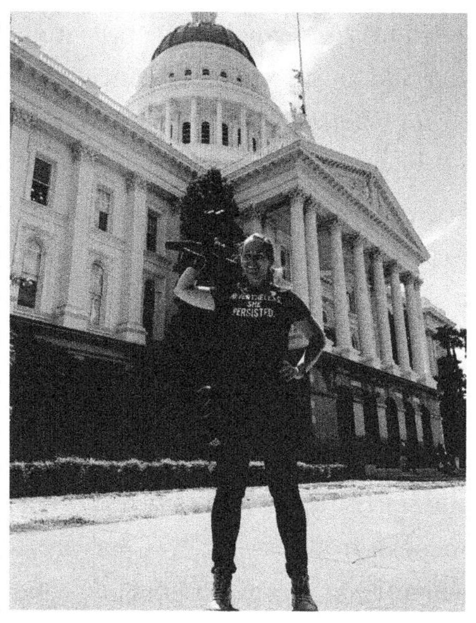

Then when I was 16, my parents got me my first video camera. It was a silver-and-purple Sony Hi-8 camera with AMAZING settings like slow motion, sepia tone, and night vision—I was off to the races. That camera was my birthday, Hanukkah, and Christmas gifts all rolled into one, and I think to this day one of the greatest gifts I've ever received. It was the camera that stood beside me as I put together my very first documentary in high school; the camera that captured silly music videos with friends long before YouTube (thank goodness); and the camera that solidified my passion for filmmaking.

Repeatedly over my career in television and film, being able to set up, shoot, and effectively use the camera has been a tremendous asset. When I started working on *Dancing with the Stars* as a story assistant, I was only 21 years old, fresh out of college, living in a new city, and suddenly working in the "Hollywood" I had heard so much about. My job was to take notes during the dance rehearsal shoots leading up to the live performances on Monday nights. I was paired with a field producer whose job it was to shoot, run audio, conduct interviews, and more. If there was anything I could do to alleviate their stress, I would do it. Rather quickly I was able to jump in and help out shooting a second camera, help troubleshoot when things went wrong in the field, and proved myself a reliable shooter. Before I knew it, I was promoted to associate producer and then field producer, with my own camera package to use week to week. I know with certainty my ability to shoot helped me get promoted quickly, and I ended up training other (often older, male) field producers who were hired on the show.

I enjoy these skills so much that I teach workshops about camera, audio, and lighting basics. It has been so rewarding to demystify some of these basic camera concepts so that anyone can go out and shoot. I am not pretending to be a cinematographer, but especially in documentary filmmaking, you don't always have the budget to hire a full crew of people for a shoot. Sometimes you need to just pick up the camera and go. I also find that when filming documentaries, you want to create an intimacy between you and your subject, especially when capturing sensitive material. Sometimes it doesn't make sense to bring in a whole other person to shoot, when you yourself can get exactly what you need. My intention here is to empower you to feel like you can get started—that there isn't a barrier to entry simply because you're not a camera-whiz. I'm not either, but I know enough to jump in and shoot something when needed (for budget, or other reasons). It has been an incredible skill to have that I want to pass on to you.

So here we go, basic camera concepts to understand that are universal to all cameras. Once you understand these, I promise it's just a matter of finding that setting or button on the camera you're using, and you're good to go. Since we don't have a camera in hand to demonstrate these concepts, I would recommend testing these out on a camera and getting familiar with it before you go out to shoot for real. Practice really does make perfect, and it's worth practicing on content that doesn't matter before shooting content that does.

Tripod

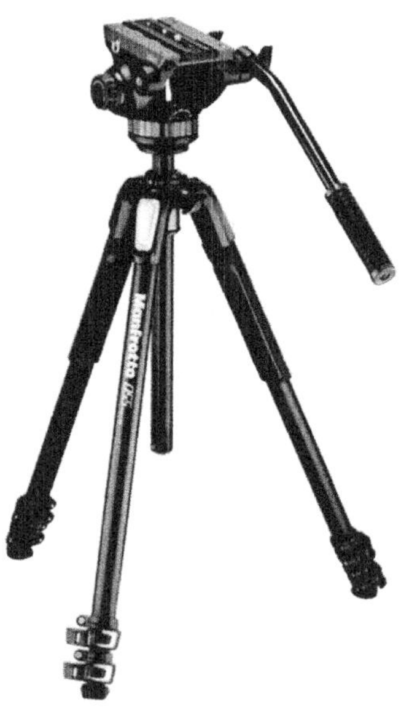

First things first, you're going to need a good tripod so that you can work effectively. Once you take the tripod out of its case, spread the three legs apart, unlock the legs, and start to raise it up. Ideally the camera lens will sit at eyeline with the subject you're interviewing, but give yourself some room to adjust once it's up. Once all of that is ready, it's time to attach the camera to the tripod. There should be a removable plate on the tripod which attaches to the bottom of the camera via a screw. Always keep a key or a quarter or some kind of multi-tool with you on set for this very reason. Pay attention to the side of the tripod plate that says "LENS" with an arrow. Point that side towards the lens, screw it tightly to the camera so that it won't move once on the tripod. Next you're going to slide the tripod plate (which is now connected to the camera) on to the tripod and lock it in place so that it doesn't slide off. You know you've done it correctly if you can pick up the camera and the tripod comes with it, and doesn't slide or fall. Now that the camera and tripod are one unit, you can unlock the tripod arm and practice panning and tilting the camera and adjust the fluidity (if it's a fluid head tripod) of the movement.

Pan is a movement of the camera left to right or right to left.

Tilt is a movement of the camera up and down or down and up.

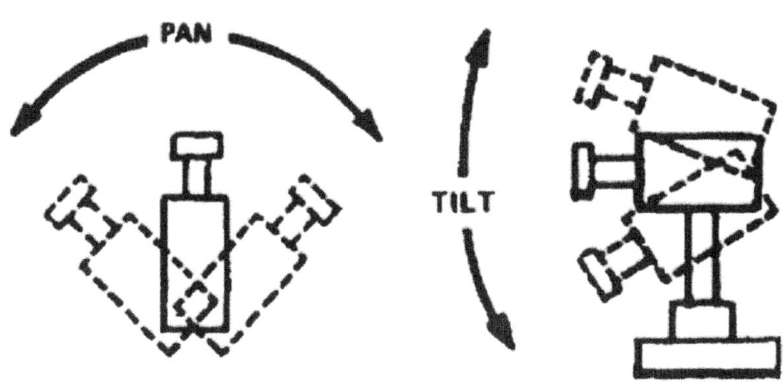

You are also going to want to make sure the camera is level on the tripod. If it's a fluid head tripod, look for the greenish/yellowish bubble, like you'd see on a level. Loosen the head by unscrewing underneath the tripod and moving the camera around on the tripod until the bubble is within the circle on the level (or two lines). You may need to adjust the level of your camera when you set up each shot, as the ground could be uneven. You can also adjust the pan, the tilt, the distance from the subject, the height of the camera, and more. Setting up the camera means constantly tweaking things until the shot what you want. Once you're done with the tripod, remember to remove the plate from the camera (unless you're doing more shoots with the same set-up), and keep the arm and head loose if traveling so that things don't get stuck. If you're buying one, invest in a solid, fluid head tripod.

Now onto the camera itself!

The first concept you should understand about the camera itself is the **iris or aperture**. This is a setting that controls how much light is let into the camera. The unit of measurement that accompanies this concept is called the "f-stop." When you hear someone ask what the f-stop is on the camera, the numbers they are referring to will give a reading of how much light is being let into the camera. Some example f-stops are:

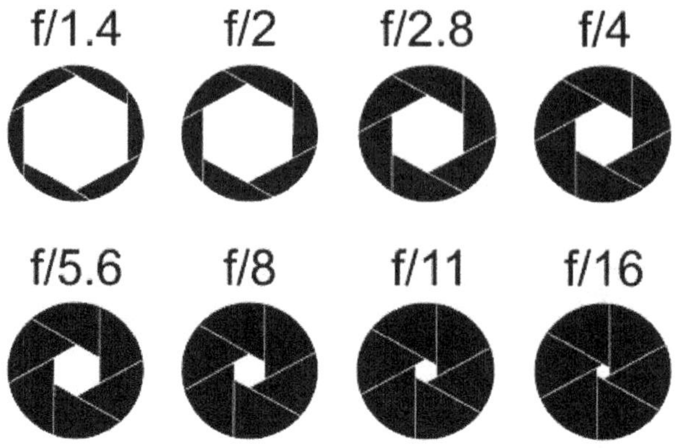

f/1.4, f/2, f/2.8, f/4, f/5.6, f/8, f/11, f/16, f/22

And as you can see in the diagram, the lower the f-stop number, the more light is passing through the lens, and the larger the f-stop number, the less light is passing through the lens. A practical example of this would be if you are shooting at night, you're going to want to let as much light in as possible to see your subject, so you'd likely need the aperture to be open to an f/1.4 or f/2. Contrastingly, if you're filming in the bright sun in the middle of the day, you have plenty of light, so you might be more in the f/11, f/16 or f/22 range—letting less light into the camera. Make sure to play with these settings when setting up your camera; watch the frame getting brighter and darker as you adjust the iris.

Frame rate is the speed at which images are captured by the camera. It's usually expressed as *frames per second*, or FPS. Each image represents a frame, so if a video is captured and played back at 24fps, that means each second of video shows 24 distinct, still images. Typical frame rates are 24, 30, or 60fps. I almost always shoot 24fps because it has a more cinematic look to it, whereas 30 or 60 has a more "soap opera"/video feel to it. But it's up to you! Play with it, see what you like, and stick with it for your whole project to maintain consistency. The amount of detail that the camera can capture is called the **resolution**, and it is measured in pixels. The more pixels a camera has, the more detail it can capture, and the larger pictures can be without becoming blurry or grainy. Typical resolutions are 720p, 1080p, and then Ultra HD, or 4K. In terms of pixels, the standard sizes are 1280 x 720, 1920 x 1080, or Ultra HD, which is 3840 x 2160. These are frame sizes in pixels (width x height). Most broadcast quality content is 1080p, but many people are choosing to shoot in Ultra HD or 4K. This gives them a broader range with color enhancement during edits, and allows them to stay ahead of the technology curve.

I always think I'd rather start with better quality content and downgrade if needed, rather than being stuck with an original image that isn't strong . Having the 4K information was very helpful when making *Losing Sight of Shore* because so much of the footage came from the rowers. They wouldn't shoot enough cutaways during a scene, so we often had to create our own cutaways by "punching in" on the footage in edit. (That means we took footage that was a wide shot, and made it in to a medium shot or close up in post by punching in or zooming in ourselves.) We wouldn't have been able to do that without 4K information; it would have been too grainy. Keep in mind, however, that shooting in higher resolution takes up more space on a memory card and will cost you more in hard drives. You'll want to consider that as you create your budget for the whole project. The resolution may alter how you edit as well. Once you pick a resolution, you usually want to stick with it for the whole project.

ND filters (which stands for "neutral density") are something you will use to cut out light when filming outside, or if you are shooting indoors with a large window and you don't want your subject or the window to look blown out. ND filters can typically be found as a button or switch on the camera in a 1/4, 1/16, and 1/64 increment, or 0.3, 0.6, and 0.9 grade increments. You can toggle through them to see what looks best. If you use an ND filter, you may need to adjust your iris again, since the light is now different. You always want the person's face you are filming to be the most well-balanced and well-lit part of the frame.

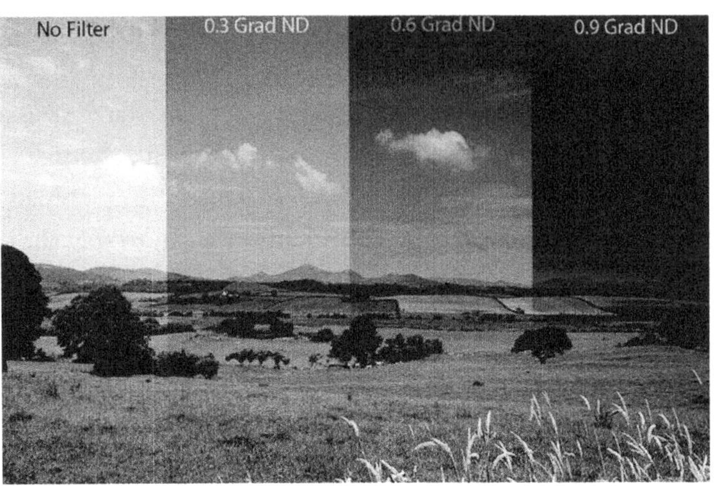

White Balance

We talked about how much light is being let into the camera, but what color is that light? I want you to look around in your daily life and notice the color of the lights you see in the world and in your house. The sunrise or sunset is a warmer, often more orange tone, whereas inside your house might be fluorescent lights with a greenish tone to them, and outside during a sunny day has a bluish tone to it. Often in documentary filmmaking, you are working with available light, so I want you to start to notice the light sources around you and how to work with those. (We will talk more about lighting tools in the chapters that follow.)

Basically, with the white balance setting of the camera, you need to show the camera what white is in your given lighting scenario, so that it can color balance all other colors based on that. Every environment in which you shoot may have a different white balance, so this is something you are often re-evaluating and adjusting as you move from location to location, and especially inside to outside. A lot of prosumer cameras have an "Auto White Balance" setting, which will likely do a decent job, but I also want you to understand what the setting is doing so that you can adjust it and make your frames look even better.

With white balance, the unit of measurement here is Kelvin. And there are three main numbers I want you to remember: 3200 kelvin, 4700 kelvin, and 5600 kelvin. Those refer to a standard color temperature reading. If you only remember and understand those three numbers, you'll be generally good to go. 3200 kelvin is a typical reading to use inside for tungsten light; 4700 kelvin is a reading to use more in the fluorescent lighting range; and 5600 kelvin is good to use in daylight, mostly an outdoor reading. Remember that our eyes are very good at balancing light sources and color temperatures, but the camera is not. It needs to be told what white light is in any given environment, so that it knows how to balance the color. That's why, if we were to set the white balance to 3200 kelvin, walk outside, and turned on our camera, the image would look very orange tinted. But if we adjust the color temperature to closer to 5600K, everything would look more normal again.

Color Temperature	Light Sources
10000 - 15000 K	Clear Blue Sky
6500 - 8000 K	Cloudy Sky / Shade
6000 - 7000 K	Noon Sunlight
5500 - 6500 K	Average Daylight
5000 - 5500 K	Electronic Flash
4000 - 5000 K	Fluorescent Light
3000 - 4000 K	Early AM / Late PM
2500 - 3000 K	Domestic Lighting
1000 - 2000 K	Candle Flame

A quick note on **gain.** I use this setting in extremely low light scenarios when there is nothing else to do, as it adds a lot of grain to the frame. You'll typically see this setting as a 0db, 3db, 6db, all the way to 18db or more. You might also see this setting expressed as ISO. Gain is a setting you want to have handy, especially if you are a one-woman band, and shooting vérité, and don't know what lighting scenarios you are in for that day. If you can keep the gain to 6db or less, you won't see much of the grainy-ness; but if you were filming at a concert late at night and it was super dark, gain would be your friend. Gain adds an artificial light to your frame.

Focus

Next let's talk about focusing the camera. When you're shooting an interview, you want to make sure you aren't relying on the auto-focus feature of your camera. The reason for that is sometimes the camera will choose the center of the frame, and not necessarily the face of the person you are interested in hearing from. You want to make sure the eyes of the person you are interviewing are always in focus. That helps the audience pay attention to what they are saying and not be distracted by any camera or technical issues.

Here's what you can do: Ask your subject to sit down in the frame where they plan to sit, and zoom the camera all the way to their eyeball. Use your focus ring to make sure their eye is perfectly in focus. You will know by your own eyes, but also there is a feature that a lot of cameras have called **peaking**. This feature puts green or red dots on everything that is in focus in the frame. (This doesn't record to the final image, it's just there to help guide you.) Once you see the red or green peaking dots, you can zoom back out and set your frame for the interview. Now, since your subject is a person and not an inanimate object, they may move considerably during the interview, so you may need to refocus from time to time throughout the interview. You don't want to zoom in and out and ruin the frame, but you can use the peaking feature to make sure their face and eyes are in focus. It also helps tremendously to have an external monitor to use on set so that you aren't beholden to a very small LCD screen on the camera. A monitor will plug in to the camera(s) and you can get a bigger view of what your frame includes. It will be easier to see what's in focus this way and you can share the frame with your crew as well.

There's also something called **rack focus**, which is a great tool to use, especially when filming b-roll. The concept of racking focus is to switch your focus from one person or object to another without changing the frame. This is an exceptional tool you can use within your own camera that elevates your b-roll, creating a professional look. Let's say you are filming two important figurines on someone's desk. You could set up the camera so that the first figurine (Leslie Knope) is in the foreground, and the second figurine (Rosie the Riveter) is in the background. You'd set your focus to Leslie, close to the camera, and slowly shift focus to Rosie, leaving Leslie blurry and out of focus in the foreground. The objects haven't moved, but the camera has shifted focus, and in turn shifted the audience's focus from one object to another. This could be a really cool way to move the story along and reveal something about your character. It may take some practice getting the move just right, but when shooting b-roll, you often have some time to play. Give it a try!

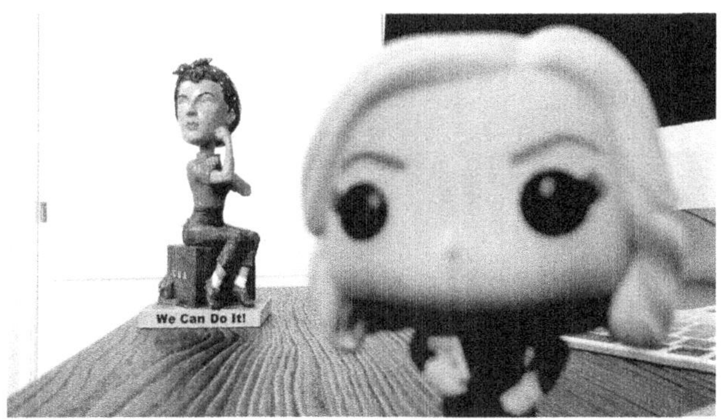

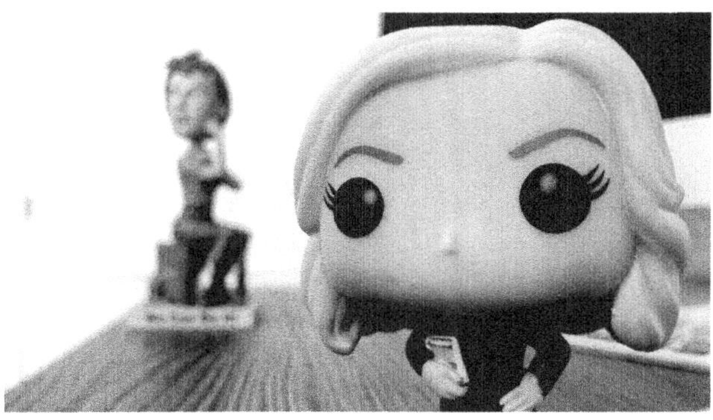

When you're **setting up your frame** to interview someone, you want to think about the "**rule of thirds**," which will help you add symmetry to your frame. I always liked the saying: "Learn the rules so you can break them." You are in charge of the visual style of your project, but it's good to know the general philosophies of filming so you can choose when to deviate from them. Basically, when you look at your frame for an interview, you want to divide it into thirds, both vertically and horizontally. This will create nine boxes within your frame. The rule of thirds is about placing the most important and interesting part of your subject where those lines intersect. When doing an interview, often the method is to put the subject on the right side of the frame, with their eyes right on the line, and have them look off camera to the left, or opposite of the side of the frame on which they appear. For example, place the subject on the left side of the frame and have them look off camera to the right. (*Your right not theirs*) You can also frame your subject in the center and have them look straight at the camera. It's totally up to you. Typically in a doc interview set-up, or the "talking head," you will frame them left or right and then have them look off camera in the opposite direction.

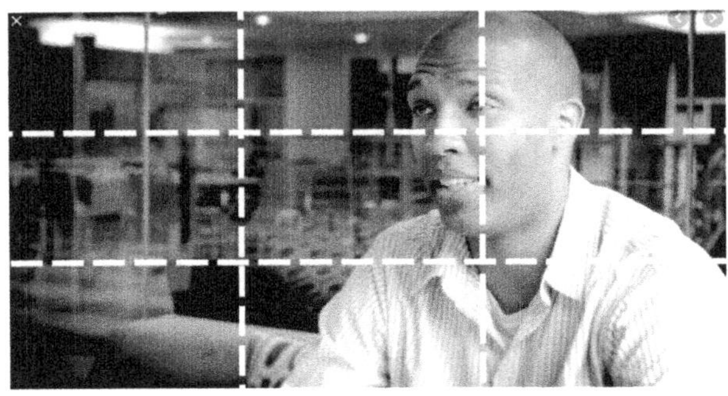

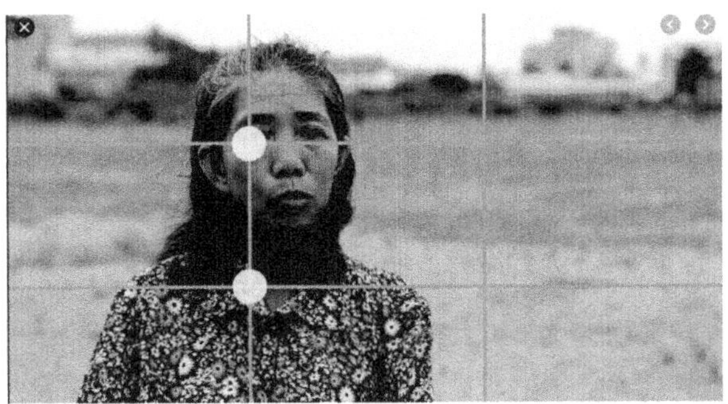

Plenty of filmmakers play with this set-up, especially for their **second angle**. I **always shoot an interview with two cameras for coverage**, unless I am limited in what I can accomplish that day. It is so helpful to have two angles for every interview so that you can cut between the two effectively, and shorten and smooth sound bites in the edit. If the two cameras can be the same, that's ideal, but not always possible due to budget constraints. If you can keep them in the same family in terms of brand, that's great too. Every brand has a slightly different sensor. A Canon and a Sony are going to have a different image quality that may be hard to match in post-production. You want to cut from one angle to the other as seamlessly as possible. If you can use a Sony FS7 as your A camera and main angle of the interview, and a Sony A7S as your second angle or B camera, those will go together pretty well. Or, if you're using Canons, a Canon C300 and a Canon 5D.

Now, for this second angle, it should not be a carbon copy of Camera A's angle. You want Camera B's angle to be different enough that you can change the viewer's perspective slightly and get more intimate. If A is a wide shot (WS) or medium shot (MS), then your B should be a close-up (CU).

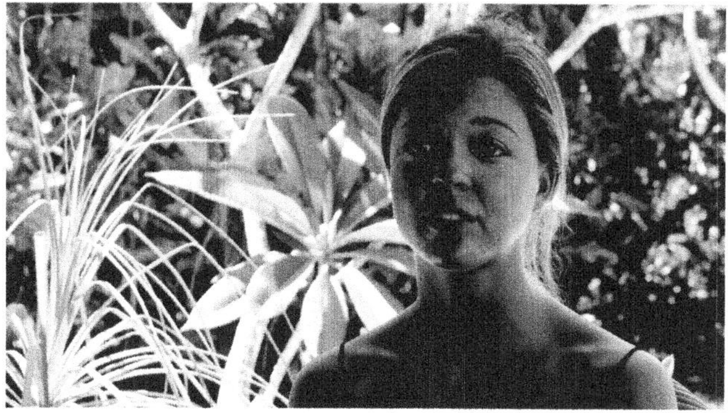

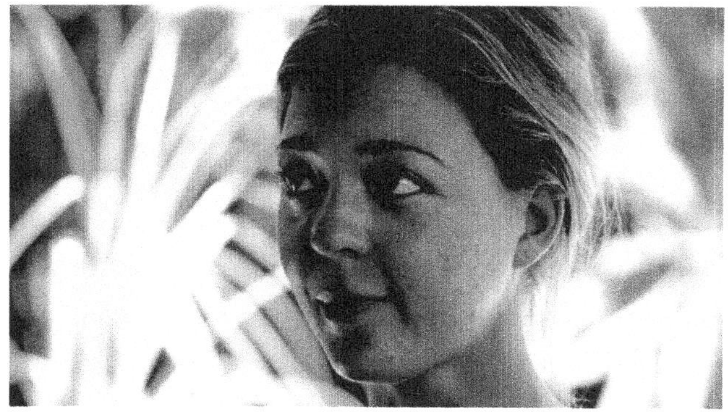

In addition, you need to keep both cameras on one "side of the line," referring to the **180-degree rule.** This is in reference to the imaginary line or "axis of action" that is drawn between the interviewer and the interviewee.

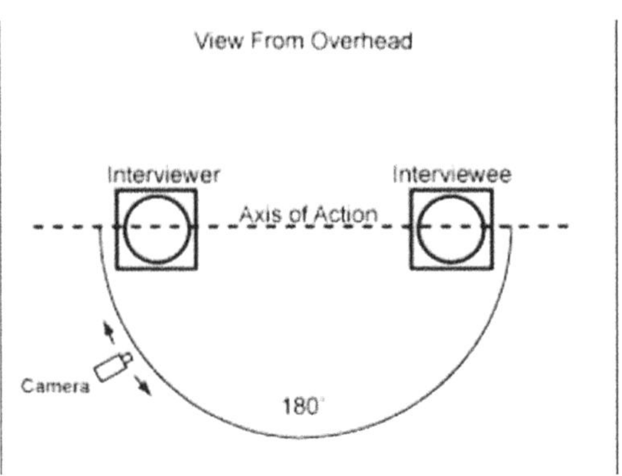

All cameras—whether you have one or five—need to be on the same side of the axis of action, within those 180 degrees. Otherwise the eyeline will be flipped, and it will be quite confusing for the viewer to process who is where. For example, if you as the interviewer are sitting with the A camera to your right, then the B camera will also be to your right. If you are sitting between two cameras, the eyeline might be off for the viewer.

Now, the exception to this would be if one of your cameras was used only for inserts. Let's say your C camera is catching hand movements only, and not focusing on the interviewee's face—then the camera can be on the other axis of action. In addition, you might have a C or D camera that is capturing behind the scenes of the shoot, and in that case all bets are off as to where the camera should be. That camera could even be in motion on a Steadicam, or on a dolly.

When you're not shooting interviews, and you are shooting more of a vérité scene with two or more people talking to one another, you need to make sure you **shoot coverage** of the scene so you can condense and cut it together effectively. That means, if two people are having a conversation, and if I'm limited to one camera to cover this scene, I want to shoot multiple aspects of this scene so that I can edit the pieces together, creating a more comprehensive depiction of the conversation. If I'm only filming one person on a stationary tripod, I won't have any footage of the other people reacting to what's being said, or speaking as well, to round out the scene. You want good "coverage" of these different elements.

Let's say two people are sitting on a couch talking to one another about a topic that is important to the film, and I want to cover the scene. I would establish who will be doing more of the talking (person 1), and who will be doing more of the reacting and responding (person 2). I could start with a wide shot so I can see both person 1 and 2, and establish where they are sitting. Then I need to get a **single** shot of person 1 talking without person 2 in it at all. This could be an **over the shoulder** (OTS) shot, meaning shooting person 1 over person 2's shoulder; it could also be from a profile angle, depending on how much I can move around. Then I'm going to need a **reaction shot** or **cutaway** from person 2 *not talking* in order to cut this together. You need footage of each person not talking in order to have the pieces to put this together. Why? If you only show both people talking the whole time, then you have no way to condense the conversation. I'll try to get at least five to ten seconds of person 2 not talking, and nodding or reacting to person 1. I might stay there if they are going to respond in some way. Then I might come back to a **2 shot**, or a wide shot, of the two people on the couch and repeat as needed.

Also, whether I'm shooting or directing a camera, I am listening very closely to the conversation. If they start talking about something completely unrelated to the topic I need to cover, I can use that opportunity to get cutaways until they come back to the topic that's most interesting for the film. I could shoot inserts of their hands, their jewelry, their pets, the photos on the mantle, I could try some rack focusing, I could go outside and shoot through the window. When the content is unrelated, I will take that time to get what I need. That way, when they come back around to the subject I need to capture, I can be completely focused on those words. I'm making a mental log of all the pieces I have in place so far, and I won't stop shooting until I have all the components I need.

It's a delicate rhythm to find as you listen, react, shoot, or direct all at the same time. Hopefully, within that time you have, you can truly capture the emotional truth of that scene. I learned a lot of this while working in reality television. The same techniques have helped me a in documentary filmmaking, especially when it's "run and gun," as they say. You are following what's happening as it's happening. If you have access to two cameras, then the above scene I described will be a bit easier to cover, as one person can be assigned to each camera, and you can completely cover the scene from two angles. You will want to make sure one of your cameras is capturing cutaways in order for it to work in edit. A lot of this is trial and error—getting out there and shooting a scene without disrupting the action. Typically, shooting handheld is going to work well when dealing with vérité, as a tripod might be too clunky to easily lug around, but you will find what's most comfortable for you.

All in all, the camera is a wonderful tool at your disposal, and not something to be afraid of. Just like anything in life, it takes practice, and you can absolutely handle it if you need to. There is something so satisfying about personally creating a beautiful image that you use in your film. The best way to learn is to pick up a camera and try these concepts out before you get on set and the stakes are high. Invite a friend over and play with the camera until you feel comfortable with the flow, with holding it, with trying the settings in a few different environments. And, you look way cool holding a camera, no doubt about that.

CHAPTER NINE

Audio Basics

Continuing on with our technical knowledge, having good sound during production of your film is going to make your project that much more professional. People often think simply having a beautifully crafted image is going to make the film great, but sound is truly equally important to immerse the audience in your story. You don't want to give your viewers any reason to check out, and bad sound is a surefire way to do that.

In this chapter, we're going to discuss production sound, and the tools you can use to capture great sound on set, especially if you are working with a very small crew or flying solo. If you have the budget, hiring a sound engineer is a great option. They will monitor your sound levels and you can focus on the interview, the b-roll, the camera, the location, and literally the 10 other things you might be worrying about at that moment. There is also post-production sound, which can be a real lifesaver to clean up the less-than-ideal sound clips.

Who are you looking to hire?

If you have the budget, I would highly recommend hiring a production sound person, or sound engineer, especially one that has their own sound equipment. You would pay them a day rate, as well as a kit fee to rent their gear for the day. They know their gear inside and out, and they run almost independently from you and your crew. They would likely bring a sound mixer, which is the device used to monitor the sound levels of whoever is mic'd up, whether it's one person or six people. When I say "mic'd up," that means individual people featured who are given a lavalier microphone to wear on their clothes, so that we can clearly hear what they say. Let's talk about what sound equipment you need on set for a typical documentary shoot.

Lavalier microphones, or lav mics

Lavalier mics are perfect for interviews. Once you put them on your subject, they should deliver clear sound and need little-to-no adjustments. Lav mics can be connected directly to the camera (wired), or they can run on a wireless system, which allows the subjects to roam free (which is the preferred route). The camera is connected to the receiver, and the subject's lav mic is connected to the transmitter. The transmitter and receiver are communicating wirelessly through frequencies, and they have to be set to the same frequency in order to work and provide clean sound.

It's important to know where you're going to be filming, as some areas in dense cities have very crowded frequencies, and you could experience some interference and hear a crackling noise during your interview. Prior to setting up for the interview, you could check with the equipment rental house and find out what frequencies are supposed to be clear in your area for that microphone. It's also helpful to test the sound before your subject arrives. It is perfectly normal to have to change frequencies during an interview, just make sure you do it as soon as the problem arises, instead of half an hour later when all of that sound has been compromised.

You also need batteries for both the transmitter and receiver, so make sure to have those on hand in case the interview runs long and you need to swap them out. There isn't much warning before the batteries die on a microphone, unlike the camera, which has a beeping sound when the battery or memory card are running out. The sound will just cut out, and you will have to quickly pause the interview and change the batteries. Try to replenish batteries on a break so that you don't have to stop and start while shooting.

Lav mics work best when clipped close to the speaker's mouth. They are **omnidirectional**, so they pick up sound from every direction, no matter which way the mic is pointing. However, if the subject turns their head to the side while speaking, you lose a little audio quality with lavs. The closer the mic, the less likely this is to be an issue.

Also be aware of where the lav mic is placed on the person. Be on the lookout for clothes that could rustle up against it, or a necklace that would knock the mic. Ideally, your subject will remove any problematic jewelry, or you can place the mic in such a way that the necklace doesn't affect it, but you have to be aware of the sound quality. People also have the tendency to touch the mic when they touch their chest or shirt while speaking, which also affects the sound. Gently remind the person you're interviewing to try not to touch the microphone. Your subject will not be thinking about any of this, so it's your job, or your sound engineer's job

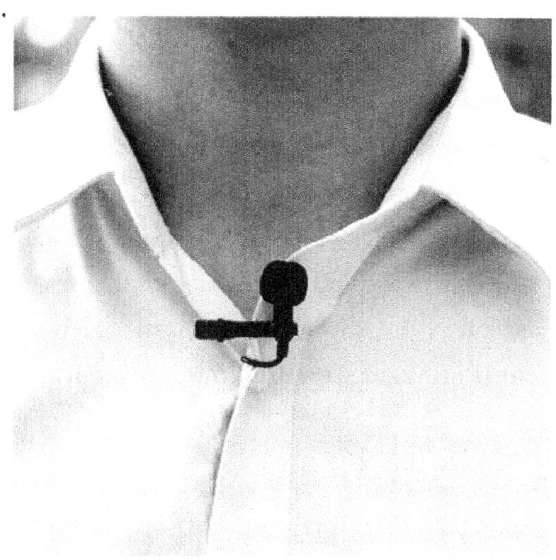

Hide the lav mic on your subject the best you can, so the camera doesn't see it. Nothing looks worse than a black cord and lav mic on top of an interviewee's clothes. That screams amateur or lazy, and it's distracting for the viewer. If possible, run the lav up the subject's shirt (they can do it, or politely ask if you can help). The clip and mic will emerge at their neck, and you can find a place to discreetly clip the mic so it's less visible, or not visible at all. You can use special tape to secure the mic to the inside of someone's collar or shirt. You can also use special mic clips that are less obvious. My favorite is the vampire clip—it has two big silver teeth and hooks into someone's shirt from the inside, making it it's easier to hide.

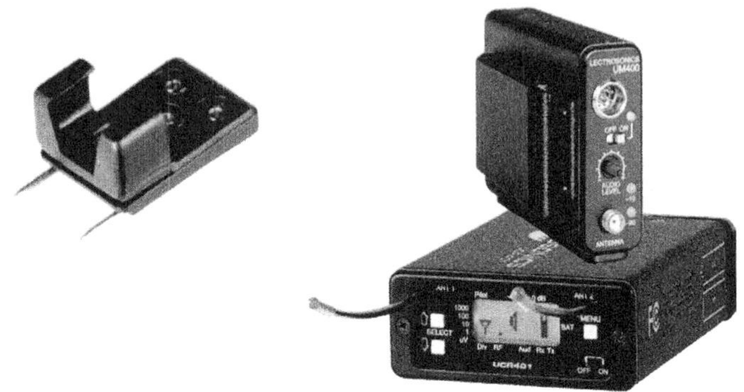

When I worked on *Dancing with the Stars* as a field producer, we used the Lectrosonic 400 series mic system, which I really liked. We would digitally scan for open frequencies, pick the open channel, and use a tweaker to physically adjust the frequency on the receiver. There were sound issues all the time, but I knew the system well enough to troubleshoot and help my colleagues. Find a mic that you feel comfortable using and stick with it, or hire great people you trust. I am constantly renting sound gear, as microphones are quite expensive. This sound system costs well over $2,000, and you likely need two for a shoot, especially if you want a backup. Only purchase equipment if it makes sense for your budget and long-term use.

The sound engineer will also bring (as long as you request it) a **shotgun microphone**, a **boom pole**, and XLR cables to connect the boom to the mixer. This set-up is often called the "boom mic." In actuality, any microphone attached to the boom pole is a boom. The shotgun microphone is typically the microphone at the helm of the boom, but it can be used for other purposes. Shotgun microphones are highly **directional** mics, meaning they get the best sound in the direction they are pointing (unlike the omnidirectional lavalier mic). This microphone is great for situations where you subject is moving around a lot, like walking down the street. It is also helpful when two people are talking with each other, and the boom operator can bounce from one subject to the other and get clear sound. In the best case scenario, the subjects have individual lav mics, and a boom microphone is being used, so you're getting two different channels of audio for each person. Each microphone is good for different sound scenarios.

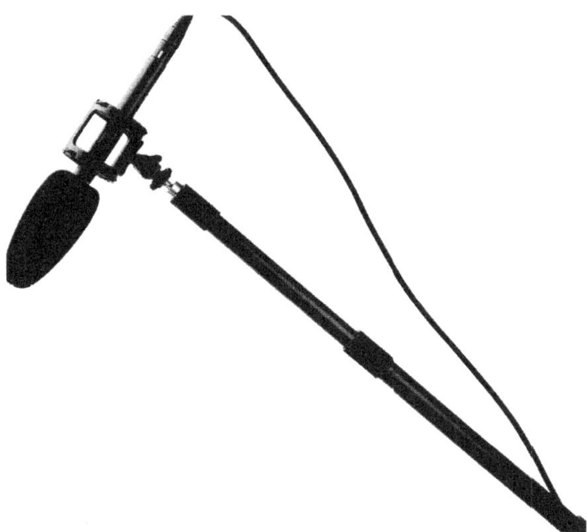

If a plane flies overhead, it might be less loud on the boom microphone, as it is typically pointed down towards the subjects. By using different microphones, you ensure the best sound quality, no matter what happens while filming. Having different sound options is also useful for your post-production sound editor.

When using the boom pole, you want to make sure you have plenty of slack with the XLR cable, which is attached either to the camera directly or to a mixer. If you have a boom operator or all-in-one sound engineer, they will make sure their XLR cord is wrangled, and they will move about the scene keeping everything in order as they follow the action. If you're using a boom in a seated interview, I'd highly recommend using a mic stand so that no one has to hold up the boom pole for an extended period of time. Sometimes you have to be your own boom operator! Someone should always be wearing headphones to make sure you are hearing the sound that is being recorded, not the sound your ear is hearing. The important thing to remember is if there is a sound issue, you are the one in charge of speaking up and saying, "Hey, can we get that again?"

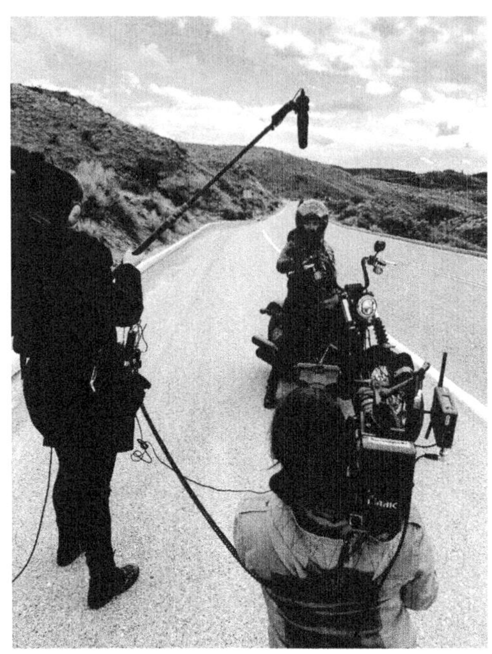

Shotgun mic

A shotgun mic is also an excellent mic to plug into your camera directly and use for b-roll shoots, and as a back-up audio, since the mic is so directional. A shotgun mic is essential for documentary filmmaking. With it already attached to the camera, you can be ready for anything. They come in different sizes and brands, so find a shotgun mic that works for your set-up.

This RODE mic is great for when you're shooting with a DSLR camera, as it plugs into the mini plug rather than an XLR. The sound quality is great. Make sure you do a test to hear the difference between a mic like this and simply recording from the in-camera mic. Big difference!

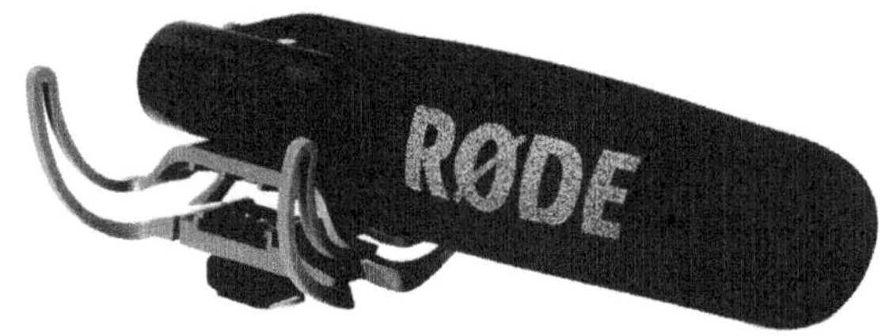

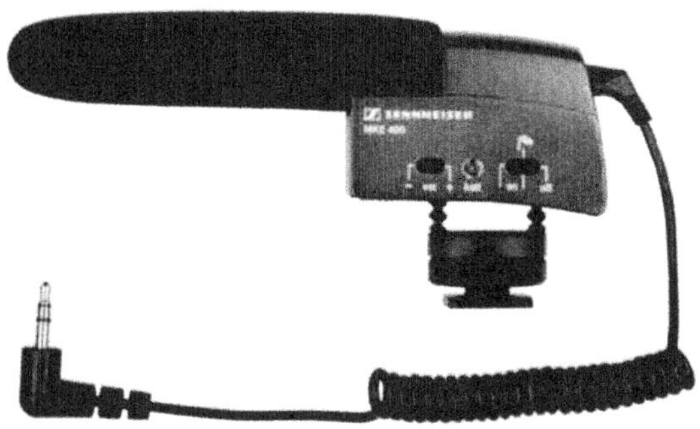

This is a Sennheiser MKE 400—a very small shotgun mic that attaches via mini-plug and runs on a AAA battery. This mic is small and mighty—I used it for the entire journey across the Pacific Ocean in *Losing Sight of Shore*. Every interview, every sound captured on the boat, came from this tiny mic. I loved it because it was directional, but easy to use. All the Coxless Crew had to do was turn it on via the switch, and it was always plugged into the camera. The batteries lasted a while, and I provided them with many replacements in case they accidentally left it on. I showed them how to check audio levels on the camera. If there were none, they would remember to turn on the mic, or change the battery. It worked beautifully in a scenario where I needed great sound, but I couldn't be there myself. I didn't want to bog them down with a lav mic or a boom pole, and there would have been too much room for error.

When I shoot a typical sit-down interview, I have:

1. A lav mic on channel 1/input 1 through my main A camera

2. The boom mic on a stand running into channel 2/input 2 on A camera

3. On my B camera, I have a shotgun mic as a back-up if anything cuts out

I am always recording sound. This set-up works really well for me because I can manage it on my own, if needed. When solo, I keep my headphones on for the whole interview, so that I can hear if any problems arise, like rustling clothes, a lost frequency, or a dead battery.

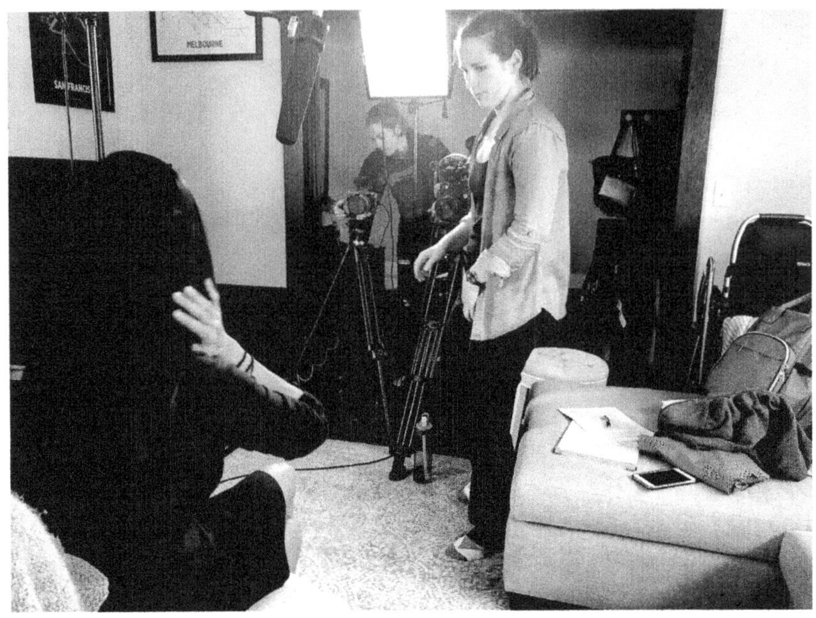

Zoom Audio Recorder

If you have a sound engineer on set, as we've discussed, they will likely provide their own equipment including a sound mixer where all the microphones will be input. Or you might plug the XLRs directly in to the camera like listed above. The other option, especially if you are on your own or have a small crew is to plug the XLRs from the lav and boom in to a Zoom Audio Recorder. This is a device that is battery powered, separate from the camera (This also works well with cameras that don't have XLR inputs like a DSLR) that can record up to 4 channels of audio on to an SD card. At the end of your shoot you will download the audio files from the SD card alongside the footage from the camera. It's a great device that's user friendly and relatively inexpensive. It's great for small crews and "run and gun" shoots.

If you're going to use two cameras and multiple microphones, you need to make sure you utilize a **slate**, or at the very least, **a clap sync**. When you get into post-production, you need to sync up the audio and video of both camera angles and multiple audio sources. Once it's all synced, you can toggle between the medium shot and the close up, with clean, usable audio for both. In order to do that, you need to align the sound of the slate clacking, or the sound of someone clapping clearly (preferably your subject, who is closest to the microphones, with no other noise in the background). That means your second angle/B camera needs to be recording some form of audio, even if it's an on-camera microphone. The second—or frame—the slate connects, or the clap is heard, is where the two shots can be synced, and then you can use either angle throughout editing with uniform sound. Without a slate or clap, it's going to be a lot harder to sync the two angles, as you will need to find a word or sound that your subject makes to sync the subject's lips moving on both angles.

Audio Levels

As you prepare the sound for your interviews you want to make sure it is not being recorded too loudly or too quietly. You and/or your sound engineer on set need to be monitoring the audio levels throughout the shoot. If the audio levels are turned up too high, the sound might come out over modulated or you may hear some audio distortion, if the audio levels are too low, you might not be able to boost them enough in post-production to hear them well enough. We measure sound in **decibels (db)**. Generally, you want to keep your audio levels in the range of -12db to -10db. You do not want to exceed 0db on the number scale as that is where audio distortion happens. On the camera LCD screen or the external monitor you can often see the colors of the audio levels, and you want to stay in the green range, out of the red, leaving room for when your subject may get excited or emotional and speak louder. It's helpful to test your audio levels before you start recording to hear how loudly your subject generally speaks. It helps to ask them to count to 10, or ask what they had for breakfast so you can hear if there are any issues and adjust. You might even want to record that initial sound test and play it back, listening to it on the headphones to make sure everything is working before you officially begin.

At the end of every interview set-up, you also want to capture **room tone.** Room tone is as it sounds—recording the sound of the room without anyone talking. You will ask everyone in the room or home to be quiet for about 30 seconds so you can record this room tone effectively. Some people wave their hand over the camera or place their hand in front of the lens to indicate room tone is being recorded. The point of this is to have the clean, ambient noise of the location you're in, in the event that you need to fill in the background during post-production of this interview. It's important that if an air conditioner was running throughout the interview, then the air conditioner should still be running during room tone. And conversely, if no a/c was running during the interview, wait to turn it back on until you record for 30 seconds. If you are shooting outside and there were airplane noises, record the ambient noise of the location with and without airplanes. Your sound editor will thank you for supplying them with options in post.

I am certainly no audio expert, but I have managed to get by knowing the basics of audio, and what tools to use. I hire audio engineers when I can, but I can also run good sound on my own, if needed. I ask questions all the time, especially when I don't know something, or I search Google for solutions to problems I'm facing. The true measure of my sound success is working with an amazing sound engineer in post-production to clean up and amplify the sound recorded on set, to add sound effects, and to make everything we did 10 times better. Don't be intimidated by sound. Use it to make your film that much more immersive and captivating.

Sound good?

CHAPTER TEN

Lighting Basics

The third technical element we're going to discuss is lighting. Once you have the basics of camera, audio, and lighting, you'll be ready to go out and shoot. Lighting is often overlooked, but it can add so much production value for not a lot of cost. The cool thing about lighting is there are options: you can use the **practical** lights of your location, you can bring your own rented or purchased lighting equipment, or you can use no lighting at all. It all depends on the scenario. In truth, with documentary filmmaking, there are instances when there's no time or space to put up lights. Instead, you have to manipulate the camera through the tools we discussed—like ND filter, aperture, white balance, and gain—to control the light you have available. There are many instances in which setting up a light is distracting or prevents you from becoming a fly on the wall and truly capturing someone in their element. But chances are, at some point during the making of your project, lighting will be essential to improving your frame.

When you walk into a space you're going to be filming, whether it's inside or outside, I want you to notice the natural light sources. If it's outside, the main light source during the day would be the sun. But is it a cloudy day? What time of day is it, and what time of day will you be shooting? The sun at noon versus the sun at 5 p.m. are very different. Is the sunlight bouncing off the surfaces around you? If you're shooting inside, the main source of light might still be the sun coming through the window. Are there other lights available in the room, like a desk lamp? Are there fluorescent lights overhead?

Once you see what kind of light is available to you, you can start to determine which you want to work with, which you don't want to work with (the fluorescent light overhead might not be the best addition), and which need shaping or manipulation.

The first thing I do is fire up the camera and take a look. You can adjust the ND filter if you're filming outside or near a bright window. You can also adjust the aperture to see what kind of range you have in this lighting environment. Move the camera frame around until you find what you're looking to shoot. Let's assume you're looking to set up for a sit-down interview, which will last an hour or more. If possible, have someone sit in a chair to test the frame. Whether that's your cinematographer or production assistant, or even you as the director, in which case your cinematographer can take a screen grab and show you what it looks like. Everyone working on this shoot needs to know what the frame is before they can properly light it. Is the subject sitting on the left side of the frame looking at you off camera to the right? Or is it the opposite, the subject is sitting on the right side of the frame looking at you off camera to the left? (Refer back to framing and composition, and the rule of thirds in the Camera Basics chapter for examples.) Or, is the subject framed in the center looking directly down the barrel of the lens? Once you generally have the frame you're looking for, it's time to cut out light, add light, and shape light so you can get rolling.

Cutting out light

Cutting out light can be as simple as turning off the practical lights. Try turning the overhead lights on and off and see what they add. Ideally, you'd have someone sitting in the chair, properly framed, so you can test these things out. If there is a window providing daylight, what does it look like to cover it? Close the curtain, or if you have tools like a physical ND filter or duvetyn, you may be able to reduce the daylight, or eliminate it all together, depending on what you need. This process really is it trial and error. It's a dance of elements—the camera, the frame, and the lighting. And if you have a crew with you, your cinematographer and gaffer will be leading this charge, but it's good for you to understand the process, in the event that you need to set up lights on your own.

Adding light

You've generally determined what your frame is, turned off the lights you don't want to use, and now you have a more accurate picture of what you need to add in order to make this frame look great. Your canvas is clear and ready for painting. First thing you need to do is determine what the **key light** is for your subject. The key light's purpose is to highlight the form and dimension of the subject. You're going to want to place this light first, because it is the most powerful and will dictate the other lighting. The other two lights support the key light. Also, if you want to sound like you know what you're talking about on set, before you turn on any light, inform your crew that you are about to do so by saying, **"striking!"**

My favorite light to use in documentary filmmaking is called the Diva-Lite. It's easy to set-up, it provides even lighting, and they give you daylight and tungsten bulbs, so you can adjust it to meet any lighting scenario, inside or outside. Remember our color temperature from the Camera Basics chapter? This is where it comes into play. If a window is your main source of light (daylight), then you want to match the color with this Diva-Lite. Use daylight bulbs, and set the camera to daylight white balance, or 5600K. Conversely, if there are now windows, or you aren't using them, and your Diva-Lite is using tungsten bulbs (3200K), then set the camera to a 3200K white balance to match. Make sense?

This light is very flattering for the subject. Also, the light and the bulbs never get very hot, so you don't often need gloves, and can put up and tear down quickly. Other lights need to cool considerably after being on for an hour, and you absolutely need gloves to wrap up.

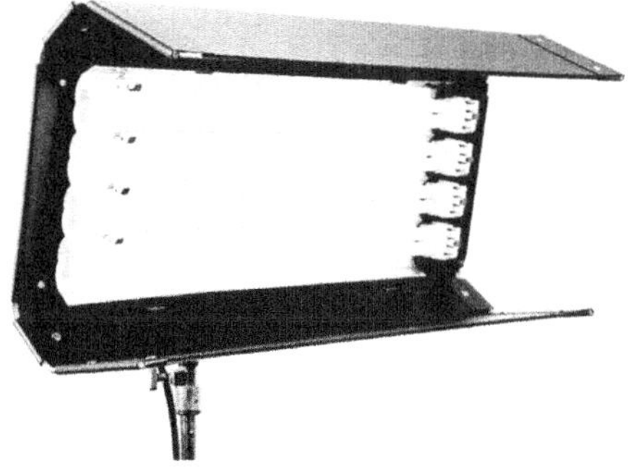

Next up, you need a **fill light.** The fill light's purpose is to fill in the shadows created by the key light, preventing them from getting too dark. The fill light is often less bright than the key light, and it's positioned on the opposite side of the key light.

We are slowly building a three-light setup known as **three-point lighting.**

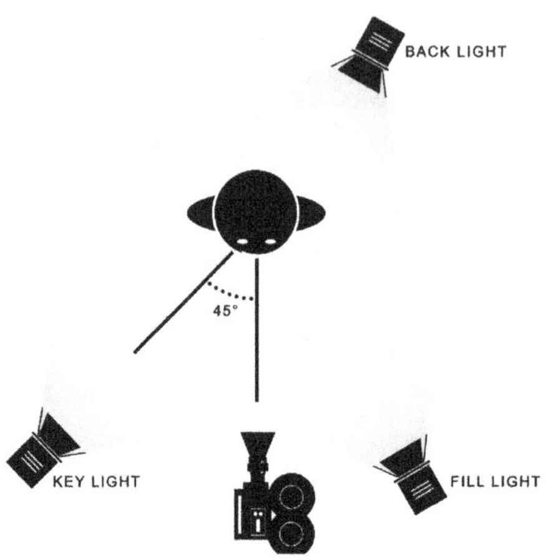

In this drawing, the key light is to the left of the camera. You can also flip this diagram, depending on which direction your subject is facing. Typically, the fill light is on the opposite side of the camera as the key light. This gets a little tricky when you have more than one camera, since you ideally won't see any of the lights or light stands. Again, set-up is a dance!

Unlike camera set-up, lights can live on both sides of the camera. There isn't the same 180-degree rule. In fact, you generally want to set up the frame first, then add lights around them.

The third light in our three-point lighting is the **back light.** This light is often the least powerful and is meant to separate the subject from the background, creating more depth of field. I often use a small "pepper" light—it's 150 watts, and can be set on a small stand either below and behind the subject, or from above and behind the subject. This light is often used to create a "halo" effect around the subject's hair, separating them fully from the background.

Finally, **shaping and adjusting light** is the last part of this equation. You have your frame, you've cut out light, you've added light, and now you may need to shape the light you have set up. This is often the most difficult and skilled part of lighting. This is where having a gaffer is incredibly helpful. Here are a few accessories I've found incredibly useful to know and understand, putting the finishing touches on your lighting set-up.

Diffusing the light refers to softening the light, whether it's the key light or fill light. Attach thin sheets of gels to a light with clamps or clips. (Clothespins on set are called C47s, for the film school nerds!) You can also achieve diffusion by using what has been nicknamed a "diaper" for the Diva-Lite or a "soft-box" for other lights.

Gels. You can also use colored gels to achieve different color temperatures and colored lighting effects. Gels are often used to change the color of the key light or fill light. You might need to add blue or orange to match the white balance in the room. Or, depending on the vibe of your film, you can use a green gel or a pink gel to achieve a more colorful look.

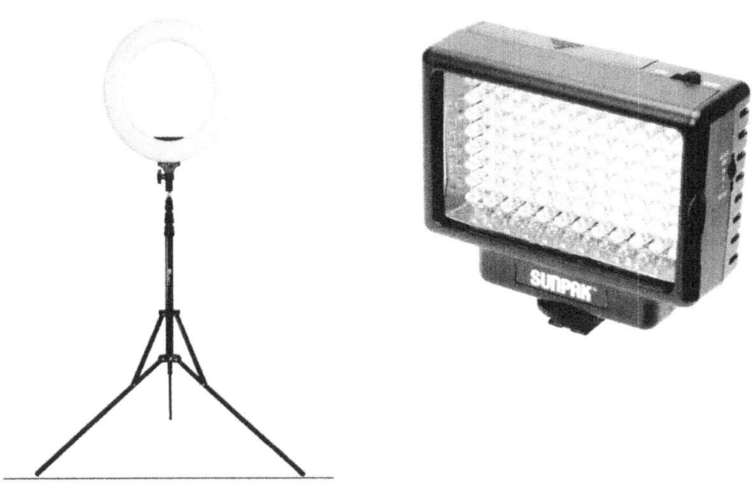

Outside of three-point lighting, portable lights are useful when you're "running and gunning," and you don't have the time, space, or bandwidth to set up three lights that require power. I would also recommend a battery-powered **lite panel**, especially one that can be attached to the **hot shoe** of the camera. They come with filters for daylight and tungsten light, so you can use it indoor/outdoor, and it's very cheap compared to the other lights mentioned. It would be great to have a light like this at the ready for any scenario.

Another popular light is the **ring light.** They can vary in price, but there are some affordable options, thanks to the demand from social media influencers. What's great about this light is it accomplishes nice, even lighting for the face without the heat—or cost—and it has daylight and tungsten options. Ring lights are typically used when someone is looking directly at the lens, and the interview is more of a first person account.

The last piece of easy-to-use equipment I would recommend is a **bounce board.** If you place or hold the bounce board underneath the subject (there's often a silver side, a gold side, and a white side), you can use the sun's reflection to bounce light up on someone's face. It instantly adds light and shine to an otherwise shadowy set-up. Bounce boards are great for a super quick reflective pop of light, especially when you're filming outside on a sunny day. No power, no stand required. Just make sure you don't have your subject squinting too much from the reflection, it can be intense!

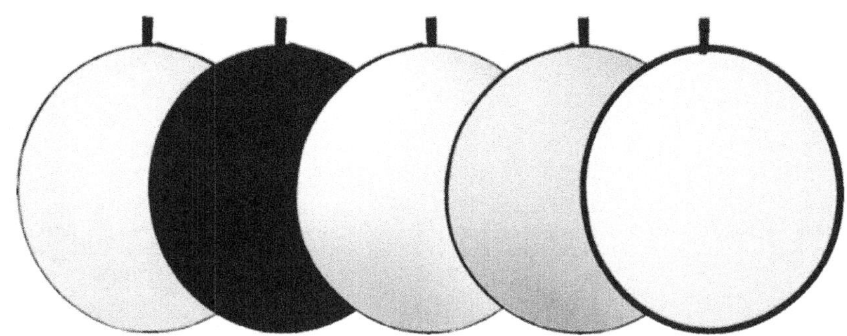

There are many other lights to use in filmmaking, but for the purposes of this book, I simply want you to understand three-point lighting, how to shape and cut out light, and the basics, so that you can work with exceptional cinematographers and gaffers as well as function on your own if needed. As the filmmaker, your ideal role is to help guide your crew on lighting, but not be solely responsible for it. Remember, while all of this is going on, you're prepping the questions for the interview, making sure your subject arrives seamlessly, thinking about the next shoot, where are you going for lunch… there are many hats to wear on set. But the best leaders know a bit about each role and can jump in and help when needed.

Light it up!

CHAPTER ELEVEN

Interview Techniques

Within my 10+ years of working in film, television, and digital content, I have had the pleasure of interviewing a pretty wide range of humans. From second man to walk on the moon, Buzz Aldrin, to NFL Super Bowl Champions, Olympians, platinum-selling artists, A-list celebrities, and also just as important, refreshingly normal, ordinary (but also extraordinary) everyday people. As the interviewer I've been ignored, doubted, glossed over, harassed, blown off, and disrespected, all within the confines of an interview context, but I've also cried alongside people, I've laughed my ass off (and had to stay comically silent while doing so), and I have felt the deepest well of empathy for the human condition. I've had epiphanies; I've felt enlightened, encouraged, discouraged, and devastated and hopeful, all within an hour. With each interview I've done, I feel better prepared for the next one. No matter what happens, I always feel like I've grown and learned by the time I say, "Cut."

The interview space is sacred, and it is a responsibility I don't take lightly. I often marvel at the nature of being a filmmaker and how people you would never otherwise meet invite you into their lives, their homes, and their truth, to serve the greater purpose of sharing their story with the world. As a filmmaker, you can really be a jack-of-all-trades by learning a little bit about a lot, and from a lot of incredible people. And your job is to be curious, to ask the questions others might not think of to ask, or others might be too scared to ask. You also have to be of two minds during an interview: you need to be conversational to keep your subject feeling comfortable, perhaps even sharing insights from your own personal lived experiences, but you also need to think about how this will be edited together, and the technical aspects of how it's being filmed. You want to leave the interview knowing you got what you needed.

There's a lot to think about simultaneously during an interview, especially if, right as you're getting to an emotional breakthrough, you suddenly hear a plane barreling through the air overhead, ruining the quality of the sound you are recording. It happens, and if you're interviewing a seasoned professional, they will know to roll with the punches and start again, but if you're interviewing someone who doesn't have experience like this, it's up to you to kindly ask them to pause until the plane has passed, and then repeat themselves. Any way you slice it, it's ultimately your responsibility to come back with a well-lit, well framed shot, good sounding audio and, most importantly, an interview that has informative, interesting, and emotionally truthful content to add to your film. *No big deal right?*

In documentaries, the interviews serve as the backbone of the film. They are what make the audience feel fully immersed in the story, event, or world. It's often the first thing you plan for in pre-production, the first thing you execute in production, and the first thing you work with in post-production. You may need only one interview for your film, or you may need 100 in order to fully tell this story. That's for you to decide based on your content.

Doing interviews is often my favorite part of the filmmaking process—it's truly where the film takes shape, evolves, and can surprise you—if you're truly listening. But filming a sit-down interview with someone is not easy—it is a skill that needs to be developed. Over time I've realized that the best interviews I've been a part of are the ones where I am fully present in the moment, and I don't even look at the questions I have prepared. I'm listening as intently as possible and letting the interview shift and move based on the responses I'm getting. The interviewee and I are building something together, instead of a black and white, back and forth, question—answer—question—answer. So how do you do that? How do you make someone feel comfortable enough to open up and be vulnerable? What follows are my top tips for conducting a masterful interview you'll be proud to use in your film.

Do Your Research

People love to be flattered and to feel important. When approaching anyone to be interviewed, it's helpful to do some research on that person so that you can give a specific and pointed compliment about their work, or their perspective on the issue you are spotlighting. You need to be very clear as to why this person is vital to the completion of your film, and what their story and views will add. Read up as much as you can about this person prior to reaching out, so that you are familiar with their work. Your familiarity will make them more likely to say yes to the interview, and they will feel more comfortable with you.

You also want to research the event or social issue you are delving in to. When I was doing interviews about sexual harassment for my film *Nevertheless,* I needed to have a working knowledge of the current events and stories of the #MeToo movement, and basic term definitions so I could keep up. With that said, you may also want your subject to define certain terms for the viewer, even if you know what they are. Not everyone may know what "quid pro quo" means, or what "cisgender" refers to, and it couldn't hurt to have someone defining it for the audience, just in case.

Pre-Interview

Not everyone is meant to be on camera. Some people are better writers than they are in real life, and you don't want to find that out when the camera is rolling. If you have the ability to do a pre-interview phone call or Zoom call, I highly recommend it, especially if this person is potentially going to be one of your main characters in the film. You need to know how they are on camera before you spend a cent on their travel, or renting gear and hiring crew.

Pre-interviewing came in to play for me with *Nevertheless.* Especially with such sensitive subject matter, I wanted to make sure I built a foundation of trust with each of the people agreeing to speak on camera and hear a bit about their story and experiences with sexual harassment ahead of time so

I knew what to anticipate. Some people are experts at sharing their story in a cohesive, emotional way. Some people need encouragement, and some people you will only get their genuine tone and feeling one time – whether it's on camera or not.

I also found it tremendously helpful to pre-interview the people I was acknowledging as "experts" so that I could understand what broad range of topics I could cover with that person and prepare my questions accordingly. This doesn't have to be super formal, it can be more conversational so you start to build a rapport with this person. This is also where you can share your intentions for making this film. Explain what you're doing, what you're hoping to create and the impact you hope to have. That way, your experts or interview subjects can feel like they are a part of the process and understand what they're agreeing to when they show up on shoot day. Anything you can do to make your shoot days run smoother you want to be proactive to do, and pre-interviewing is a part of that.

Write your interview questions

Even if I end up not using them, I typically type up and print out interview questions for every one of my interviews. It helps me organize my thoughts and stay on track with what I'm hoping to get out of our time together. Keep in mind, you could have an incredibly in-depth interview with someone, but if it gets off topic and you don't get to ask what you came there to ask, then it wasn't really a success. It's up to you to use your time with your subject (this could be anywhere from five minutes to five hours, depending on their availability) and get what you need to tell a complete story. At the beginning of each and every interview with someone new, I ask them to state and spell their name, and what their preferred title is. That could be their relationship to your main subject, or it could be their profession, depending on the context. This is also a great opportunity to get any audio or camera issues fixed before the interview truly begins. You may make a few adjustments after this section, and you haven't missed any of the content.

From there, when writing interview questions, I try my best to not ask any "yes" or "no" questions. I want to give then the opportunity to elaborate on their thoughts with open-ended questions. Use words like "Describe" or "How did it feel when..." instead of "Was that hard?"

Here are some sample interview questions I used with the Coxless Crew once they made it to the island of Samoa, after 97 days on a 29-foot ocean rowing boat:

Coxless Crew Questions - Samoa

- *What does it feel like to be on land?*
- *Samoa like? Tell me about your time here?*
- *Describe what it felt like to row up to shore for the first time in 97 days.*
- *Tell me about showering and eating for the first time.*
- *If you can sum up your experience in the second leg of the journey, what was it like for you?*
- *What was the journey like as a team?*
- *Describe the moments where you wanted to quit or give up, how did you cope?*
- *What were some of the hardest things to deal with at sea?*
- *Tell me about crossing the equator.*
- *Tell me about having to ration your food because of the extra time at sea.*
- *What were some of your favorite parts of the journey?*
- *How did you cope mentally? Physically?*
- *Was it harder than you imagined to complete? Why?*
- *How does your body feel now?*
- *What has been the most gratifying part about being back on land?*

- *Are you proud of yourself? Why?*
- *What is the agenda in Samoa, what needs to get done before you depart?*
- *Tell me your thoughts about getting back in the boat for the final leg.*
- *Is there any part of you that wishes this was the end of the journey?*
- *Who did you think about when you struggled?*
- *What did you learn about your teammates that you didn't know before the row?*
- *What did you learn about yourself?*

These are a great start, but I definitely add in more and take some out as I'm doing the interview. As I've gotten better at interviewing, I look at my questions less and less, sometimes not at all. I'll look them over at the end of the interview to make sure I covered everything, and most of the time I've more than covered the content I prepared.

Here is the actual transcript from part of that interview with one of the rowers Natalia Cohen. I've bolded what I think of as usable sound bites from this part of the interview:

	Q: How does it feel to be on land?
00:29	N: Strange. **It's really strange to be back on land**. Uh but this time it was necessary to get back to land. I felt like I was out on the ocean a little bit too long. Um **it's great to be back on land, but for some reason, I still feel the ocean calling me. So, I'm not ready to stay on land.**
	Q: Did you worry about how your body would feel?

01:03	N: Yeah. The, the main thing for me this leg has been my skin. Um **so after about day 80, all – all sorts of strange things have started happening to my skin.** Uh all of our skins, to be honest. Uh lots of dry skin, lots of chaffing, so many salt sores and pressure sores. Um I got something specific on my underarms that was really uncomfortable, which made rowing like every stroke really, really difficult. **(01:29)** Um our bums are just destroyed. Uh I was concerned that a week wasn't going to be long enough to allow things to heal, to be honest, before heading off on the last leg. Um at the moment, they're starting to heal, but they're – they definitely haven't healed yet. So, **there is a little bit of a concern going into leg three for me, because I think everything that we're doing to our bodies and our minds, to be honest, with the sleep deprivation, I really feel like it's cumulative.** Um it was more difficult in leg two than it was in leg one, and I think that **leg three is going to be the most challenging in, in all respects. (02:02)**
	Q: What was the welcome like coming into Samoa?
02:09	N: **The welcome we had in Samoa was absolutely incredible. Uh I could never have imagined a better welcome.** And for me, it has always been a place that I've wanted to come, Samoa, and I think the main reason is that there's such a, a strong and deep culture here that is so in twined with the ocean, and that's a big reason why I had an interest in Samoa. And hopefully, on Saturday I have a day off, I'm going to learn a little bit more about the culture. **(02:38)** And then we're going out with the Oceanic um society as well to try and find out a little bit more about the, the background and the, the old ways of navigating. So, no, **it's amazing to finally be here.** Yeah.
	Q: Describe what was going through your mind getting to land

04:34	N: Um, **I think the first few steps are always the strangest when we get off the boat, and the strangest thing is that the second we're on land, I feel like I've been on land.** It – it (Interrupted) N: **(05:26)** Yeah. I think after nearly 100 days at sea, stepping on land was always going to be strange. Uh **it felt a lot weirder arriving in Samoa than it did in Hawaii I think because we'd been out even longer.** And walking definitely needed support. So we actually automatically gravitated two and two together and sort of linked arms because we just felt like we needed a little bit of help. Or, maybe we're just used to being so close. I don't know; one of the two. **(05:54)** Um we sort of stumbled and zigzagged our way to the, the welcome area and then luckily we got to sit down straight away. Um but then standing up after sitting down was, was quite a struggle. And **the last sort of few days – or the first few days on land have been just physically quite demanding because we're doing so many movements that we're just not used to doing.** So it's been interesting.

Maintain good eye contact

This may seem obvious, but you'd be surprised how many interviewers I see fail to do this. I have been interviewed a fair amount as well, and when the interviewer isn't maintaining eye contact, I feel more disconnected from them and don't know where to look. Especially if I'm asked a personal question, and then I have no one to engage with, it takes me out of the momentum. You want to make your subject, your guest, feel as welcome and comfortable as possible. You want them to feel like what they have to say is important and worth sharing, and eye contact is truly the best way to do that.

By the way, your subject might not be great at maintaining eye contact either, but for eye line and framing purposes, the more they have steady eye contact with you the better, so it's also up to you to set the tone. You don't want them looking at the camera and then you, as their eyes will appear shifty and uncertain. You may want to gently remind your subject to look at you the whole time and forget the cameras are even there. In some cases, of course, you may opt to have your subject look right down the lens to answer questions as part of your visual style for the film. And in that situation, you may want to rent or buy a piece of hardware that would still allow you to make eye contact with your subject, even though they are looking straight to camera. One example of this would be the Eye Direct, which is essentially a series of mirrors allowing your subject to look at you through a mirror, but it reads and records as though they are looking straight down the lens. This can be a really powerful tool aesthetically, adding dramatic effect.

Using your questions in their answer

Because the audience won't hear your voice asking the question, you want your subject to use your question in their answer, so the audience knows what they're answering. This technique a tricky one, and people either get it or they don't. Especially for the novice, it can be hard to get used to, but it is essential to you walking out of there with usable content. I always give the same example to help illustrate this point. I'll say:

"I'm sure you'll be a total pro at this, but as a reminder, please try to use my question in your answer, because no one is going to hear my voice. So, for example, if I asked you, 'What's your favorite color?' instead of just saying 'blue,' you would say, 'My favorite color is blue.'"

They usually understand the request with that example, but from there it's totally up to you to police this and make sure they are in fact using your question in their answer. You may need to ask them to re-phrase certain answers if it was a good sound bite, but not a complete thought. You need complete thoughts in edit to piece this all together. Without a complete thought, you may need to use your voice subtitled on the screen to help explain the answer. That's not a bad thing, but it may not be the style you were going for.

Instead of feeling bad for reminding them, know that you're helping them. Every interviewee wants to look and sound good on camera. This is your way to help your subject come across as articulate as possible. Nine times out of ten, people are willing to say something again to make a complete thought if they didn't initially. One final tip: don't jump the gun in asking them to repeat their answer. Sometimes people may not start their answer with a complete sentence, but they come around to it by the end of their thought. Listen for that before interrupting. People tend to say things best the first time around, rather than repeating themselves per your request.

Try not to overlap dialogue

It's a delicate balance, right? You want the interview to feel conversational and casual, so that your subject is relaxed and disarmed, but you want to avoid overlap for audio purposes. If you're asking a question and your subject starts speaking before you're done, and they say something great, the audio isn't quite usable without the clean beginning of their sentence. Kindly ask that your subject pause for a beat before answering your question so that there isn't overlap. Luckily, you are not mic'd up, so your voice isn't heard as clearly on the audio waves, but it still isn't ideal to be talking over one another and will be hard to remove in sound editing.

Let the interview evolve and flow

In some of my best interviews, something is revealed that I didn't expect. If I hadn't been listening and open, I would have missed interesting information about them. This goes back to prepping interview questions and doing your research, but also being an empathetic human being and listening in the moment. Hear what this person wants to share. Maybe it's something you couldn't have found online or they didn't mention in the pre-interview.

Here is an example from an interview I did for *Nevertheless*. This moment stands out because it told us so much about this woman's background, and was poignant in its emotion. This is with Patricia Brooks, a 911 Dispatcher who experienced sexual harassment while working.

00:04:33	***Q: What makes one good at police dispatching?***
00:04:39	Patricia: I don't know. You just have it. It's one of those things you just have. And it's um – Statistics show um – After, after my assault, and I went through therapy, um I had seen um Dr. Flynt who was uh a specialist and he dealt with um police officers and he also did the background (Stutter) psych checks a lot of the Contra Costa and other areas. **(00:05:06)** And through one of my conversations with him, I had asked himw you know what – you know what do you look at when you're, you're doing the backgrounds. And he said well, every agency will tell him what criteria they want within the scope and he said **statistics show that majority of people in police work either came from alcoholic families or um domestic violent families or they had some history in their past (00:05:37) and you know a lot of them want to um you know help people. You know make it – make a difference?**
00:05:47	***Q: Is that true for you?***
00:05:48	**P: (pause) Yes. (tears up)**
00:05:52	***Q: Do you want to share that part of your life?***
00:06:02	P: I always had this um – I don't – I don't um – I don't know how to articulate it, but ever since I was a little girl, I always had this um – I'm the youngest of three. And our father was very uh heavy-handed um and my brother was the middle child and he got the majority of it and then I got what was left over. **(00:06:34)** My – My sister really didn't get any. But um I always had this um, I don't know – And I still have it. It's um something inside me. Um a good example. I think I was in 1st grade and joined brownies. And a little girl had moved into our school. I didn't know that they were poor, that they couldn't afford you know anything. And it was a Friday night and I had brownies and I had her stay over and we went to the brownie meeting **(00:07:04)** and because the application segment had passed, they wouldn't let her come in. And I was like "Well, you said we're

00:06:02	supposed to be, be nice to—you know we're supposed to help people." "Well, she can't join." So I took my little sash off and I threw it on the ground and I said, "Well, now I'm not going to be in it." And we marched back to my house and my mom's looking at me. I told her what happened. Well, it wasn't until years later that I found out (Clears throat) that my mother had saved the grocery money to buy me my brownie uniform and the little sash. **(00:07:35)** And then in one moment, I'm just like (Sound effect). You know? But that's been uh – I don't usually you know – it's gotten me in trouble and it's gotten me out of trouble, so it's just part of my personality.

Now this is a case where I might actually use the sound of my voice and subtitle it in the film, because it didn't feel right to ask her to rephrase this for a succinct sound bite. It was an emotionally authentic moment, and if I hadn't been listening, I might have missed it.

Finish Strong

I end every interview the same way. I always ask the subject if there's anything they'd like to add, anything they feel like we didn't cover. This gives you both an opportunity to take a breath and reflect on what you've just done together. They might be so exhausted that they're just ready to get out of the hot seat and say, "Nope, all good." But there might also be some magic that comes out, if you allow for it. There might be something your subject didn't get to discuss yet and it's on the tip of their tongue, but you didn't know to ask about it. It's always good to create that extra space for additional details or stories that you don't expect.

Practice

You will get better with time. Some interviews will flow effortlessly, like you're talking with an old friend, and some will feel so sticky and awkward that you're not sure if you came away with anything usable. It totally depends on the person you're interviewing and the energy between the two of you.

Give them respect, maintain eye contact, actively listen, and make them feel comfortable in your environment. This will give you the best chance at a great interview. Your interview skills will get better over the course of your project, and over the course of your career. It's ok to be nervous, and it's ok to share your experiences and be vulnerable too. And once you get into post-production and actually need to use these interviews to help tell a story, you will see firsthand how you can improve for next time.

Practice, practice, practice!

Helpful Exercise:

Interview a friend or family member. Ask them questions you may not have asked before and see what kinds of usable responses you get. You can record it on your phone, or set up a camera on a tripod next to you so you can focus on the content. Once you feel good about it, move on to someone you don't know so well, as most of your interviews will be with people you just met. Load the footage into an editing program if you can, and try to cut it together into something. You will learn a lot for next time!

Checklist:

- *Did your subject use your question in their answer?*
- *Did they say more than yes or no?*
- *If you remove your voice when editing this together, would you have complete thoughts and sentences to use?*
- *Did you ask them if they had anything to add?*
- *Did they state and spell their name and tell you their preferred title or occupation?*

Who would be your ideal person to interview, and what would you want to ask them?

CHAPTER TWELVE

B-roll and the Visual Language of Docs

Building off of the Production chapter, here we will dive a bit deeper into the visual tools available to you when you're in production and post. You have a blank canvas at the start of production, and now it's time to paint. Conducting a well-rounded interview, and telling the story in a crafted, effective way, certainly is the backbone of a documentary, but the genre is exploding with a visual language we haven't seen in decades past. You want to be able to articulate your artistic vision when pitching the project to funders, and part of that includes seeing beyond just interviews and b-roll. How can you make your project stand out? How can you fully immerse the viewer in the experience of watching? Especially if there's a lot of information to explain, how can you keep the audience engaged and paying attention? These are questions you will be repeatedly asking yourself throughout the process of making your film. I would encourage you to be open to the visual possibilities of your film. We often think of the narrative genre as the visual art form, but documentaries can be just as artistic and narrative in style.

B-Roll

When I'm going into a filming scenario for an interview, I'm looking around, thinking about what visuals I can capture in the environment to help me with b-roll. If you've brought your subject to an interview space, then chances are there won't be much to film, since they aren't in their natural environment. If you're in their home, there will be items that you couldn't have predicted, but want to see in use. You can plan and plan, then on the day, you have to go with what works. If I'm going to be in someone's home, I'll come prepared with a list of potential b-roll to capture, and then during the interview, I'm listening closely to see if there's footage to add to my list.

Let's say I'm doing an interview with a mother named Carla in Memphis, Tennessee who loves her cat and religion plays a big role in her story. A sample list of B-roll I would have prepared for my shoot with Carla would be:

- *Establishing shot of house, trees, street signs*
- *Family photos framed on the fireplace*
- *Clock on the wall*
- *Cat sleeping*
- *Carla praying*
- *Carla making coffee*
- *Carla looking out the window*
- *Carla and her son watching TV and talking*

And remember, Carla is not an actress to play a role. This is a real person, and we are in her space. So it's up to you as the filmmaker to explain to her what b-roll is, and how you want to capture her in her natural environment doing what she might normally do. Some people feel quite uncomfortable with being on camera, so you may need to disarm them a bit and hope they forget the camera is there. It's your job to capture a variety of shots of Carla in her daily life, from various angles, so you can use it throughout the interview and potentially throughout the film. We discussed coverage and cutaways in the previous chapters; it's very important here that you get footage of Carla not talking, as well as some natural moments of her talking to you or to her son. Cutaways or quieter shots of her will be tremendously helpful in the edit, as will natural moments and exchanges with Carla showing you around her house and talking to her son, praying, etc. If Carla is not into any sort of staged b-roll shots, then you will need to stick around to capture genuine fly-on-the-wall b-roll by being present in her daily life.

You may also want to utilize **slow motion** on some of these shots. This is an effect you can add in post-production, but sometimes it's nice to use in the moment to create a more dramatic effect. Perhaps you use slow motion to capture Carla walking down her street, or looking up at the sky. Slow motion adds a nice tone and texture to a b-roll shot. Every camera is going to have a slightly different way it creates the slow motion effect, but in essence you are speeding up the frame rate to 60 frames per second (fps), for example, which gives it the slow motion effect. The camera is taking more pictures per second, thereby elongating the movements on screen and slowing things down.

I'm going to jump slightly ahead here to when you're in post-production (which we will talk about in the next chapter) to talk further about the visual language of documentaries. When your film starts taking shape in post-production in terms of a stringout, or first cut, this is where you can let your brain wander into the creativity of how to visually reinforce the words that are being heard. First, I see what b-roll I was able to capture on the day, or throughout the shoot. Does any of it potentially apply to what's being said? B-roll can quickly feel out of place if it doesn't make sense for that dialogue. In our example if Carla is talking about a location—*"I grew up in a small house in Memphis, Tennessee."*—then we need to see some kind of establishing shot of Memphis, Tennessee. That could come in the form of a "Welcome to Memphis" sign, a shot of her actual house or neighborhood, a sweeping drone shot of the city, a graphic map of the United States and zooming in on Tennessee, etc. (We will talk about tools for finding footage of locations if you weren't able to shoot them yourself in post-production.)

What about something a bit less obvious? Let's say the sound bite from Carla is: *"As a child, I was endlessly curious. I would chase fireflies and walk along the train tracks until my mom called me in for dinner."* What are our potential options here?

- We could simply stay on the subject for this line, especially if her facial expression is interesting or reflective, and cut from one camera angle to another.
- We could use establishing shots of her neighborhood in Memphis that don't necessarily pair with what she's saying but could still work.

- We could use some b-roll we captured when we were filming with the subject of her walking along train tracks, or go back and film that once we know we need it.
- We could find some train tracks to film and get some b-roll to use here, or we could license footage of train tracks from a third party site.
- We could commission animation of this scene and see a girl chasing fireflies and walking along the train tracks. That would be especially effective if the same style of animation is used throughout the film.
- We could hire a child actor to re-enact this narrative scene and have her chase fireflies (which are likely added later as a visual effect) along the train tracks. We could also hire an actor to play her mom to call her in for dinner from the house. We would storyboard the scene to plan it, and then shoot it hopefully alongside other re-enacted shots. (This option, and animation will likely cost the most to produce.)

In the options listed above, some will be doable, and some will be out of your budget range. But creatively, you have so many options, way beyond this list. You want your brain to open up to the creativity that the visual language can provide.

It's exciting to think about this other layer in your film. How can you take your viewer to another level of your storytelling? As you watch other documentaries, see what elements they use to tell the story. What works and what doesn't? When does your attention start to fade and when do things get interesting? Do you find yourself wanting more out of some films you watch?

Re-enactments

We often think of re-enactments as something incredibly cheesy from one of those true crime shows, but more and more documentary filmmakers are using re-enactments to bring their stories to life and immerse the viewer. It's not even a re-enactment—it's stylized, narrative b-roll added into the film to bring the viewer deeper into the story. You can use this technique once you have your interviews done, or mostly done, so that you know what you need to capture. Ideally, you would have at least a few scenes cut together ahead of time so that so you can map out shot for shot what you need in order to tell this story. You will need to hire actors (who ideally look like the person who is talking in the film); you'll need to find locations that match the time period and setting of the events being described; you may even need to source props from that era. Then you can create a shot list based on the slots you need to fill, hire a crew that can help you execute your vision, and bring those scenes to life.

A great example of skillful narrative re-enactments is the 2018 film *Three Identical Strangers*. Three baby boys are separated at birth and find their way back to one another in adulthood, and try to find out why they were separated in the first place. The narrative re-enactments really make the film larger in scope, bringing the audience seamlessly into the story. Without them, the story might have been quite slow and less engaging. And since it was looking back on the 1980's, they had to secure a car from that era, clothing from that era, and an actor that looked like the triplets enough to photograph as him from behind. They never actually show the actor's face. It's so well done and cinematic.

If you're interested in doing re-enactments, take a look at documentaries that use them well, and use that as a jumping off point to inspire you for your film. Think about why you are doing it. What does it add to your story? Is it the best way to bring the viewer into this world? How can you make them as seamless as possible? And finally, do you have the budget, or can you include it in your budget when pitching to funders?

Graphics

I would also encourage you to use graphics when possible to illustrate a concept or point. Even if the speaker is very clear in what they're saying, a graphic can help drive home a point and reinforce it for the viewer. In *Nevertheless,* we had a lot of complex social issues to discuss, so I used graphics whenever I could to define a term and make it more visual for the viewer. Graphics can be a part of your visual language, especially if you have a uniform look to them. The VOX/Netflix show *Explained* is a great example of using graphics in an effective and stylish way. Each episode has the same theme of graphics. They are easy to understand and a bit whimsical, even though the information is often serious and important. It helps break it down for the viewer, and it helps move the story along.

You're not going to hire your graphics person until you are pretty far along in your post-production process, as you don't want to burn through budget trying things out graphically and then having to make many changes. The graphics artist will want to know exactly what information to share. Especially if you are sharing statistics and factual information, you need to have all of that ready to go before they officially come on board.

Animation

In the same vein, you want to wait to add any animation to your film until you know exactly what you're looking for. Is the animation going to be interwoven throughout the film? It's always nice when there is a theme or style established at the beginning of a film and we as the audience can rely on it throughout the story. A great example of this is the documentary *He Named Me Malala*, which is about the story of Malala Yousafzai. As she describes the history of her name, we are swept away into beautiful animation that tells the ancient story. It was like a Pixar movie interwoven with a vérité documentary. Animation is very expensive to use, but if you have the budget for it, it can certainly make your film stand out and add a beautiful layer of visual language. Animation can help you illustrate a story for which you may have no b-roll or archival footage. Animation can help bring an abstract concept or story to life, or serve as a metaphor for what's being said.

One stand-out example of the use of animation and re-enactments is in the documentary *Tower* from 2016 about the first school shooting at the University of Texas at Austin in 1966. The filmmaker Keith Maitland used a **rotoscoping animation** technique that is incredibly well done and gripping for the viewer, making it all feel like a narrative film. From the first moment of the story, it draws you in. The filmmaker conducted sit-down interviews with the survivors who remembered that horrific event. Then he hired actors to play the roles of the people being interviewed, and those who had passed. He shot most of the footage in his own backyard with actors acting out scenes from the script he wrote based on the interviews (he wasn't allowed to film at the University of Texas). He then utilized this rotoscoping technique to animate on top of the footage of the actors, placing them in the setting where the shooting takes place and mixing it with archival footage from that day. It's an explosion of creativity for the genre, and if he had made a more traditional film with talking heads and news clips from the day, it wouldn't have been nearly as effective or impactful for the viewer.

Archival Footage

Archival footage is used a ton in documentary filmmaking. It refers to footage that was not shot for this specific production. It is obtained from a film library or archive, and so often now, via the internet. Archival footage can show historical events, without the need for re-enactment. This often includes news clips, newspapers, audio recordings, legal records, and much more. If your film has a historical element to it, you are going to need to do a deep dive into archival footage to see what's available. If you can uncover a piece of archival footage that no one has seen before or has been recently released for the first time, that could make your documentary even more special. If the musician you're following has an album they never released, or you obtain never-before-seen home videos from a celebrity that passed away, you're making a case for your access, and for this film to be different than anything else.

Where can you find archival footage? It depends on what you need, and from when. There are many libraries, databases, websites, news archives, and sometimes the piece of footage you need is from someone's personal collection (i.e. in their garage or storage closet from decades ago). It can be quite a search to find what you need, and it could make sense to bring on an archivist or research producer. Both do these searches for a living.

Beyond the footage itself, what can you do to liven it up and add artistry? Instead of just showing a photo on screen, you can slowly zoom or push into it; or the opposite—slowly zoom out or push out, so that it has some movement. An advanced technique that has recently become popular is called **parallaxing.** Parallax scrolling is a technique in computer graphics where background images move past the camera more slowly than foreground images, creating an illusion of depth in a 2D scene, and adding to the sense of immersion for the viewer. It brings photos to life and can be done in Photoshop and After Effects using motion graphics techniques. There are also many incredible graphical templates you can use in Adobe After Effects to liven up archival photos, add text, and create an introduction and credits sequence for your film.

There are so many tools available to bring these stories to life. Gone are the days of switching from talking heads to b-roll. Audiences want more. Documentaries are an exciting form of artistry, in addition to being educational and informative. Take a look at all of these methods, watch other films that inspire you, see what your budget can afford, and get creative! Bring something new that can draw your audience in and shine a light on the story and this genre in a different way.

The sky's the limit!

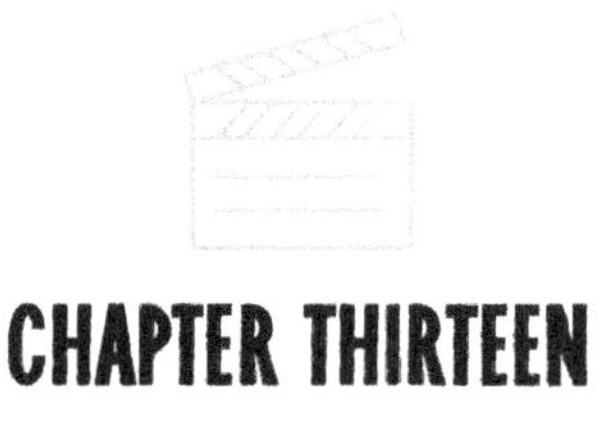

CHAPTER THIRTEEN

Post-Production

We've come to post-production! Woo hoo! EDITING. This is a phase of the filmmaking process I used to dread, but now I have come to love and embrace. Documentary films are made in the editing room. It's fascinating to think that 10 different directors with the same 10 hours of footage would make 10 very different films. You start this phase with hard drives full of footage, and now somehow, they need to be turned into a cohesive film that people would want to watch. Oh, and it's not like in narrative film where you have a script to follow and you are choosing the best takes and angles. There is no script at first. You are writing the script with every choice you make. Post-production is made up of thousands of tiny decisions each day that add up to the final product in the end. Some days you may feel stuck, or that no progress has been made, and then other days pieces are finally fitting together and flowing. Editing is a long process, especially for a feature-length documentary. It takes months, and sometimes years, to finish.

In this chapter, we're going to discuss best practices for you, the director or producer of your project. This is assuming and hoping you will have the budget to bring on an editor to help you through this phase. This is not meant to serve as an extensive guide for editing. This is about how to be a supportive player and set your editor up for success, and lead your team to the finish line.

What is your intention with the film?

Beyond these technicalities of editing, you need to be super clear as the director what your intention is with this film. Truthfully, that will guide all of your decisions from here to the end of post-production. If you aren't clear on what story you want to tell, especially now that you've shot the whole thing (or most of it), then editing could take forever. The clearer you are with yourself, the clearer you can be with your editor, and the easier you can work together. That doesn't mean the film won't evolve as you edit—you will discover new pathways every day—but you need to start with an intention or a philosophy for the film before you can truly begin.

The first conversations with your editor need to be about the big picture. What is your goal in making this film? How do you want the audience to feel after watching it? What do you want the audience to take away? Where and how it will be shown? All of these answers will help dictate how to cut the film, the pacing, and the flow. For *Losing Sight of Shore*, although the story seems to be about four women setting off to row across the Pacific Ocean, I never honestly cared much about the rowing part. To me, this was a story about friendship, perseverance, and the power of the human spirit. It happened to be set against the backdrop of the Pacific Ocean and on a rowboat, but I didn't want the focus of the film to be about the sport of rowing. That direction helped dictate the edit. We placed notecards with these main philosophies in our editing suite to help guide us. I remember we had: THIS IS NOT A FILM ABOUT ROWING on one card, and WE WANT THE AUDIENCE TO FEEL LIKE THEY CAN DO ANYTHING AFTER WATCHING THIS on another. When it came time to consider including more of the technical aspects of the journey across the Pacific, less was more, since we knew that wasn't our focus. This film was to be for everyone to enjoy, not just professional athletes or rowers.

What are your strengths as the director?

People often ask me if I can edit, and I typically say I'm not an editor, but I can do basic editing to get a project set up. I have edited projects in the past, but I know my strengths, and editing is not one of them. Giving feedback, notes, and ideas in editing are a strong suit of mine, but being the one to actually edit is not. It takes a tremendous amount of skill to edit efficiently, but also with creativity and vision for the entire project. Be honest with yourself about what your strengths are at this stage. Chances are you are the expert in the story and footage, and will be a tremendous asset when it comes to shaping the film. You want to keep your editor happy, as these projects almost always take longer than expected. That brings us to one of the most important points of this chapter:

Finding the right editor

If you're making a feature-length documentary, choosing your editor is a lot like entering into a marriage. You are going to be spending a LOT of time together and need to make sure you are on the same page creatively. You are looking for someone who is efficient, who has great ideas (not simply a button-pusher), and who's worked previously in a style or subject matter you admire. Every editor-director dynamic will be different, but chances are you will have major discussions about the themes of the film together. If it's a social issue, like sexual harassment, those conversations can get personal or intense. You both need to approach the content you are working on with professionalism and a sensitivity for the people on screen. It's a tall order, and I have seen many friends and colleagues switch editors halfway through their projects. It's so different from a day-to-day director-DP relationship, which is important too, but the amount of time spent together most likely doesn't even come close to that of an editor and director in documentary filmmaking. Your editor is perhaps your most important creative partner on your journey to making this film, and you've already come so far! Choose wisely. Do not undervalue a good editor, or the editing process. An editor can truly make or break a project. You want to find someone who matches your sensibilities when it comes to working together. I find this more important than credits on their resume. Is this an editor that wants you there with them each day, or do they work better on their own? Many editors I know do not want someone over their shoulder each day. They may want you to come in a few times a week to check in and brainstorm, but they largely want to work on their own. They need time with the footage to form their own opinions and make their own creative choices. So it's also about finding an editor who is on the same page as you about how and when to get things done.

When I was making *Nevertheless*, I prioritized working with as many women as possible behind the camera and in post-production. However, when it came to editing the film, I really wanted to balance it with the male perspective because ultimately, that was the audience I was trying to reach. So I worked with the editor from my previous film, Peter Saroufim, who is also my film school pal. We already had a great working relationship and friendship. I valued his point of view, and knew that we both would treat the content with sensitivity and respect. There were many days where we would have intense, personal discussions about sexual harassment, sexism, racism, and so much more, and I know the film is better because we challenged each other in the editing room. I fought to keep certain sound bites in because I knew how meaningful they could be to a woman, and he did the same for what he deemed important for men to hear. There were many days where I felt like we had so far to go, and we might never climb out of this pit of footage. The content was a lot to handle. But there were also days that felt light and effortless, and progress was finally in focus. Our post-production process for two feature documentaries together has averaged about six to eight months. After three feature docs, that seems to be my typical timeline. It's short enough to be efficient, but long enough to have some time to marinate on the footage and themes.

How do you find an editor?

There are so many ways you can start your search for an editor for your film. Hopefully by now you have at least dipped your toe into networking and finding contacts in the documentary film community, which is the ideal place to start.

- Ask your friends and contacts in the documentary community. Who do they recommend?
- Find similar films to yours and take note of who edited those films. Try reaching out to see if they would be available and interested

in taking on your project. Even if they aren't similar films, but you appreciate the pacing and style, reach out anyway!

- If you went to film school, is there someone from your class that you know and trust to help you?
- Post on Facebook in specific groups like "I Need An Editor" with a short description of what you're looking for and who to contact.
- You could go through a production company or post house and hire them on to help you throughout post-production—not just editing, but also color correction, sound, graphics, and more.
- If someone helped you edit your sizzle or work sample, is that someone who could be good for the full film?
- You can also start editing on your own and hire someone when you've done some of the groundwork, so they don't start from scratch. However, a good editor wants to see all of the footage they will be working with, whether the film is just starting or halfway complete.

*It's important to note here that a lot of these options are based on the assumption that you have a budget to work with. All of the people and groups above are not likely to work for free, or deferred payment. So if at this stage you don't have the money to pay an editor, I would suggest you focus on fundraising. Do as much of the prep work as you can in editing, so that when you can afford an editor, you have a clear picture of what you need, and they can hit the ground running.

**It's also important to note here that there are inherent biases and privileges built into the suggestions listed above. If you are mainly dipping into a film school or previous work search, chances are the candidates you might get are rather homogenous (read: white and perhaps male). It's essential that you take an active role in seeking out editors that are BIPOC, LGBTQIA+, especially if your subject matter is dealing with any issues present in those communities. You need to hold yourself accountable to ensure the people behind the camera are representative of the story and community you wish to spotlight. I, as a white, cisgender, straight woman, always need to do a better job of this too.

Get Organized

Next up, once you've found your editor, or even if you are in the middle of your search, start to get organized with your footage. The first thing to do is to make sure your hard drives are organized. This will help when you're in your editing software. If there's a lot of footage, how is it categorized? Remember that your editor will likely have very little context as to where things are in the project, so you need to make it as easy as possible to locate footage. We talked about this in the production chapter. If you weren't organized in production, it's going to be that much harder in post.

Additionally, you need to choose an editing software before you start organizing your footage. Adobe Premiere, AVID, and Final Cut X are the most widely used software these days. Make sure your editor is on board with the software you want to use, or vice versa. You are not going to want to switch software in the middle of your project. They don't often play nicely with each other. Personally, I like using Adobe Premiere. I find it very user-friendly, and I have it in my office as well, so if I need to do some remote work here and there, my system can communicate with my editor's.

Back to organization.

You could organize by:

- Phase of the project or journey. For example, in *Losing Sight of Shore*, there was Leg 1, Leg 2, and Leg 3 of the linear journey across the Pacific.
- It could be by city you filmed in.
- It could be by the person you interviewed, with separate folders for each person.
- It could be by month or date.

- It could be by topic discussed with that person.

Come up with a system that is easy to explain so that down the road, when you are looking for footage, you will be able to find things. Not only do the hard drives need to be organized, but the imported footage within the editing software needs to be organized in a similar fashion. The media browser or bin where all the footage lives in the editing software needs to be clear so an assistant editor or editor can fire up the project file and find things with ease.

A quick note on **assistant editors**: They can be incredibly helpful to hire when setting up a project and getting it ready for an editor. They typically come in prior to the editor and get the project organized. Sometimes footage from production needs to be transcoded in order for it to be viewable in the editing software. Also, most of your interviews will need to be synced up, since you likely shot with two or more cameras. You need the sound from Camera A to match the sound from Camera B. An AE can help with that tedious process and create new sequences for each interview so that they're ready to be edited. If you aren't able to hire an AE, then the editor will absorb a lot of these responsibilities, which takes time away from the actual edit. In a perfect world, your editor will recommend and hire an AE that they love working with.

Logging Footage

Beyond the sit-down interviews in a documentary, you may need to log the other kinds of footage you've shot, like vérité scenes with your characters (by "log" I mean add detailed notes and categorize). In *Losing Sight of Shore*, the polished, sit-down interviews only happened when I was on land with the rowers, for about a week each time. The rest of the nine months of footage was all scenes on the boat that needed to be logged. As the director, since I wasn't physically on the boat, I took it on as my responsibility to log those hundreds of hours from the boat, so I could truly know the whole story of what they experienced at sea. (Or at least, what was captured on camera). I considered it part of my preparation as director, and let's face it, I did not have the budget for an AE. I watched through each clip and summarized what was going on, used a system of keywords to categorize moments. Keywords like: FRUSTRATED, TEAMWORK, SUNSETS, GOOD SHOT, etc. so I could refer back to those moments if I needed to later. Then I would transcribe, or at least paraphrase, what was being said in a confessional-style interview to camera. I bolded the moments and sound bites I thought were really good. I'm so glad I did it all this way, as it helped my editor. He didn't have to watch through every frame, but to be able to read what happened each day and each week on the boat.

Here is an example of one of my logs from Leg 2 of their journey:

LSOS LEG2 WEEK 5 HAWAII TO SAMOA

Sony C0013

Lizanne confessional inside the cabin at night. SEASICK / TIRED / LOW ENERGY

Liz: Hi Sarah! ***It's Day 34 and I've still been seasick. I'm sick of being sick. Today has really got me down. It's been a long time now, my energy levels are low. I can't really keep food down; my appetite has gone to pot.*** *I'm eating the sweets but energy is short lived and then I get the energy drop afterwards. (00:38) It's just getting really frustrated. The girls have been amazing. Absolutely incredible and helpful. But I don't want them to do everything for me all the time. They do the logbook and they stop me from having to look at the screen which is really thoughtful but (1:04) reality is I've got to get on and do it anyway. I'm trying to push through and yeah luckily being out on the oars is better. If I need to be sick then that's fine, I'm sick and then back on it.* ***The only frustrating thing is I know I can give more. I'm pushing really hard and I'm giving all my energy to rowing cause we're stuck in a current and we need to get out of it. Like everyone I want to get to Samoa.*** *(1:57) Pushing on, but I'm just getting me down and I, the only medication that seems to have worked so far we ran out of which is why the last few days have been worse for me. (2:21) There's nothing to take it away and keep it off. Which is ironic. Yeah, so I'm just having a bit of a bad day. Anyway, onwards and upwards.*

C0014

Outside on the oars, the water is SO BLUE. Rain clouds can be seen in the distance and heavy rain too. The clouds are electric blue! The waves are choppy.

GOOD SHOT / WEATHER / FORESHADOW RAIN

C0015

Laura confessional in the cabin with the BAM wall. DEFINING MOMENT / CONFIDENCE / ONCE IN A LIFETIME OPPORTUNITY / WORKING AS A PHYSIO

Laura: Hi, so this is in answer to some of your questions. How is the row a defining moment for me? Without a doubt yes, the row is a defining moment for me. (00:22) ***I think I remember when I first heard about the row, for me that was as if I had to do it... And in particular it's kind of a confidence building thing as well. (1:43) Naturally I'm not the most confident of people and some people might say that's not true. I'm confident in something once I've got more experience in it. I tend to love chucking myself in the deep end and I learn and adapt and take everything on. (2:07) And it's only after I've done something and I've been out of my comfort zone and I've built something in my confidence.*** *And I've had an impact on me. (2:30) How it compares to other defining moments in my life. I was trying to reflect before about key defining moments for me. There's a few and you can reflect on different decisions that you make and opportunities that you take. And I think (2:57)* ***living a life never being left with 'what if' is very important to me.***

Transcripts

Next, you need transcripts, if you haven't already procured them. For every interview—whether it was one or 100—you will want a written transcript of every word (unless you know you won't need to use it somehow). Transcripts are documents that allow you to read each interview word for word, so you can create a paper cut and get organized further with how you are going to shape this film. You can use services like Rev.com or Temi.com to get automated transcripts within a day, or you can hire a transcriber to spend a few hours transcribing each interview and pay them for their time.

The second option often leads to the most thorough and accurate transcripts. However you acquire the transcripts, organize them all into a folder, or print them up and put them in a physical binder. For me, I like having the transcripts physically printed a binder. I highlight the sound bites I like, and bring the binder with me to edit, so that I can quickly find things. But you can certainly keep it all digital and search words or phrases to quickly find things too.

Paper Edit

Some filmmakers like to create an entire paper edit of their film before they start actually editing the footage. This is, in essence, writing the script for the film now that you've shot it. The paper edit will include the visuals as well as the audio, and in some cases the entire voice over narration will be written and recorded (or recorded temp) before the edit begins. This has never been my personal style, but I do see the value in this process. Your editor might prefer a paper edit, or you can send it to your investors or funders ahead of the actual edit to keep them in the loop. A paper edit may also save you time and money with your editor, as you can take the time to map out the whole film before they get started.

When creating a paper edit, use your transcripts and pull sound bites to create a cohesive script, including the timecodes of the sound bites. You may also include the b-roll or the vérité scenes . You can do this by creating columns in a Word or Google Doc of **VIDEO** and **AUDIO**, along with the timecode and clip number so the editor can find it. Tell us what the viewer is hearing and seeing throughout the film. You can then give that to your editor to create the first assembly cut.

Creating Sequences

Once all of the footage is loaded into the project file, transcoded if needed, transcribed, synced, and organized, you may want to start categorizing the footage into sequences. In *Losing Sight of Shore* this was so helpful for us, since so much of the film was moments from the boat at sea. My editor, Peter, and I created endless sequences of footage. We had a whole sequence of sunrises and sunsets; we had a sequence of wildlife they ran into on the boat, like whales and sharks and mahi mahi; we had a big waves sequence; we had laughter and silly moments, frustrated moments, tears, and much more. Some shots lived on multiple sequences, but as we combed through hundreds of hours of footage (that wasn't sit-down interviews) we wanted to categorize the events happening on the boat in a cohesive, searchable way. That way, later in the edit, when we needed a sunrise shot to serve as a transition from scene to scene, we knew exactly where to find it. You have to find a way to make sense of your mountain of footage, to the best of your ability.

For *Nevertheless*, the process was quite different. The footage was mostly interviews, no vérité moments or wildlife. So we made sequences based on topics and themes. We made a masculinity sequence, a victim blaming sequence, a legal system sequence, gender roles, intersectionality, and transgender rights sequences. Then we had a sequence for each of the seven portrait stories featured in the film, so we could shape those separate from the experts. We made far more sequences than we could ever need, and eventually were able to distill those themes into larger sections, and combine them as we combed through. There were so many days when we'd watch hours of a sequence, pull interview sound bites from several people discussing sexual harassment, and then we'd talk through the essence of what we were trying to say, and find the best sound bite based on that.

Create a rough schedule

Work with your editor to create potential deadlines. Working backwards is a good way to go. When do you need the project done? Choose that date first (knowing you might need more time), and walk back from there to what we call **picture lock.** Although a lot happens between picture lock and the finished film, your editor's job is mainly done at picture lock. Picture lock means the visuals of the film are locked in and ideally will not change. Audio can shift a bit if needed (additional sound effects, music, and more will be added), but the edit of the picture is done. This milestone is important because then your other artists can officially get started on the film. Your sound editor, sound mixer, color correction, original score, graphics, and other artists can move forward confidently knowing the film won't change.

Everything becomes extremely precise at this stage, which is why the picture lock is an important checkpoint.

Backing up further, you can set a fine cut deadline, a rough cut deadline, a first assembly, and more, depending on the scope of your project. Here's the general order of cuts:

First Assembly – *This is the best first guess at the film's structure. It will be much longer than the final film, but you will know if a viable film exists at this stage. Do you need to shoot more?*

Rough Cut – *With the rough cut, the structure is mainly in place, and we are getting closer to the ballpark of the final run time, though the film still lacks finesse. This version could be shown to an audience for a test screening. You may be using temp music or graphics to show the whole scope of the film.*

Fine Cut – *The length of the final cut should be very close to the final run time. This cut includes some of your graphics, music, and any visual effects to make sure they're working. The film's structure is completely in place now, and you can do another test screening at this stage.*

Picture Lock – *The picture lock is the finalized structure of the film, including the total run time. Now you can move on to color, sound, music, and final graphics. You will also add in opening titles and closing credits.*

Final Cut – *The film is done! Color, sound, music, graphics, credits, everything is complete.*

Final Exports/Deliverables – *Depending on the requirements of your distributor, you will deliver the film in the format you need.*

Keep in mind there can and will be multiple rough cuts, fine cuts, and assemblies, but these are the main checkpoints to hit. Prior to the first assembly, you might want a smaller deadline to hit, like a stringout of the whole film (a stringout is basically roughly placing clips together in an order). Whatever your structure is, these are important check points to have so that you can complete this film in an efficient time frame. Also, the artists who will do their work after picture lock want to know when to expect that version of the film. As your deadlines shift, make sure you keep them informed as well.

Test Screenings

Deep breath. Test screenings are a great way to check in with audiences before you are done editing the film. I would suggest hosting at least one, if not several, test screenings of your film at various stages of the edit. It's easy to get too close to the film and the footage. Neither you nor your editor can see what the audience sees. Even if it's a small group of trusted colleagues and friends, you need to know what's working, what's unclear, and if this film is shaping up to be any good. I like to hand out surveys at a test screening and have each audience member write down their answers so I can reflect on them later as well. Then, you can facilitate a discussion (which might even turn into a brainstorming session) that hopefully gives you and your editor some concrete ideas on how to problem solve from here.

Yes, these test screenings can be hard to stomach. You have been so in it and working so hard that you just want to fast forward to the part where everyone loves the film. As time goes on, you also want to populate your test screenings with people you don't know, so they aren't biased to give you good feedback, as your friends can be. You also want to show the film to your intended audience and see how they respond to it. If the film is meant to be seen by students, then show it to a group of students and get their thoughts. If it's a film hoping to represent and honor the transgender community, make sure you have some transgender individuals watch a cut of the film and give notes. You cannot finish this film in a vacuum, and I promise you have blind spots. If everyone says something is unclear, then it's unclear, and you need to fix it.

Here is the test screening survey we gave out for a rough cut screening of *Losing Sight of Shore*:

- *What is working well in the film?*
- *What is not working as well, or missing, if anything?*
- *What do you think of each of the characters?*
- *How did the movie make you feel?*

- *Who do you think would want to see this kind of movie?*
- *Who would you recommend it to?*

Other notes/reactions:

You don't want to ask leading questions, or "yes"/"no" questions. You want to leave room for them to have their own reactions and thoughts. You can keep it anonymous as well, so that no one is afraid to tell you the truth. These surveys were so helpful for us to know where we were headed in a good direction, and to smooth out the parts of the film that people found confusing. There were a ton of moments that we had to leave on the cutting room floor. A nine-month journey had to be boiled down to 92 minutes! But hearing from a test audience was tremendously helpful, and it gave us the energy to keep going knowing we were getting close.

You may also want to take this opportunity to conduct some market research and ask your audience where they typically consume documentaries. Where might they expect to see a film like this? As you move into distribution, you also want to know how people are perceiving your film. Maybe someone even suggests something you hadn't thought of yet. Be as open as you can to seeing these screenings as helpful, not painful. Plus, wouldn't you rather get this feedback now than when the film is done and you can't fix it?

Giving Notes

This brings us to how you can effectively support your editor when things get tough and you have problems that seem hard to solve. It's up to you to be the leader, even if you're not the one editing the film. There will be days where you feel stuck, and it seems like the film is going to suck. We all have those days, or weeks even. It's up to you to be a good collaborator and give helpful notes and feedback to your editor to move things forward. But take a break when you need to! I like to point out what's working well and what is speaking to me, in addition to what I'm struggling with. You don't want to just say something isn't working without explaining why. Try to come up with a solution to go with it.

Maybe you watch other films together to see how other filmmakers creatively solved problems like the ones you're having. Maybe you take a day or a week to let it marinate and see if a path becomes clear. Maybe you hire an editing consultant to come in and give ideas for a week. Maybe you need to go out and shoot a bit more to bridge a gap. There are many workarounds when times get tough, and they will. Editing is a marathon, not a sprint. Give yourself grace, and honor how far you've come to even be able to sit in that chair alongside your editor. Chances are you had to fight to raise money, traveled all over to capture this footage, and put endless time and effort into this. It is totally normal if there are moments when you want to quit, or feel lost.

Sound, Color, Music, Graphics

Once you hit picture lock (which is a huge cause to celebrate!), you can move on to a really exciting phase of post-production: sound editing, sound mixing, color correction, music licensing and composing the original score, as well as any final versions of graphics and animation. Think of each of these as layers added to your picture lock. It's amazing how each of these components make the film even better and bring it to life. Ideally, you have lined up these artists prior to picture lock, and you've shown them an earlier cut of the film. You want to give them time to think about what sound issues may arise, what music to compose, what graphical themes might be best, and what color palette makes the most sense for the film and your vision. All of these artists are turning to you for guidance, and are also bringing their immense talents to the table. You don't have to know a ton about sound design or music composing to react to what they give you, and provide feedback. Same as giving notes to your editor, can you explain why you feel something isn't working? Do you have an example of something you want to emulate as a reference? I have felt impostor syndrome many times during this phase of post-production. It's easy to feel out of your wheelhouse talking about musical instruments or the saturation of a particular color, but this is a great opportunity to step into someone else's world and see what creativity they bring to your film.

Here are some of the things that might happen at this stage, and basic information about each:

Sound Editing

You and your editor will deliver all of the sound files from the film, as well as a reference video of the picture locked film, to your sound editor. Your sound editor will also want the original sound from the cameras, in case there are better or usable tracks than what's on the picture lock timeline. Usually you will have an initial **spotting session**, where you watch the film together, and you point out any sound issues or request specific work on the audio layers. The sound editor will ask questions about what to add in, what to take out, and if you have better audio for certain spots if it isn't sounding great. They will ask about production and how you recorded sound and on what kinds of microphones.

In the weeks or months that follow, they will go through each second of the film and clean up the audio as best they can. They may add sound effects to liven up certain moments; they may need to record additional sound if there is something missing in the film; they will try their best to remove interfering noise in an interview, like a plane overhead or static on the microphone; essentially, they will work their magic to make sure this film sounds the best it possibly can before they deliver the final sound files back to you.

Sound mixing is the act of determining how loud the music should be versus the dialogue versus the sound effects. The ratio of volumes is important and delicate work. Sometimes one artist can do both tasks of editing and mixing, but ideally you can hire separate people to work on each part. Sound mixing also typically comes after the music has been composed or licensed, and is ready to be placed in the film. You as the director will want to hear the final sound mix in a sound proof studio so any other outside noises don't interfere with you giving notes.

Composing music or an original score

Your composer will need the picture locked film, without any temp music, and a version with the temp music you and your editor placed so they can understand your initial vision and tone. The composer will write music for the entire film based on the tone you've discussed and the feeling you want to create. The composer might play their own instruments or use a digital library of instruments to come up with each piece of music. You'll start with another spotting session with the composer, where you discuss: where you want music to come in and out, where you might not want music to be heard, and what kinds of music you are looking for throughout the film. It's ok if you don't have working knowledge of music. Your job is to give initial thoughts and gut feelings, and your composer will come up with ideas. It will be a back-and-forth discussion, lasting weeks or months, until you both agree it's done. Your composer will share pieces of the music with you along the way, and you can react to those before they fully compose a whole track. You might want to change the key of the music, the tempo, or an instrument, each of which can drastically shift the feeling. This is a really fun phase of post-production, as music is such an important part of bringing feeling and emotion to your film. If you have other music scores you love, make sure to reference those. Or even if you like piano over guitar, share that in the beginning.

You also need to specify if you're going to be licensing any tracks for the film, so that your composer writes music only for the necessary sections. Some editors like to add temp music while editing, and it may be that you end up feeling attached to a few of those tracks and want to pay to license them instead of having the composer write something new. There are lots of music licensing sites with great music, like Audio Jungle, Epidemic Sound, and many more. Typically, licensing fees for each track depend on how you plan to distribute the film, but always reach out and negotiate the price, especially as an independent filmmaker. There are also royalty-free music sites where you can download and use free music that's public domain. If you're interested in licensing a popular track for your film with vocals, perhaps for the end of the film or the credits or trailer, that will cost significantly more, and you will need to reach out to the record label and the publisher to get clearance and negotiate the fee. The more popular the song, the more expensive it will be. You will also need to articulate your plans for distribution. If you don't know, I would recommend licensing it worldwide in perpetuity for this film, so that no matter how you distribute the film, you can use the music.

I was set on licensing the immensely popular song "Rise Up" by Andra Day for the ending of *Losing Sight of Shore*. I couldn't imagine any other song encapsulating such an impossible, triumphant moment. I worked with a music supervisor who helped me navigate the choppy waters of licensing a popular track from a major record label. After a few months I ended up spending about $10,000 total to license that song for the film worldwide in perpetuity. Expensive yes, but the only song I wanted for that moment. Worth it.

Color Correction

I'm always pleasantly surprised by how much life color correction brings to a film. You get so used to seeing your footage raw, or with a general filter over it, that when someone sits down to carefully color correct your whole film, it makes everything pop. It also makes your cinematography look even better! For this phase, you and your editor will deliver all of the video files in their original form to the colorist. These are by far the largest files that have to be delivered, and may need to exist on multiple hard drives. The colorist needs to work on the original images, not something exported or compressed. The colorist will go through frame by frame, shot by shot, and color correct every single one until the film is done.

You will have an initial meeting with them and share any thoughts or details about what you're going for in terms of a color palette. Do you want the whole film to be de-saturated, or warm and very saturated? Maybe the re-enactments should look more out of the 1980's, and the rest of the film should look true to current life. It's a painstakingly tedious process, but it's also fascinating to watch an artist essentially paint on top of your images and make them look the best they possibly can. In this phase, you can also work to remove any imperfections in an image (like a speck of dirt or dust on the lens), even out a white balance, or make a window darker. Once the entire film has been color corrected, your editor will help you bring all of those files back into the project so that they will play in the locked film. Color makes a huge difference!

Final Graphics and Animation

At this stage you should have some kind of temp graphics and animation in your picture lock. Or, at the very least, the accurate space (down to the frame) in the timeline where they will be. Once you hit picture lock, you need to solidify and finish all graphics and animation for the film. You will deliver a picture locked film to your graphics artist, and they will deliver back files that perfectly fit the spaces you have reserved. Review the graphics carefully. Make sure that they flow well in your film, that everything is spelled accurately if there are statistics or words on screen, and that you have no further notes to give. Your graphics artist will deliver a folder of the individual files, and you and your editor can incorporate them into the project file for the final exports.

Final Exports and Deliverables

This is it! Somehow, someway, this part is always stressful. It's like you're so close to the end you can taste it, and that's usually when a computer or hard drive decides to start acting up. Based on your distributor's needs, your editor will help you export the final film with all elements and files back on the timeline, often referred to as the **online edit.** Once it is exported, it's up to you (typically this falls to you, as you know the film best) to watch through the entire film very closely and make sure everything exported properly. It's normal for something to be off, like a file that didn't fully import, or a glitch of some kind. If so, you will need to re-export. If you have an upcoming deadline for a film festival or screening, make sure you give yourself plenty of time to export the film (which could take several hours, depending on the file size), and also to watch it through and make sure it's 100% done before you start sharing it. You will end up watching your film a million times.

Listen, editing and post-production is really hard. It's a thousand tiny decisions every single day that add up to the final film. Keep going. Keep trying, keep questioning and pushing until you feel in your bones that it's done. Documentaries are made in the edit. This is where the real directing happens. You will be so proud when it's complete.

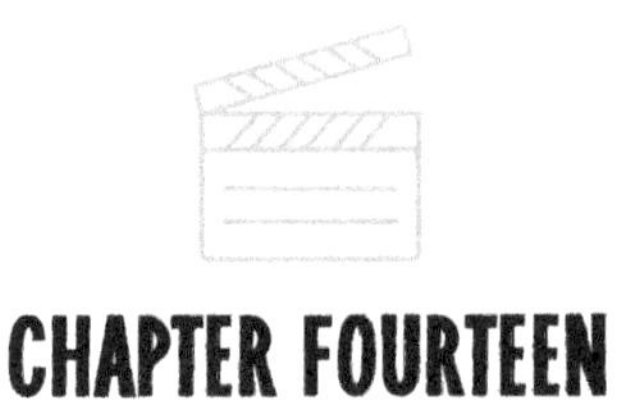

CHAPTER FOURTEEN

Defining Success for You

If you are nearing the end of post-production, it's time to start seriously thinking and planning for the next phase which is...(drumroll please)... distribution. Listen, I know you're tired. I know, you've come so far. When is someone else going to swoop in and help you, seeing your film for what it is? A masterpiece. I know, but look how far you've come, largely on your own drive, your own merit, your own permission. This next phase is no different. This can be an empowering time for filmmakers, but also a frustrating one. You've worked so very hard to get here, and yet there is more work ahead?? No thanks. But hang on! This is where a lot of that hard work pays off, not only financially but emotionally as well, so keep going. Don't stop now; this new phase is upon you, and it needs your full attention.

In the next chapter we will dive further into the pathways and revenue streams available, and the nitty gritty money side of distribution. This chapter is about empowering you to determine the right next step for your film.

First things first, I want you to take a deep breath and think about your **goals** for this film. Now, I don't want to hear what everyone else's goals are, I want you to truly think about what **success** would mean to you **for this film**. Not for your last film, or your next film, but this one. The clearer you can be about this now, the clearer you can be with a sales agent, a distributor, your team, and ultimately your audience. Are you focused on winning awards?

Which awards, and why? Are you aiming to get into as many film festivals as possible, so your poster is packed with laurels? Do you need to pay back investors, so your most pressing goal is the highest sale possible? Are you focused on impact—passing legislation, changing hearts and minds, using the film as a tool for change?

That's a lot of options, and truthfully, you could want none of those things, all of them, or some combination. Whatever the goals are, you need to be laser focused on what really matters to you, because if your goals aren't firmly in place, distribution can carry you away in a direction you didn't want to go. Everyone else will claim to know your goals, but you're the only one who can truly define them.

I have made three feature-length documentaries, and each one has had a different definition of success for me. With *Losing Sight of Shore*, I saw this story of four women rowing across the Pacific Ocean as the hero's journey and something anyone could enjoy and be inspired by. Getting the film on a worldwide platform like Netflix was always my #1 goal, from the start of that film. They reach over 160 million subscribers in 190 countries, and everyone seems to have a Netflix account, so I aimed high. I also had investors to pay back, which certainly adds some pressure, and made revenue another priority. Netflix could check two boxes for me: worldwide audience, and return on investment. **And it did.** I was able to pay back my investors in full (including myself, as I had invested all the money I could) plus interest. We even entered the elusive profit stage of revenue, which is very rare in documentary filmmaking. And on top of that success, people from all over the world could see a film I had worked so hard to make. Goals achieved, and then some!

For *Nevertheless,* everyone assumed I would get the film on Netflix, as if I have a direct line to the CEO. But that was never my goal for the film, and of course, Netflix is never a guarantee. It's not like once you get a film on Netflix, all of your work gets on Netflix. I wish it was that simple. And although I loved being on Netflix, and hope to have many more films distributed that widely, I also could see the flaws up close, especially for an independent filmmaker. For example, the algorithm wasn't truly supportive of *Losing Sight of Shore*. The film was categorized as a "sports documentary," which I suppose it is, even though I never saw it that way. But because it was categorized that way on the platform, the people who were coming across it on their Netflix queues were already prone to watching documentaries about sports, or extreme sports. Netflix has defined my audience for me, even if it wasn't the best fit. For three years, I felt like millions of men and women would never know my film existed, even though they might have absolutely loved it. It's about so much more than rowing or sports.

In this screen grab, the second row displays movies that Netflix determined are "More Like This."

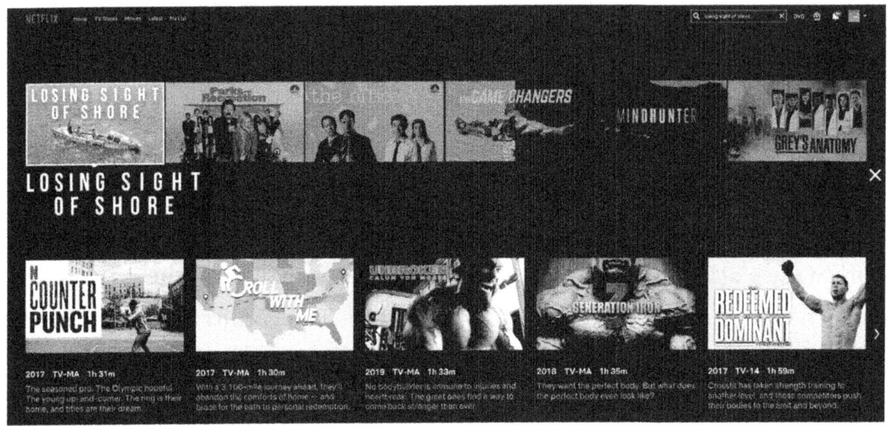

It's almost comical how Netflix paired a film about a team of women rowing across the ocean with these films about extreme (male) athletes. The key art for these films is literally the buffest men. Masculinity is being used to market those films to the extreme.

I digress. But you can see how, as a filmmaker, you can feel quite powerless to the algorithm. Even though you got what you wanted, it's still flawed. And when you don't have a huge marketing budget for your project (like I never seem to), there's not a ton you can do to promote your film so that your audience is widened. And don't get me wrong, reaching those people was a success too, but I always felt like the film was more universal than a sports film, and anyone could enjoy it, whether you cared about sports or not.

With all that in mind, when it came time to think about my goals for *Nevertheless*, a film about sexual harassment in the workplace, I knew instinctively that a platform like Netflix would immediately classify it as a "women's film" or "women's issues" (which kind of makes my blood boil) or "feminist content." It *is* those things, but I knew in my heart that the only way the film could make actual change in the world was to spread it more widely. I didn't want to release it only to the people who largely agreed, but rather find a way to get the content in the hands of people who needed it the most: workplaces. That's where real policy and procedures can actually change. Putting it on a major platform wouldn't help that goal, at least not initially. I certainly intend to bring it to streaming platforms in the future, but for now I want to stay true to my initial goal which is to use *Nevertheless* as a tool for sexual harassment trainings in workplaces and schools.

I also know a bit more about sales at this stage, and because the film doesn't have a lot of splashy headlines or never-before-heard stories about a well-known person, it likely wouldn't make a huge sale on a streaming platform. In terms of revenue, I am willing to play the long game over time with this one, and build up our revenue over the next few years with the help of our educational and community screenings distributor, Indieflix. There is significant revenue to be made in workplace and school screenings, but it takes a lot longer. I will dive deeper into this in the distribution chapter ahead.

At this point in my career, film festivals have never really warmed to me and my work. I don't know if I'm not playing the game right, or if I don't have enough connections at film festivals, or if I'm not making "festival films." Whatever the reason, getting accepted in to festivals and winning awards at festivals has never really been a part of my definition of success. It would be lovely, but it rolls off my back these days to not be a part of that club. Having several laurels on your poster or your website is nice, but for me it has never made me feel successful or fulfilled. I have screened at some lovely film festivals that are smaller or more regional, or niche (I guess "films about women" is a niche somehow still) but I have found my own successful path outside of the film festival circuit as a part of my strategy. You may have noticed there is no film festival chapter in this book.

Do I want to win an Oscar someday? Of course. But I have peeked behind the red curtain enough to see how much MONEY it takes to even be considered as a nominee. You have to do a theatrical release in LA and NYC, which costs tens of thousands of dollars, even if no one shows up, get reviewed in the LA Times or NY Times, and if you *are* lucky enough to get all that done, that's where the real money comes in. It's costly and near impossible to get the film from one of 170+ films in consideration, to shortlisted, to nominated, to winning. This happens through serious ad campaigns, parties, networking, travel, expensive marketing materials, celebrity endorsements, and more. I see myself as a practical dreamer. I will save that dream for when I have a huge streamer or broadcaster behind me to foot that bill, and who can use their connections to help. For now, I will sit in awe like the rest of the world and listen to the speeches and cheer on my favorite films and filmmakers.

My definition of success has shifted and morphed with each film, and simply with age and perspective. My goals now are to make work I'm proud of, and that can help change the world in some way. I want to pay myself a salary, or be paid a good salary while I'm making the film. I want to make significant revenue over time so I can sustain a career in documentary filmmaking and help support my family. I just want to keep making good work that inspires people! When you're clear about your goals, every decision or fork in the road is easier to manage. If you're unsure, or you let other people decide for you what success and fulfillment should look like, it winds up feeling empty.

Please take a deep breath, release any other peoples' expectations of you, and think about what your goals are for this film.

What does success mean to YOU for this film?

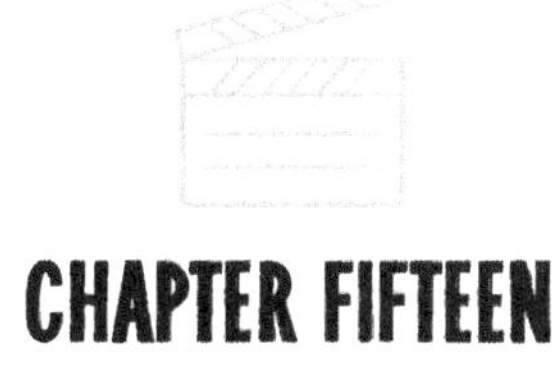

CHAPTER FIFTEEN

Distribution for Independent Film

The best part about filmmaking is that these projects can live on well past the day you finish working on them. Making a film is like pushing a boulder up a mountain. It gets a little easier with time, but it's still effortful, until finally one day, you don't need to push it anymore. Think of it as the gift that keeps on giving. This film that you've worked so hard to create, sacrificed so much for, finally stretches its wings and finds its place in the world to serve others. Hopefully, you get to sit back and collect revenue while observing its impact. That is the power of distribution.

In this chapter, we will be diving into strategies you can use to achieve your goals, including a general understanding of all the avenues you can take with distribution. I hope you can empower yourself with the information that follows, so that you can be an active participant in the distribution of your film, and not just sign on the dotted line and wait to collect checks. Truthfully, if you do that, those checks may never come. Although releasing your film can happen through a distributor, your film needs to be guided by you through this process with the same care that went into making it.

First things first, what is distribution, and what is a distributor? **Distribution** is the commercial process by which you get your film out to the world. A **distributor** is a company that helps you achieve that through a built-in pipeline to an audience. They help manage your release strategy.

An important concept to mention as part of your distribution strategy is called **windowing.** This is the process by which you divide up and maximize the rights of your film so you can generate the most revenue. Typically, the first window for your film is a **theatrical release**. Your World Premiere may have been at a film festival, and then you acquired a distributor through a sales agent (we will discuss those shortly). Your distributor secures you a theatrical release, meaning people around the country, or in select cities, can buy a ticket to see your film in an actual theater.

Well, things have changed significantly since the pandemic in 2020. The state of movie theaters is uncertain at best, so you may need to reimagine your theatrical release. In addition, documentaries, unless they have a massive marketing budget and following, don't often do well in theaters. This window for documentaries is shrinking. However, this window could be very important for your goals, and you want to make it happen. Or, if you are interested in an Oscar nomination, a theatrical release is a typical requirement, and holds a certain amount of prestige.

Next, you might want to think about a **TVOD** platform—transactional video on demand. This is a place for people to buy or rent your film, and they pay per transaction. iTunes and Amazon are good examples of common TVOD platforms. On a TVOD platform you make money per transaction for your film, so the more people who watch it and rent or buy it, the more money you make. Keep in mind, iTunes and Amazon take a significant percentage of each sale, and you might have a cut to pay your distributor on top of that. The profitability of this window is directly related to how much effort and marketing dollars you put into it. When you stop marketing the film, the sales will likely stop too.

Following that, you might choose a **SVOD** platform—subscription video on demand. On these platforms, people pay a monthly subscription fee to watch content in this platform's library. Netflix, Disney+, Hulu Plus, and HBO Max are all prime examples of SVOD platforms. With a SVOD platform, you either sign an **all rights deal**, meaning your film would become a "Netflix Original" or a "Hulu Original," and the only place people can watch your film is on Netflix or Hulu (you cannot pursue other windows).

With this option, the SVOD owns all rights in perpetuity. The other option is for the film to be an **acquisition.** That means Netflix is acquiring your film with three distinctions: 1. The rights represent a certain territory—North America, the US, worldwide; 2. The rights are for a certain period of time—one year, two years, three years; 3. And it's for a set **licensing** deal—that could be $10,000, or it could be $1 million, depending on the scope, quality, and buzz about your film. Is it a Sundance darling? Is it a story that's never been told? Is it about a well-known person people are dying to know more about? Those are some of the factors that would increase your price tag. But the important distinction here is that the licensing deal on an SVOD platform is set at the start. So no matter if 10 people or 100 million people watch the film, you make the same amount of money. And by the way, platforms like Netflix don't often share their data, so you will probably never know how many people have seen your work, which can be kind of maddening. (I will never know how many people watched *Losing Sight of Shore* on Netflix.) This window of SVOD is the most popular right now for documentaries, as more and more people are getting their content almost exclusively from streaming platforms. If this is your main goal, focus on this window and build the others around it. SVOD platforms seem to be more interested in all-rights deals than acquisitions these days since there is such fierce competition for viewers and more players crowding the landscape every year. They want to own as much content as they can in perpetuity. But for you the filmmaker, if you license the film instead of sell it, the difference is you still own all the rights to it, and one that term is up, you can turn around and license it somewhere else.

Another window to consider is **AVOD**—ad supported video on demand platforms. These platforms allow the viewer to watch your film for free, with the inclusion of ads throughout. Hulu would be a prime example of an AVOD platform. Revenue made within the AVOD space are determined by the AVOD service's ability to sell advertising during a given period of time. Filmmakers who take advantage of AVOD platforms reap a percentage of the advertising revenues based on the number of views for their particular title. The more views you have, the more money advertisers will pay to access those viewers. The AVOD model is quickly becoming a great source of ancillary revenue.

The **broadcast** window can be a very important part of your strategy, especially if you are interested in applying for awards and interested in serving a built-in audience. Similar to SVOD, the broadcaster will pay a licensing fee to the distributor or filmmaker for a length of time on their channel. Examples of a broadcaster would be PBS, National Geographic, Discovery, Lifetime, and hundreds more. Today the broadcast window and SVOD windows can go together, or they can be at odds with one another. Some broadcasters don't want you to also have your film on Netflix at the same time, so it's important to work out your windowing strategy. You might want to have your PBS run first, and then go on an SVOD platform. These platforms all have to play nice with each other and agree to these windows, which can be difficult.

The last window we'll talk about is **non-theatrical or educational,** a window that is often overlooked and yet can be incredibly powerful for a documentary. This window can also include DVD sales of your film. This is the process of distributing your work to schools, workplaces, organizations, libraries, prisons, churches—the sky's the limit with "non-theatrical." This window can go on throughout the life of your film and not be restricted by other strategies (unless you've signed an all-rights deal). In fact, I would highly encourage you to "carve out" these rights from any contract you might sign with a distributor, so you can use this window to your maximum advantage for impact and revenue.

For my first film, *The Empowerment Project,* we stayed in this window for three years before we did any of the above windowing strategies. We realized the film was best utilized in a classroom, in a girl scout troop, or in a workplace. If we had put the film on iTunes right away, we would have made about $10, and the life of the film would have probably been over very quickly. Instead, we kept it special. We worked hard with our distributor, Indieflix, to create a film-based curriculum. We licensed the film to well over 700 schools, groups, organizations, brands, and corporations. Over the past six years, the film has grossed hundreds of thousands of dollars! No one would have expected *The Empowerment Project* to make such an impact, and to create so much revenue.

Here's how our non-theatrical window worked: the film was only available through our educational distributor, Indieflix, for the first three years. A school, group, organization, or corporation could request a screening of the film. They would pay a $500 licensing fee, and with that fee included the ability for them to screen the film up to two times in a 24 period. We would ship them a DVD, which included access to our discussion guide of questions, discussion topics, activities, school curriculum, and even an award to honor an extraordinary woman in their community. When the event was done, they would ship the DVD back. The school or workplace could also request to have myself and/or Producer Dana Cook at the event for an additional appearance fee, plus travel. We would attend the event, answer questions post screening, take part in a panel, deliver a keynote, or whatever was required for that specific event. At schools, we led assemblies with students after seeing the film. We asked students to come up in front of their classmates and declare out loud what they would do if they weren't afraid to fail (that was one of the themes of the film). It was an incredible way to connect with audiences firsthand. Even with Indieflix as our distributor, it all felt very grassroots, and like a team effort through and through. We planned and organized national screenings tours, and we also worked with sponsors like Nordstrom, American Girl, Charles Schwab, and Microsoft to host screenings around the US and around the world as well.

All of this is to say, you are in charge of how you want to use the windows. Every film is different, and so are every filmmaker's goals! Once you know what you what to accomplish, you can pursue a window strategy that makes sense for you and leverages what's currently available in this changing landscape.

Finding the right distributor for you

Let's talk more about finding the right distributor. I'll start with the mistake a lot of new filmmakers make: looking for a distributor to sweep you off of your feet and solve all of your problems. Yes, there are exceptions where a multi-million dollar deal is made for a hot new documentary fresh out of the snow at Sundance, but for most of us that is not the reality. I want you to go into distribution with renewed energy and purpose because it is a marathon and it doesn't usually happen overnight. To quote Emily Best, CEO and Founder of Seed & Spark, and someone I really admire, "Distribution is not something you *get,* it's something you *do.*" That means you need to realize you are an active participant in this phase, and you should be. You know your film, your characters, your issue, better than anyone else in the world. There is no way someone could come in, fully understand your vision, and distribute the film perfectly on your behalf. You have been the leader up till now, and that leadership is needed even more than when you were working on the film.

I also want you to avoid teaming up with the wrong distributor and signing a multi-year deal that makes you unhappy. Unfortunately, I've seen many of my peers end up in that mess. When someone is interested in your film, it's exciting. It feels like being courted or wooed, but for a lot of these deals, that magic and courting ends as soon as the ink is dry, and you don't hear from them again. Here are a few ways you can protect yourself before signing with any distributor or sales agent. This should help you identify red flags.

Talk with other filmmakers that have worked with that person or company

Look up their roster of projects. They should have a website where they show off the projects they have sold or distributed. Do some research and find out who the director was, then reach out via LinkedIn, Facebook, Twitter, or through a mutual contact. Ask for their honest opinion about working with that company with questions like:

How long was the term of your deal?

Did you make real money?

How communicative was the distribution company?

What kind of marketing expenses did they claim, and were they reasonable?

Anything to look out for or avoid in the contract?

Knowledge is power, and if you know this distributor agreed to a smaller percentage or shorter term with another filmmaker, you can use that as leverage to negotiate better terms. If they are claiming it's a seven year deal for 35%, and this filmmaker told you their deal was five years for 30%, you can use that information to your advantage. You can ask the distributor for references as well, but chances are they will point you to the happy customers rather than more honest, comprehensive feedback.

Consult with a lawyer

Yes yes yes! We talked a bit about this in The Legal Side Chapter. Unless you have a law degree, distributor contracts are hard to understand on your own. They're LONG. And complicated. You need to make sure someone is looking out for you and your film. You can communicate to your lawyer about what is most important for you to maintain or to avoid, and they will mark-up the document with notes and can go back and forth with the distributor. This is totally normal, and the distributor will expect you to have notes on a multi-year contract. You might have a lawyer on retainer, you might have a friend who can help you, or you might need to pay a lawyer by the hour to get this done. I have found a good entertainment lawyer costs anywhere from $300-$500/hr. But hopefully they won't spend more than a couple hours on this, and believe me it's worth it to make sure your film is not tied up in a bad deal for years.

Take note of the term

Ten years is a long time, so is seven years! Try to get the term down to as low as you can, in the event that the deal doesn't go well. Or make sure there is a clause in the contract stating that you can re-evaluate halfway through the term and make sure everyone is happy to continue on. Make sure you include payment terms you are comfortable with. Meaning, how often are they going to pay you out? Yearly, bi-annually, quarterly, monthly? Quarterly is probably the most common.

Marketing expenses

Every distributor is going to take on some kind of marketing expenses to get your film sold to an SVOD platform or broadcaster or wherever, but you need to make sure there is an expenses cap in the contract. This means your distributor can't wildly spend whatever they like and simply charge it to your project's revenue as "marketing expenses." This happens a lot to filmmakers.

For example, let's say distributor X secures a $20,000 licensing deal with a broadcaster for your film for one-year. Hooray! But then, when the quarterly report comes in, you're only receiving $5,000 of that $20,000. If their cut is 25% of all deals, and you receive 75%, technically you are owed $15,000. But you see this mysterious line item on your report that says "marketing expenses" totaling $10,000. They could have used that for flights to a film festival, lunches with potential clients, social media marketing, anything they want to claim as marketing expenses (and in truth, those could have nothing to do with your film), and you are left with $5,000. It's not fair, and it happens all the time.

What happens if the company folds or gets bought?

This is happening more and more. In your contract, with your lawyer's help, you need to make sure there is language that addresses what happens if this distributor gets bought by another company or goes under. In that instance, you want your rights to revert back to you, so that you can find a new distributor. I have had many friends find themselves in the impossible position of their distributor folding, and the rights to their film are tied up in that mess. You do not want to pay the legal fees to fight to get your own film back in court. And in truth, when you sign a seven to ten year deal, this sort of thing is bound to happen. The landscape of film is constantly changing, as are the distribution companies.

Carve out rights

As I mentioned above, if you work with a distributor that wants to get your content out to multiple platforms, keep in mind that not every distributor is going to be great at all of these windows. Especially with educational rights, a typical distributor, unless they are focused on educational rights, will not know what to do with that window and you may be leaving money on the table. Mainstream distributors don't see the revenue potential in the educational market because it takes a long time to build up a database of schools and organizations, so they might find an educational distributor to whom you grant those rights, and they'll still take a cut. Don't be afraid to carve out the rights you want to exploit on your own or with another company. If you want to sell DVDs and merchandise through your website, for example, you need to carve out those rights in your contract so that you are free to do so in perpetuity.

Sales Agents

Another important part of this ecosystem is **sales agents.** A sales agent is like other kinds of agents in that they represent your film to make a sale to a distributor. They take a percentage of the sales they secure, typically anywhere from 10-25%, with an average of 15%. Sometimes they also take a flat fee off the top of a sale—$10,000 plus 15%, for example, but that is taken only if a sale is made. That incentivizes them to be proactive in selling your film, whereas if you pay them a salary or fee up front, they won't have to work for that money. Sales agents can be advantageous because they know the players and the marketplace better than you do.

They can help strategize about your distribution, including who might want to buy or license your film. You want to make sure they understand what your goals are, because your goals and their goals ($$$) might be quite different. A typical sales agent wants to do as little work as possible and make the highest commission possible. They want to be able to call up their friends at Netflix or Hulu, send over the film, and make the deal. They can't control if Netflix or Hulu will want your film, but they can get your work in the right hands to make that decision. And that, on your own, could take months or years, or might never happen.

Yes, you can secure a distributor on your own. A lot of these companies take submissions, or you can reach out through a filmmaker you know who has worked with them, but sometimes working with a sales agent is the best way to go, especially when aiming high for an SVOD deal. They are likely to negotiate a better deal than you could negotiate for yourself. For example, my sales agent knew to negotiate for Netflix to pay for the subtitling of *Losing Sight of Shore* in 25 languages. That would have cost me upwards of $50,000!

How do you get a sales agent?

There are a few ways—you can be referred by a friend who knows a sales agent and can push your email to the top of their inbox. You might meet a sales agent at a film festival or film market who is out looking for new projects to represent. You can also find a sales agent by researching the other films they've represented, and reaching out via their website or social media to see if they will watch your trailer. If they are interested, you can then send the full film. Keep in mind: not every sales agent is meant for every film. I was turned down by two sales agents before I found the one that helped me license *Losing Sight of Shore* to Netflix. If you're going to work with a sales agent, it should be one with a great track record who has sold films like yours before and knows exactly how to help you strategize. And ultimately, the sales agent doesn't control whether your film sells. They might have all the relationships in the distribution world—they may have sold many films like yours—and still for some reason they might not get offers. They still need the gatekeepers to say yes.

Self-Distribution

If all of this gives you a headache, you are not alone! I also want to make sure you understand that you are in charge of what happens to your film. If you made this film independently, then you own most, if not all, of the rights to it. You get to decide how to distribute it. You can also pursue the path of self-distribution, meaning you act as your own distributor and you don't sign with anyone. You can act as your own sales agent, your own publicist, your own educational distributor, your own advocate. It can be much harder, slower work, but it could also be the best thing, given your film and your goals. Beyond that, if distributors and sales agents aren't responding to your film the way you'd like them to, self-distribution is a great way to go. You can build your own audience, keep 100% of the profits, and not have to consult with any other company or person on what to do. You can do the research, continue to build the audience you've been building all along, and find a way to get your content to that audience at whatever price you want.

Maybe you do a combination of all of these methods. Maybe you self-distribute educationally, but then you bring a distributor on board to get the film on a streaming platform. Maybe you want to sell your own DVDs out of your house, but you have an educational distributor to help you get the film into schools and libraries. There are so many ways to piece this together.

If you do this right, your film can be the gift that keeps on giving years after finishing it. Don't get overwhelmed, take this step by step, and stay active in the process because it's your hard work that got you here! As of now, I'm going on year six with *The Empowerment Project*, year three with *Losing Sight of Shore*, and we are just getting started with *Nevertheless*. I see a long future ahead.

CHAPTER SIXTEEN

IMPACT

Hopefully by now you've been thinking more about your goals for the film and how you'd like it to exist in the world. Documentary films often lend themselves nicely to the world of social impact—you're showcasing a person, a group, an event, or an issue that people can learn from. Documentary filmmaking has the incredible ability to not only entertain people, but to help them see the world differently and possibly change their hearts and minds. This of course doesn't happen by accident; it's due to the deliberate and intentional work of the filmmaker.

To create impact, ask yourself how you can ignite audiences to take action after seeing your film. That action could be internal, causing someone to question their own biases, privileges, or inherently racist beliefs, for example. Or that action could be external, getting people to sign a petition, helping instate legislation, or changing their recycling habits to improve our planet. Whatever the call-to-action, it should be clear in the film, as well as in any supplemental materials you distribute with it. As you approach finishing your film, consider how impact can be incorporated in your distribution strategy. In fact, the sooner you think about impact the better. In the best case scenario, you were able to build an impact campaign budget into your original fundraising. But more often than not, filmmakers are looking for the money to fund an impact campaign later in the process, since they had so many costs prior to this stage. However you got here, now is the time to plan out what sort of impact you'd like your film to make, including attainable goals both large and small, given your timeline and budget.

So how do you figure out your goals for impact? First, think about how you want your audience to feel after watching your film. Your greatest moment of engagement with your audience will be when the credits roll. Hopefully your film is followed with either a call to action on screen, and/or a panel discussion or Q&A to reinforce and further the emotional tie to your film. What do you want your audience to do now? The further they get from your screening, the duller their passion and enthusiasm becomes. Right now, you have their attention.

Some concrete goals could come in the form of:

- Signing a petition
- Marching in a protest
- Donating money to a cause
- Purchasing merchandise where part of proceeds benefit the cause
- Calling local or federal representatives in government
- Reducing carbon footprint
- Hosting their own screening of the film in their community
- Taking a pledge acknowledging that they saw your film and learned from it
- Encouraging people to vote
- Dismantling internal biases and recognizing privileges
- Encouraging allyship and bystander intervention
- General awareness of an issue or group of people

Impact Producers

If this is all very new to you and you are looking for help in this arena, you may want to consider hiring an impact producer, or a company that specializes in impact campaigns, so you can effectively generate and reach your impact goals together. Impact producing is, in short, an individual or a company that can help you achieve the impact-related goals for your film, no matter what they are. They can help you organize a screening tour, manage your impact campaign, help you design and implement supplemental materials that go with your film and message, line up partnerships and sponsorships for your film's campaign, and help you produce events. Typically, an impact producer comes to the table with a database of contacts within this space, or can help you build up your contacts within this particular social issue. Picture Motion is one of the leading companies in this space.

Funding for Impact

If you weren't able to factor an impact campaign into your original budget, now is the time to start thinking about how much you need to achieve your goals. You can draft up a new and separate budget for things like: working with an impact producer for a certain number of weeks or months; organizing and implementing a screening tour; creating a screening packet or discussion guide; and much more. There are also specific impact grants. When you apply, you will need to specify what you plan to do with the funding, who your intended audience is, and what measurable impact goals you have for the film. You can also try going back to some of your previous funders for the project, update them on your progress, and see if they are willing to put in more money for an impact campaign. They too will want to know how you plan to spend the money and what you are hoping to do. You could crowdfund once again, or even work towards creating some revenue from the film first and then using that to fund your impact campaign. And if you just aren't in the position to raise any more money, you can work towards your impact goals on your own, and spend your own time on it.

Designing a Discussion Guide

For all three of my films, having a discussion guide or screening packet has been incredibly useful when bringing a film out into the world. The purpose of a guide is to empower the person or organization who is hosting a screening of your film. You want to give all the tools they could need to make sure this is an impactful and effective event for everyone, especially once the credits roll. Discussion guides take the best of the film—including images, quotes, and takeaways—and consolidate them into a multi-page packet. In some ways, it's your film in document form, with extra resources packed in. If you can, I would recommend working with not only a great designer to create the guide so that it looks great, but an expert in the field of the issue you are covering to help you with the information. If your film is about mental health, and you yourself are not a mental health professional, you want to consult with one for your discussion guide to make sure it's accurate and useful for other professionals in the field.

A discussion guide can include many things, such as a letter from the director explaining why making this film was important to them, a glossary of terms from within the film so that everyone is on the same page when it comes to this new vocabulary. The guide could have discussion questions; it could also have essay questions for students to answer so that school administrators could use the film and guide as part of their curriculum. It may also include activities for students or parents to utilize within their homes and communities. You could expand on the stories featured in your film, and expand on the information presented by experts. You could include a quiz to test the knowledge of your audience after watching the film. You could provide more context about statistics, charts, and graphs featured in the film. This guide can be a couple pages, or it could be 50 pages, depending on what you want to provide and accomplish. You may want to create multiple versions of the guide—one for schools and one for workplaces, or one for students and one for parents. This is where you connect the dots between your film and impact.

Who is your role model?

@EmpowermentDocu / facebook.com/Empowermentdocu

For *The Empowerment Project* screening packet, we pulled inspirational quotes from the film that people could cut out and put up on their wall. We provided activities for middle schools and high schools to encourage their students to stand up in front of the class and share: *What would you do if you knew you would succeed?* and *Who is your role model*? Teachers could print cards on which students could write their answers, and then post them up in their locker or add their card to a mosaic on a school wall. We also provided an award that schools could present to an extraordinary role model in their community. We got a lot of great feedback from teachers across the country saying they enjoyed our materials and would use the guide to facilitate homework assignments and special projects after seeing the film. In six years, we have seen perhaps every iteration of what a screening and follow-up assembly or event could look like for that film. It has been amazing to see how passionate people can use a film that compliments the lessons they are bringing to their community.

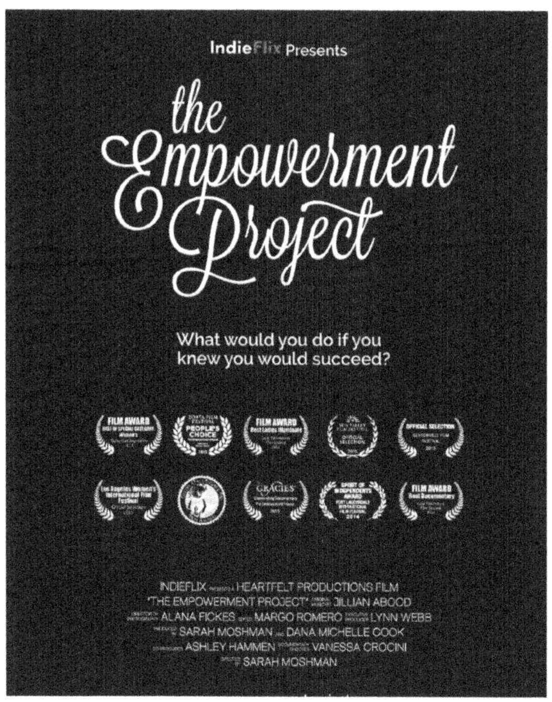

The Empowerment Project

what would you do if you knew you would succeed?

CERTIFICATE of Appreciation

is presented to

____

Thank you for being a positive role model in our community.
You inspire us every day!

________________	________________
Date	Signature

HOW TO BE AN ALLY AGAINST SEXUAL HARASSMENT

For our *Nevertheless* discussion guide, we went a lot more in-depth with our resources, statistics, questions, and activities. We wanted to make sure it would be an effective tool for workplaces as part of their sexual harassment trainings. We also had a version for schools to help empower students with this knowledge before they entered the working world. In the discussion guide, we break down all seven stories featured in the film and follow-up with questions for further study. The guide is 31 pages, took about six weeks to complete, and I worked with an impact consultant and graphic designer. For reference, it cost about $8,000 to create, which felt like a lot of money, but I know it brings our film to a new level as a film-based program or curriculum, rather than just a film.

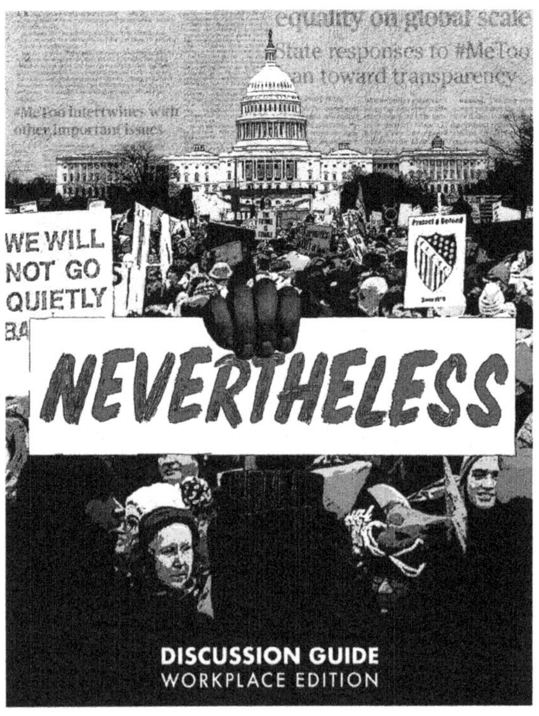

What is Sexual Harassment?
Sexual harassment is any behavior characterized by the making of unwelcome and inappropriate sexual remarks or physical advances in a workplace or other professional or social situation.

Partnerships

The next thing to think about is what partnerships could help you create greater impact. This will vary immensely based on your project and social issue, but in essence you want to find the people, groups, and organizations that are already out in the world doing this work. Can your film help amplify the work they are already doing? It's important you don't come to the table as if you've single-handedly solved this social issue. You need to remember that some people and organizations have been working towards this same goal tirelessly for decades, and just because you made a film about it does not make you the expert. The goal is not to invalidate or dismiss the work that's already been done in this space. You merely want your film to add to the conversation, to continue the fight, and help the movement progress.

On your own, or in conjunction with an impact producer, create a list or database of all the main players in this space. Find out whom to contact, what their latest goals are, what kind of work they are doing this year, and if they've partnered with films in the past. If you are fighting climate change, you should be contacting every environmental protection organization and non-profit with the same mission that you can find. If you are fighting racial injustice, you want every major activist in this space and every organization in this fight to know about your film, and to see it as an asset to their mission and message.

After you've created the database, you or your impact producer can agree on some kind of intro email, and start reaching out. Your goal should be to set up calls with the leaders at these organizations and listen. Listen to who they are and what they want. What initiatives are important to them right now? What kinds of events do they host throughout the year, if any? Then you can tell them about your film, share your trailer, materials, and even a private link to view the film. Your goal is to discuss how your film might support their goals. This is not necessarily a revenue generator; this is you aligning yourself with the right partners so that people in the community take your film seriously. You could offer your film as a fundraising tool for them; you could ask the head of their organization to speak on a panel after a screening of your film. You could ask that they feature you in their email newsletter which has an audience of thousands of people who might be interested in your film. You could ask for a quote about the film from the CEO of their organization, to be used on your website and marketing materials, adding legitimacy to your project. You could ask that they lend their support to your impact goals, especially if your impact goals are the same as theirs. Find ways to support each other through partnership. It needs to be mutually beneficial for this to truly function as a partnership.

Sponsorships

Another option is bringing on sponsors and sponsorships to help reach your impact goals. Sponsors can come in the form of companies or businesses that align with your mission and your message, and want to help get the film to the world in a meaningful way. Doing so, in turn, makes the company or business look good to their customers and shareholders, and can complement their annual impact goals. More and more companies are reaching beyond profits and revenues and finding ways to leave their mark on the world. Your film might be the perfect way to subtly place their brand next to a mission they want to support. This can become part of your distribution strategy, as it can yield significant revenue.

When distributing *The Empowerment Project* through Indieflix, over the course of three years we secured sponsorships from four major companies. Each was a little different, but the film stayed the same. First, we worked with **Nordstrom** (which I also discuss in the Marketing and Promotion chapter coming up next). They heard we were organizing a four-city, four-week screening tour around the US. Thanks to their relationship with Indieflix (as two Seattle-based companies), Nordstrom decided to sponsor big event screenings in each of the four cities—LA, DC, Chicago, and Seattle. They covered the event costs and paid us for the screenings. They wanted their branding on everything, they wanted to advertise the screenings in their stores, and they wanted to invite all of their customers and staff to attend. It made sense because the audience for our film aligned with their audience as well. We of course went back to them once the tour ended to see if they wanted to engage further with the film, and they declined. It was a one-time sponsorship that we loved and learned a lot from.

Then we were able to work with **American Girl**. Dana (the producer of the film) and I had made a short documentary about the Girls on the Run organization in Chicago a couple years prior in 2012. American Girl happened to be a big sponsor for that program and 5K culminating event. We thought American Girl would be a great partner for *The Empowerment Project*, so we asked our mutual contact to connect us with the PR department of American Girl. After a series of calls and proposals over several months, American Girl decided to sponsor 60 screenings of the film in all of their stores and in surrounding middle schools in the markets where they had stores. It was amazing! To see eight-year-old girls show up to the American Girl store with their dolls and sit and watch the film alongside their Girl Scout Troop was incredible. We adapted our screening packet to skew to the middle school girl, and put American Girl's branding and materials inside, so each school was well equipped for their event and discussions. We were even invited to visit the American Girl factory in Middleton, Wisconsin to screen the film and speak to the employees and see how the dolls are made. Again, it was a one-time sponsorship, but we got so much out of it, and my inner eight-year-old was freaking out.

Next, we were fortunate to work with **Microsoft**, which was a sponsorship that was more global in scope. Indieflix had an existing relationship with the right department at Microsoft, and they worked on that connection for months. Microsoft sponsored 50 screenings of the film all over the world, and their focus was expanding their reach as far as possible, so the more countries we added to our list for screenings, the better. We had the film subtitled in several languages and put out a call on social media that Microsoft was offering to sponsor screenings. Over the course of a few months, people wrote in from all over. Microsoft wanted to see measurable impact from their sponsorship, so we collected quotes, photos, and testimonials from screenings to compile and send to them. We learned so much about how far and wide the messages of gender equality can stretch, and how women and girls all over the world were hungry for this content. It was also a one-time sponsorship for that film, but the relationship continues to this day.

And finally, we had the pleasure of working with **Charles Schwab**, a financial services company. Another Indieflix contact, this one seemed to come out of left field. I couldn't believe a financial company and a doll company wanted to sponsor the same film, but they did! Charles Schwab was a bit different, as they wanted to license the use of the film internally so that all of their thousands of employees could see it, in addition to special public screenings for their community. Once again, we adapted our materials for the Charles Schwab employees. We were delighted to hear that after a year of working together, they wanted to re-up their license so they could continue using the film at internal and external events.

I learned so much from these four sponsorships, and it opened my eyes to what's possible when the themes and messages of your film align with those of a company or brand you admire. I would never have thought the missions of these four companies would have been similar, but when it comes to empowering girls and women, they are very much aligned. The way they expressed those goals was different, but they could all utilize the same film.

I should mention, for every sponsorship, there are countless meetings, phone calls, and proposals that don't come to fruition. We had many experiences where we got very close with other big brand sponsorships, and they ultimately fell apart, for one reason or another. It might have nothing to do with you or the film; it could be that the person you were talking with no longer works there, or their budget for the year has been approved, and there isn't any room for this anymore.

When pursuing sponsors, it was always a team effort between the passionate people at Indieflix, and Dana and me. It takes perseverance. It's a process of finding the actual gatekeeper at the company, instead of wasting time pitching to the part of the company that doesn't actually have the power to say yes. Sponsorships are hard to secure, and it takes a long time to iron out the details, but they're valuable opportunities to pursue alongside your other impact goals.

Measuring Impact

How can you measure your impact goals and show potential funders what kinds of change you helped create with your work? I would advise creating some kind of Google Doc to collect all of the best quotes, testimonials, photos, and social media posts that demonstrate the measurable impact of your work. This document should be continuously updated over the years. Then, when pursuing new sponsorships, partnerships, and funders for your next project, you can produce a one sheet or deck to show how your last film helped move the needle on that issue. This is called an **impact report.**

Examples of Measurable Impact to Consider:

- *How many signatures did you secure on that petition?*
- *How many screenings were hosted in schools?*
- *How many people showed up at your protest against gun violence?*
- *How much money were you able to help raise for people in poverty?*
- *How many people did you get to register to vote after seeing your film?*

Find a way to show the impact you're making in the world based on your goals. It's important, and it matters! The power of cinema is so real—these films can save the planet, change the course of an election, ignite empathy in others, and create awareness for a cause the audience may have known nothing about. That is no small feat. You worked so hard to get to this place to be able to have an impact; keep going until you do.

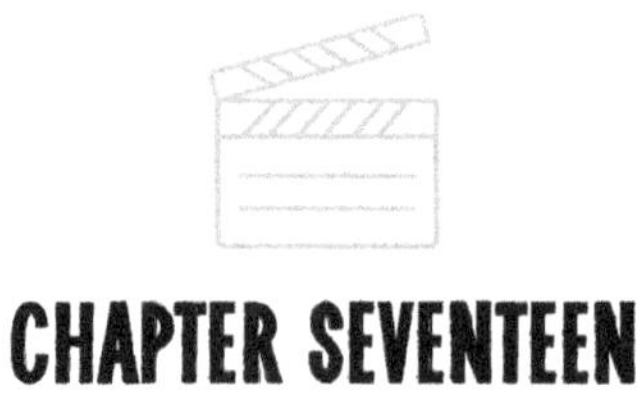

CHAPTER SEVENTEEN

Marketing and Promotion

Once your film is done, no matter who the distributor is, it needs to be marketed to your intended audience. Luckily, given everything we've talked about up to this point, this should come as no surprise. You had to think about your audience during fundraising—whether it was grant writing, or crowdfunding, or throwing a fundraising event. Identifying who will care about your subject matter is paramount to the entire process of making a film. And now that your film is done or near complete, this phase is no different. You need to know to whom you're marketing, and how to reach them.

No matter your distributor, you will need to do a lot of heavy lifting. Distributors are spending less and less on marketing campaigns for independent films. An impact campaign might be the main source of marketing opportunities for the film, but there is more you can do as the filmmaker. These options will require some budget, but truthfully, I've never had a big marketing budget, and I've gotten wildly creative to stretch a dollar. If you're like me, by the time the film is done, no matter how good of a planner you are, you're exhausted and out of money. Please learn from my mistakes and raise enough money to properly market your film when it comes out!

I'll share some of my favorite tactics for marketing and audience-building. These have worked well for me, and they don't cost a lot. Hopefully they get your wheels turning about what's possible.

Social media pages

When your film is almost done, start engaging with your social media followers, and work to gain more. That way, when you're ready for screenings, or to purchase, the news isn't coming out of nowhere. I know it's hard to maintain social media pages for your film, especially when it feels like you have nothing to say, but even dedicating 10 minutes a day makes a difference. Sign on and follow some like-minded accounts, follow back the people who have followed you, and post new content regularly. Respond to people's comments. You can use your personal social media account to boost the posts initially. For example, in Instagram stories, you can post something and tag yourself, then go to your personal page and repost it right away. Or you can do an Instagram Live from your personal account, or your film's account, to promote the release of the film, or some upcoming call to action. Make sure these social media pages are alive and tell the story of your progress.

Website

If you haven't had a website designed for your film yet, now is certainly the time to get that up and running as well. I like using Squarespace, as it's very user-friendly, but Wordpress and Wix are great too. I typically hire a designer to help me set up an account, choose a template, and make sure it's all functioning, and then I update the site myself after that with new photos, quotes, art, etc. You can also connect your social media to your website, so that every time you update your Instagram, it appears on the homepage of your site. Your website is also a great place to organize content around your film. You can include reviews, screen grabs, the trailer, how to get in contact with you, and press articles. It should be a one stop shop for your film. And you can sell merchandise here too, if you choose to! The website should be the most comprehensive place for people to learn more about the film. It doesn't have to cost a ton to be effective.

Poster design and marketing materials

This part is really fun. If you're like me, you've been daydreaming about the poster art for your film since the beginning. It will represent your film to the world. Hire a designer whose work you admire, and come to the table with some concepts or ideas. The poster is really important, as it may be the first—and potentially only—image people see from your film when deciding whether or not to watch it. If you have a platform you're hoping to get on, or a distributor in place, you can ask the designer to mock-up your finished poster on that platform and see if the art holds up. And if it's a great poster, people may even want to buy it as part of your merchandise after seeing the film!

For *Losing Sight of Shore*, I knew we needed to see the ocean and the rowboat with four people on it. We played with a couple views, but this was our final design, and I absolutely love it. This image was adapted from a drone shot of the boat that I provided the designer. We selected the font from what was used in the film for cohesion, and I had the tagline ready as well. Once you have your poster, you can ask your designer to adapt it into a square for Instagram, and isolate the title art for other materials. You can also have alternate posters, if you like. In my experience with Netflix, even as an acquisition, we provided our poster art, the title treatment file, and some screen grabs from the film. They created additional key art for marketing, including thumbnails and horizontal art like this, which I really like:

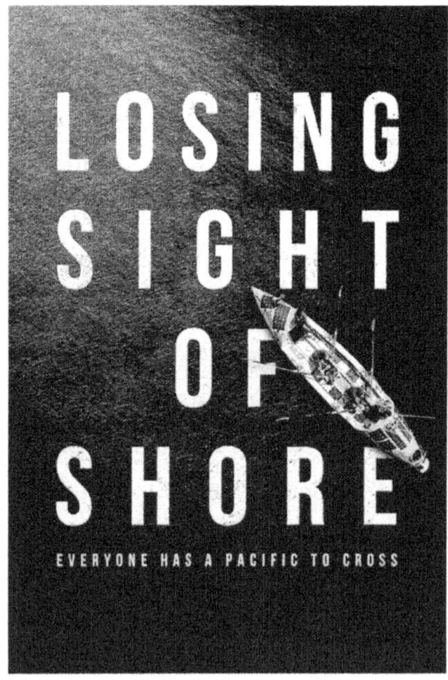

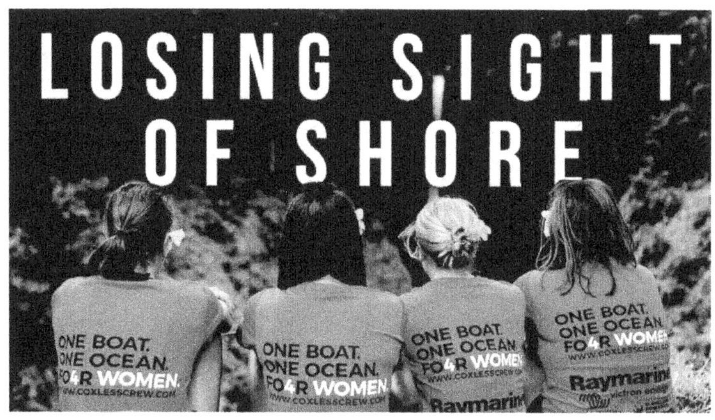

There are so many marketing materials you can design outside of the poster that won't cost you anything. I like taking screen grabs and adding quotes from the film, or reactions to the film, as a way to spread the word on social media. There are many free apps you can use like Canva, Overgram, Fotor, etc. Here are some examples of marketing materials I made for *Losing Sight of Shore* and *Nevertheless:*

"THIS FILM TRANSCENDS GENDER. THIS IS AWE INSPIRING STUFF FOR EVERYONE."

"IF YOU HAVEN'T FALLEN IN LOVE IN A WHILE, WATCH LOSING SIGHT OF SHORE."

"ONE OF THE BEST DOCS I'VE EVER SEEN. PERIOD."

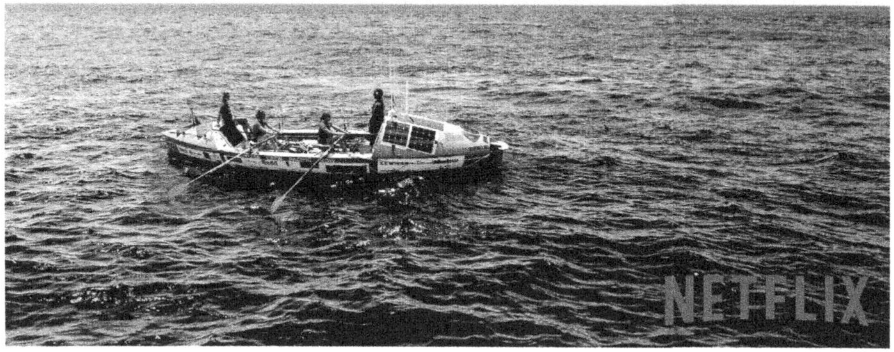

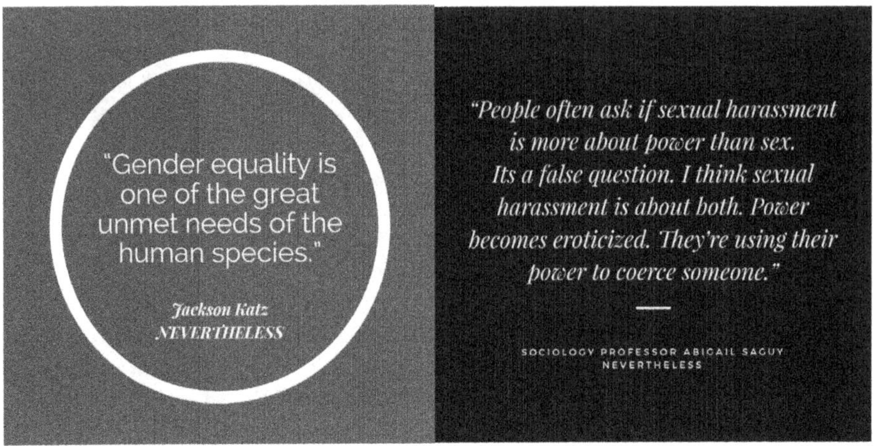

You've worked so hard to create powerful content, both images and quotes. Now you can use it all to create the best marketing materials for your work.

The Trailer

Another exciting part of the marketing process is finalizing the trailer. You may have one already cut, but alongside the poster, the trailer is the most powerful influence over whether or not people to decide to watch your film. Hopefully throughout post-production you've put some of your best sound bites and shots on a separate timeline to be used in the trailer. Even if you haven't, you can go back now and pull your favorite moments from the film. A good trailer editor is important, so if you don't use your primary editor, make sure you find someone whose previous trailers capture the tone you want. Reserve budget for your trailer. It may be the only thing a distributor sees before deciding to screen your film as a potential acquisition, and it certainly impacts whether audiences watch.

Luckily, I work with an incredibly talented editor, Peter Saroufim. He cuts the whole film with me, and we build a trailer together at the end as part of our agreement. He is an editor that is great at cutting the full film as well as a trailer or sizzle. We pull clips throughout the post process, so that when it comes time to cut the trailer, we have a lot to work with, and we're on the same page about what to do. It's still up to me to have a clear direction. You can help your editor by sending them trailers you want to emulate, and by picking music. Try to keep the trailer right around two minutes or less. Don't give away the whole film; leave the viewer wanting more. I fully believe the trailers for all three of my films have gotten me through doors, helped me build an audience, and represented the films and me so well. I'm so proud of those trailers, and I hope you will be proud and excited about your trailer too. If you're not, it's worth re-doing it.

Facebook Ads

There are many books written about Facebook ads, so I won't pretend to know all the intricacies of using their platform, but I simply want to encourage you to explore what you can do on Facebook, Instagram, and Twitter to market your film. Unless your posts have the capacity to go viral (and let's face it, that is often a fluke, and unpredictable at best), in order to combat the algorithms of these platforms, you may need to spend some money to boost your posts, especially when you have something really important to share, like the release of your film. The Facebook ad tool can be extremely nuanced and complex if you know what you're doing, but it can also be very easy and user-friendly for those of us that don't.

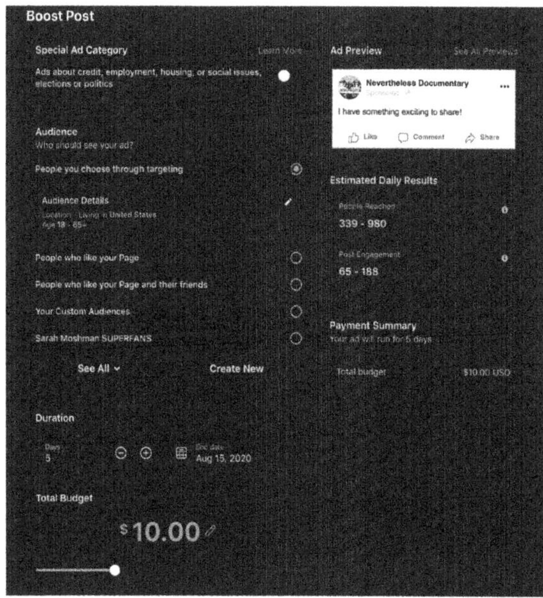

When you go to post your content, click "Boost Post," and then you decide how much money you want to spend over what period of time (a day, a week, a month, etc.). The best part is you can hyper-target your post to the people who would benefit from seeing it the most. Since I have three films, I can target my trailer for *Nevertheless* only to the people who like the pages for my other two films. I can boost the post to people who have watched (at least three seconds of) the trailer for my previous films. Or I can boost the post to women in the US between 20-65 who also like Oprah. You can tailor it however you like, and however makes sense for your audience. I never end up spending too much on this, but I like to try different options, see what happens, and then adjust the ad and try again. Since Facebook and Instagram are under the same umbrella, you can run Instagram ads through this interface as well. Again, you do not need to be a marketing expert or Facebook ads expert to promote your work effectively. If you have some budget to play with, you could hire a person or company that specializes in these platforms and stretch your ad dollars further. Before you spend money on social media promotions, ask yourself what the goal of the ad is. What do you want that $10 to accomplish? Do you want likes on your page, clicks to the website, views of the trailer, click through to buy the film right then? Whatever it is, make sure it's clear in your mind before you spend money, or wait until you have a more concrete call to action, so that you're not burning through budget. You can post on social media for free anytime, so save this tool for when you're ready to promote something.

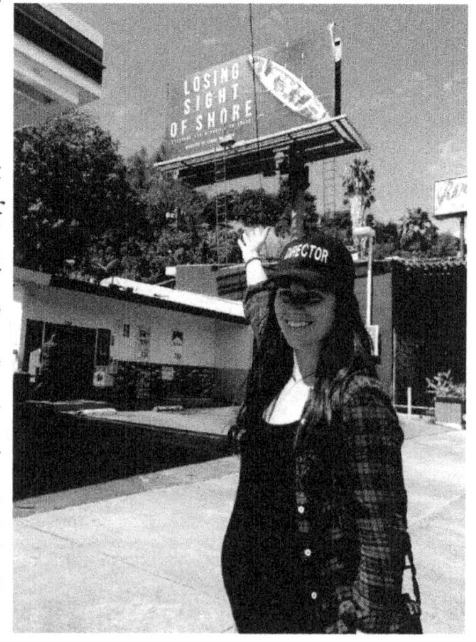

Physical Ads, like a billboard

I had this vision that I would get a billboard for the Netflix release of *Losing Sight of Shore*. Since having a billboard was my dream, I decided to take the power into my own hands and pay for my own. Since I couldn't afford a fancy red carpet premiere, getting a billboard seemed like great, tangible, shareable marketing material that I could afford. I mean, how many times does your documentary about a team of women rowing across the Pacific Ocean premiere on the largest platform in the world? It certainly felt like a cause for celebration. It didn't hurt that I was also five months pregnant at the time—everything was quite emotional. I reached out to a billboard company, asked for a quote for two weeks on one of their larger billboards in a high traffic area on Ventura Blvd in Studio City, CA, and was quoted about $1,500. I asked my graphic designer to adapt our poster to fit the specs of the billboard scope, picked a time frame, and voilà! A dream come true! You can get your own damn billboard if you have to. And I only drove by it 17 times a day.

For me, this was cooler than any award or accolade—after two hard years of work, having a film you're proud of premiering on a platform you dreamed about, all showcased on a billboard in a city you always wanted to live in as a kid...I'll take it.

Promotional Screenings

Now it's time to think about how to build up some excitement for the film itself by hosting screenings of your own, and partnering up with like-minded organizations to build awareness for the film. This could be a complement to a distribution strategy, or this could be the first part of your impact campaign, or a kick-off to self-distribution.

Regardless of where you're at, promotional screenings can be instrumental to setting you up for success. Film festivals aside, you need to collect marketing materials from audiences and hear what they're saying about your film. Sharing your hard work with people—whether that's in-person screenings or virtual events—should be the fun part! Bottom line is, you need to get people excited about your film, and the best way to do that is for people to see it! This doesn't have to be an expensive endeavor either. I'm not suggesting you go out and pay for a full theatrical release, unless it fits with your goals and budget. I have not personally done one, but I understand the prestige, reviews, press, and potential for awards that can come with a theatrical release strategy. However, given COVID-19 and all that's changing with movie theaters, theatrical releases might be a thing of the past anyway.

Screening Tours

For my three films, a grassroots screening tour was part of our strategy. It's always worked phenomenally for raising awareness, booking more screenings, getting press, and generating revenue. With *The Empowerment Project*, after a successful premiere in Los Angeles in May of 2014, and some great screenings in nearby schools, the momentum for the film dipped over the summer. We worried if that was all that would happen with the film. We didn't get into any big name festivals, and we were passionate about getting the film into schools and organizations with an educational model rather than throwing it up online. So we planned a Fall 2014 Dream Big Tour.

We picked four cities, planned to keep it cheap by staying with friends or family, and booked as many screenings as possible during the week we were there. We chose Los Angeles, Seattle, Chicago, and Washington D.C. We ended up doing over 30 events during that month—sometimes we had three screenings in one day! It was honestly so nice to have such a focused approach in our marketing and outreach. Rather than trying to bring the film everywhere, we had these set dates, these four cities, and we started cold calling and emailing nearby schools, companies, and organizations to see if they would host a screening while we were in town. We charged for most events, or did a ticket sale split. With the low travel costs, we ended up making some decent money in that month as well, which was great.

Once the train was moving, and we were deep in planning our Fall Tour, Indieflix mentioned the tour to Nordstrom. After several conversations, Nordstrom joined our Fall Dream Big Tour as the sponsor! Why? They wanted to be in alignment with the film about female empowerment, as that is what their brand stands for.

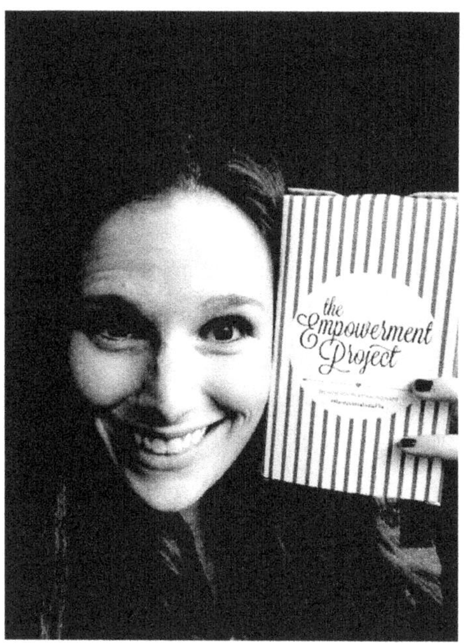

In each of the four cities, Nordstrom hosted and sponsored a screening of *The Empowerment Project*! It was unreal. We showed up to Seattle on day one of our tour, and we saw our window display in downtown Seattle promoting our screening. That night, over 1,000 people showed up in the pouring rain to see our film. There were branded popcorn boxes, temporary tattoos, a photobooth, and candy for everyone. It was the "premiere" we didn't even dream big enough for, and better than any film festival. And that was just day one of the tour! Dana (my producing partner on the project) and I spent the whole month of September looking at each other in disbelief and wonder.

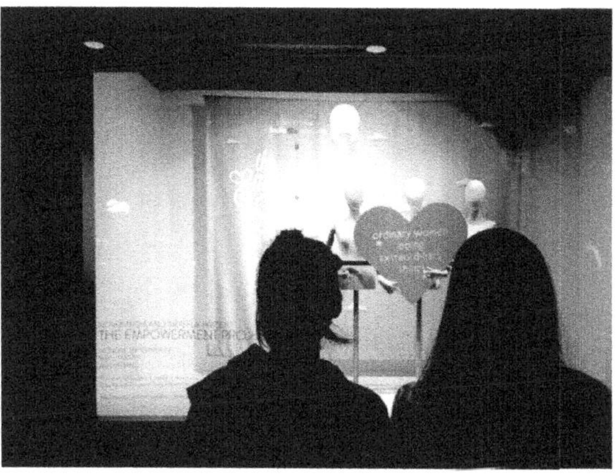

We got so much out of that month of screenings: we collected photos, quotes, testimonials from students who watched the film, teachers who saw the value of bringing the film to their students, press, awareness, and perhaps more than anything, confidence in ourselves that we had made a good film. It had value.

We ended up doing a second tour in the Spring of 2015. This time we did eight cities in eight weeks. We didn't have a formal sponsor for that tour, but we had a lot more contacts and organizations to call upon to host screenings, and we had collected so much evidence from the first tour that it was a valuable experience. We ended up being asked to speak as part of WE Day California, a global youth conference in San Jose, CA in February of 2015. We shared the trailer and spoke about the film in front of 16,000 people! It was insane. We felt like rock stars, literally. By the end of the tour in March of 2015, *Good Morning America* was interested in what we were up to. Thanks to the help of a great publicist who worked with Indieflix, we were interviewed by Amy Robach for *Good Morning America* to finish out our Spring Tour. As I'm typing these words, I still can't believe this was real! It feels like a dream. And truly, none of it would have happened if we hadn't decided to organize a screening tour to share our film with audiences firsthand. In hindsight, those tours set us up for success for years to come. As of 2020, *The Empowerment Project* has been screened over 700 times around the world, and created significant, solid revenue and impact for **six years.**

For *Losing Sight of Shore*, it was a bit different, as the promotional screening tour was really more of a marketing tool to promote our release on Netflix rather than to book more screenings. Our Netflix premiere was to be May 1, 2017, and I quickly realized that because the film was an acquisition for the platform and not a "Netflix Original," they would be doing little to no marketing outside of the platform itself. So much hard work went into making that film (and rowing an ocean!), that I couldn't pass up the opportunity to do something myself to celebrate even beyond the billboard.

I didn't have a big marketing budget, and because your earnings as the filmmaker of a Netflix acquisition aren't tied to how many people watch the film, you're not really incentivized to spend a lot of money on marketing. I decided to plan a grassroots promotional screening tour with the film and all of the rowers in their hometowns. The reason I chose their hometowns in the UK and South Africa was because I knew we could gather an audience, and maybe even get theaters to donate their space for the events. Without a huge marketing budget, it would have been hard for me to get butts in seats where I didn't know anyone, especially abroad. Work with what you have! Plus, it didn't hurt that I would love to travel to England and South Africa anytime, so I could also see the world while doing this—not too shabby.

With my husband Ryan, and my newly pregnant belly, we set off in May 2017 for a three-week screening tour all over England and to Cape Town, South Africa. Our events of all sizes sold out. We did Q&As after each event, which was perhaps the most fun part of all. I loved being reunited with the women I thought of as heroes, and had spent two years working with. It was a total dream, and the best part was being able to tell the audience that the film was available right then on Netflix worldwide, so when they went on social media to promote the movie they just saw, their friends could go watch it immediately as well. It's wonderful when your marketing efforts pass the torch to the audience to be ambassadors for your film.

We basically broke even on that tour between flights, some theater rentals, transportation, and food (we didn't have to pay for hotels since we stayed with the rowers and their families). We charged admission to most screenings, and with all of the ticket sales from the three weeks, we were able to cover our costs, which was the goal. And my husband and I got to check another continent off of our bucket list, seeing Africa for the first time.

For *Nevertheless*, we hosted our own premiere in Los Angeles in February 2020, right before the pandemic hit the US. Needless to say, we had to pivot our strategy considerably, given that we intended to have in-person screenings and events throughout 2020 and beyond. However, we have found a lot of value in doing virtual screenings, given the circumstances. Our screening tour and promotional screenings have simply switched online to Zoom. It has been surprisingly great to be able to engage with audiences virtually from all over the world during the same screening. Our goals with this film are to use it as a tool for change when it comes to sexual harassment, so finding our way into workplaces has been complimentary to the virtual model. We have done promotional screenings with Women in Film, the Geena Davis Institute on Gender in Media, Pixar, Google, Equal Rights Advocates, Human Resources Professional Group (PIHRA), Indiana University and many more. As it stands, we have close to 800 screening requests in almost 20 countries around the world, so something is working!

Bottom line with promotional screenings or a screening tour: use the tools you have in front of you. It doesn't have to cost a lot to be effective, and it can be a great way to engage with your audience, collect marketing materials that will help you for months or years to come, and be incredibly useful for the rest of your distribution strategy.

Working with a publicist

I have hired a publicist for all three of my films to help me promote their releases. Sometimes it has been fruitful and successful, and sometimes not so much. But I do find the process of working with a person or company that has great press contacts useful. It means I don't have to reinvent the wheel and get my own press each time. If you have a lot of press contacts from your career or your networks, you might not need to hire a publicist at all. For those of us who are cold emailing and sending out a press release each day, a PR company can fast track you to get the coverage you want. A publicist can cost a range of prices. I've heard everything from $1,500 to $10,000/month, depending on your coverage goals, and the length of your relationship. Publicists will use some of that time to formulate the pitch and the press release, as well as organize their list of contacts according to their relevance to your film. I find that the clearer you are with a publicist about what press outlets you're going for; the better job they can do. Press can come in many forms.

Questions to consider:

- *What is your budget for PR?*
- *What would be a successful piece of press for you?*
- *Are you aiming for film reviews?*
- *Are you looking for magazines or news shows?*

- *Are you looking to get on podcasts or write blog posts for your favorite sites?*
- *How can the publicist frame your film and your story, what's the angle?*

A publicist will help craft a **press release** to send out to media outlets, and you can help craft that pitch to make sure it encapsulates what you're trying to get across. Here is an example of a press release that went out for *The Empowerment Project* in January 2017 when we had our release date set on iTunes and Amazon:

Dear XX,

Isn't it time we had some good news for women?

A new documentary is about to be released internationally, and it couldn't come at a better time.

As seen on Good Morning America, Marie Claire, Forbes and indieWIRE, The Empowerment Project: Ordinary Women Doing Extraordinary Things is the uplifting and energizing journey of a crew of female filmmakers driving across America to encourage, empower, and inspire the next generation of strong women to go after their career ambitions.

Driving over 7,000 miles from Los Angeles to New York over the course of 30 days, the documentary spotlights 17 positive and powerful women leaders across a variety of lifestyles and industries. Watch the trailer now.

I'd love to introduce you to the award-winning filmmakers, Sarah Moshman and Dana Michelle Cook, or some of the women featured in the movie—from a brewmaster, to a professional athlete, to an astronaut—so you can find out for yourself what they were able to achieve once they let go of the fear of failure.

The Empowerment Project will be available on iTunes and Amazon beginning January 17th. I'd be happy to share a link for you to preview it!

I look forward to hearing from you.

PS. The film is available for pre-order now!

Beyond your goals, I would also say that having a very concrete call to action helps. I have learned this the hard way, and wasted money hiring a publicist when the call to action wasn't strong enough. You need an event, a date, a release, something solid to promote so that press outlets will be more likely to shine a light on your film. For *The Empowerment Project*, we worked with a publicist when we had an iTunes and Amazon release day in January of 2017. For *Losing Sight of Shore* we worked with a publicist twice—once when the rowers were going to complete the record of rowing to Australia, and then again for the Netflix release. For *Nevertheless*, we tried working with a publicist for our virtual screenings, but given everything with COVID-19 in 2020, we didn't get a lot of press at all. I can see now there were three reasons why:

1. The world was focused on much bigger problems and no one had the bandwidth to hear about sexual harassment at that time.
2. I wasn't clear enough with my goals and what press outlets would be right for it.
3. When your call to action is "host a screening in your community" it's much less catchy or concrete than "watch online now, and here's how."

We should have waited to spend the money on a PR company until the world could listen again, and when we had a more concrete call to action. Every film is going to present its own strategy, and sometimes you have to learn the hard way (aka waste money) hiring someone when it's not the right time. Whoever you look to hire as your publicist, make sure you're on the same page about what successful press hits would be and how many, and make sure you speak with other filmmakers they've worked with. Were they satisfied with what was spent and the press they received as a result? And then you can ask the publicist: What kinds of press outlets do they see pitching this to? Do they have an "in" at the show or site you are dying to get on? A publicist can't read your mind, so you need to be an active participant in this process.

Marketing and promotions are what you make them. You didn't come this far for no one to see your work. On a basic level, you need to find ways to let people know your film is done and that it's worth watching. It's up to you how much time, money, energy, and effort you want to put into this phase. Just remember that you are your own biggest advocate here; you are your own biggest fan, so you need to lead the way, no matter who is on your team. You care the most about your project, and no one is going to market it like you can.

Have fun with this part!

CHAPTER EIGHTEEN

It's Your Turn!

Friends, we have come to the end! You now have all the tools to get started on your dream documentary project. I hope you found this information helpful and empowering as you embark on making films you are proud of and care deeply about. You are fully capable of creating your own work that will catapult your career forward with its professionalism, impact, and profitability. The best part of this field is that the barrier to entry is low, and the opportunity for impact and success is high.

We need documentary filmmakers from all walks of life to bring us into communities and worlds we might never experience on our own. We need to see a social issue from your point of view so we can make sense of it in a new way. We need you to show us how to tap into our deepest wells of empathy. We need you to inspire us to be better humans, to meet characters we'd never otherwise meet, and see parts of the planet we may never be able to travel.

Documentaries help us make sense of the world, and it can be such an incredibly exciting field to work and grow in. Your projects will evolve as you do. I can't think of many other fields that require you to wear this many hats, to think creatively at every turn, to build your resilience, and that puts you on a national or even worldwide stage in the process. I think it's one of the hardest and greatest fields of work. I hope you come back to this book over and over again, like an old friend waiting with open arms. Don't be intimidated by all of the steps in front of you, no matter what phase of your project you find yourself in. Take a breath, and figure out what you need to do in the next hour, in the next day, and in the next week. Take this at your own pace—you are in control. Try not to compare yourself to anyone else. You are on your own path, and your project and your vision are different than any other.

Build a community of allies and fellow filmmakers to call on when you're stuck. I have learned so much from my peers sharing horror stories and huge wins along the way. Most doc filmmakers I have crossed paths with have been incredibly gracious about sharing their experiences, and are open to mentoring and supporting others in the field. Even on the loneliest days, I promise you are never alone. And when you have built up some knowledge of your own, please help your fellow filmmaker by paying it forward, whether it's a phone call, meeting up for coffee, or heck, writing your own book! We need to uplift one another and share our stories, not only on screen, but behind the camera as well. You never know who you might be influencing.

I hope you now have the courage to make a film you are proud of. Give yourself the permission to start, which is the most empowering feeling of all.

You got this!

ACKNOWLEDGEMENTS

This book has been yet another labor of love. I wrote this book during the 2020 COVID-19 pandemic when I couldn't make any films due to the global health crisis. It was my creative outlet in a year that felt desperate to strip away all creativity from my life. As a full-time parent in 2020, I got up at 5 a.m. on Mondays and wrote for two hours until my daughter, Bryce, woke up ready to start the day. That's all the time I had truly. I also wrote this while pregnant with my second child, my son. As my body grew, so did my urgency to complete something I started. It felt like an act of rebellion to have something that was just for me in 2020, and now just for you. In one of the toughest years of my life, it has been a delight to have this to come back to, so thank you for sharing it with me. I am proud of all that I've learned to get me here, and to be able to write these words. There are many more films I want to make in my life, so perhaps there will be more books with more lessons learned in the future.

I want to thank my wonderful husband, Ryan Morrison, without whom most things aren't possible in my life. I want to thank my daughter, Bryce, for showing me how to be present, making me smile, and reminding me that passing on knowledge to others is a gift. I want to thank my parents, Diane and Harvey Moshman, for always encouraging me to aim higher and dream bigger, and knowing they would always catch me when I fall. And to my Dad for lighting up this path of filmmaking for me at such a young age, and (whether he realized it or not) showing me how to be the best producer and filmmaker I could strive to be, regardless of my gender. Thank you to my teachers, both in school and in life, my amazing friends who are always a shoulder to cry on, making sense of this crazy world alongside me.

Thank you to JL Stermer from New Leaf Literary who represented me as a literary agent for more than three years shopping around a book proposal and believing in my vision. We never quite found the right publisher for these words, and yet she still encouraged me to self-publish. I continue to learn that sometimes your story needs to be told, no matter what. There is always another way.

Thank you to the people who have supported me along my filmmaking journey and have made a huge difference in my experience making these three films: Scilla Andreen from Indieflix, Jonathan Dana, Lynn Webb, Dana Cook, Ashley Hoff, Vanessa Crocini, Alana Fickes, Margo Romero, Peter Saroufim, Jillian Abood, Evan and Tracy Segal, Samantha Goodman, Audra and Courtney Smith, Laura Penhaul, Natalia Cohen, Emma Mitchell, Lizanne van Vurren, Meg Dyos, Isabel Burnham, and many more.

Thank you to Laura Thomas for editing this book beautifully, Mayra Toscano for designing the awesome cover and Gracie Anderson for her help in the layout and formatting.

Thank you to anyone who reads this book and finds the empowerment to go forth and make their own films on their own terms and believes in their heart they can change the world.

You inspire me.

If you'd like to hire me as a consultant or director for your project go to: http://sarahmoshman.com to shoot me an email. I would love to hear from you.

Instagram: @sarahmoshman

Twitter: @SarahMosh

Facebook: Facebook.com/SarahMoshman

Made in the USA
Monee, IL
12 March 2021